NEPAL

Publisher:	Aileen Lau
Editors:	Kesang Tseten
	Aileen Lau
	Bina Maniar
Design/DTP:	Sares Kanapathy
Illustrations:	Susan Harmer
Maps:	Rebecca Fong
Cover Artwork:	Susan Harmer

 Published in the United States by
PRENTICE HALL GENERAL REFERENCE
15 Columbus Circle
New York, New York, 10023

Copyright Sun Tree Publishing Ltd
1993

ISBN 0-671-87913-8

Titles in the series:
Alaska - American Southwest - Australia - Bali - California - Canada - Caribbean - China - England - Florida - France - Germany - Greece - Hawaii - India - Indonesia - Italy - Ireland - Japan - Kenya - Malaysia - Mexico - Nepal - New England - New York - Pacific Northwest USA - Singapore - Spain - Thailand - Turkey - Vietnam

USA MAINLAND SPECIAL SALES
Bulk purchases (10+copies) of the Travel Bugs series are available at special discounts for corporate use. The publishers can produce custom publications for corporate clients to be used as premiums or for sales promotion. Copies can be produced with custom cover imprints. For more information write to Special Sales, Prentice Hall Travel, Paramount Communications Building, 15th floor, 15 Columbus Circle, New York, NY 10023.

Printed in Singapore

NEPAL

Text by Jon Burbank

With contributions from:
Rosha Bajracharya
Wendy Brewer Lama
Morten Strange
Manjushree Thapa
Kesang Tseten

Editors
Kesang Tseten
Aileen Lau
Bina Maniar

Prentice Hall Travel

New York   London   Toronto   Sydney   Tokyo   Singapore

C O N T E N T S

INTRODUCTION

Swagat Chha! 1
The authors perspective of the country
Fast Facts 5

HISTORY & ECONOMY

From Panchayat to Democracy 7
Prehistory – The Kirati – The Licchavis – The
Mallas – The Shahs – The Ranas – Gurkhas
& The British
The Gurkha Legend 19

Wealth and Poverty 23
Agriculture – Tourism – Carpets – Imports
and Exports – Foreign Aid – Child Labour
Women in the Economy 28

PHYSICAL PROFILE

A Yam Between Two Boulders 33
The Himalayas – The Mahabharat – The
Terai – Hot Springs
Hydropower Rescue 37

Birds and Beasts 45
The Terai – The Middle Hills – The Himala-
yas – Parks and People
Environment & Conservation 48
He Is or He Isn't 51
Birding In Nepal 52

MEET THE PEOPLE

Cultural Individualism 57
North and South – Caste Hindus – Hill
Tribes – The Tharu – The Newars

Village Life 62

Tolerance & Reinterpretation 67
Hinduism – Caste – Buddhism – Tantra
Hindu Gods and Goddesses 69
The Buddha's Life 74

Festive Focus 79
Festive calendar
Folk Beliefs and Superstitions 82

Anonymous Art 89
Newar Renaissance – Thangkas – Verbal
Arts
Erotic Art 95

FOLLOW THAT BUG

Kaleidoscopic Kathmandu 101
Kasthamandap – Rani Pokhara – Durbar
Square – New Road – Kumari – Hanuman
Dhoka

**Valley Vistas – Around Kathmandu
Valley** 117
Around the Valley Rim – Changu Narayan
– Chobar – Kirtipur – Nagarjun – Kakani –
Shivapuri – Budhanilkantha – Dhum Varahi
- Boudhnath – Sankhu – Swayambhunath –
Pashupatinath

**Golden Roofs & Working Craftsmen –
Patan** 139
Patan Dhoka – Kwa Bahal – Kumbeshwar –
Durbar Square – Mangal Bazaar – Sundari
Chowk – Tusa Hiti – Taleju Temple –
Bhimsen Temple – Mahabaudha Temple –
Uku Bahal – I Baha Bahal – Bishwarkarma
Temple – Jawalakhel

C O N T E N T S

A City Of Brick & Wood –Bhaktapur
.... 153
*Bagh Bazaar – Thimi – Sidhi Pokhari –
Dattaraya Square – Golden Gate – Taleju
Temple – Taleju Chowk – Palace of 55
Windows – Bhagbati – Nyatapola Temple –
Batsala Durga – Pashupati temple –
Taumadhi Tole – Peacock Window –
Wakupati Narayan – Banepa –
Chandeswari Shrine – Dhulikhel – Paunati*

Valley Town – Pokhara Valley ... 167
*Phewa Tal – Baidam – Machhapuchhre –
Annapurna – Manaslu – Temple of Varahi
– Patle's Fall – Devi's Fall – Bindyabasini –
Bhimsen – ACAP – Tibetan settlements –
Mountain Views – Gorkha - Tansen – Butwal
Local Courtesies* 173

**Inexhaustible Riches – Terai Sightsee-
ing** 179
*Lumbini – Janakpur – Biratnagar –
Naxalbari – Itahari – Dharan – Janaki
Mandir – Birgunj – Royal Chitwan Na-
tional Park – Narayanghat – Devghat –
Central Terai – Nepalgunj – Bardiya Wild-
life Reserve*

WHAT TO DO

Adventurous Holidays – Trekking ....
.... 191
*Trekking with an agency and on your own
– weather – times – Annapurna Circuit –
Dumre to Muktinath – Annapurna Sanctu-
ary – Everest – To Gokyo – Everest Base
Camp – Far West – Rafting*
   Mangis 204
   The Khampas 211

The Thakalis 213
ACAP 217
The Captain's 218
The Sherpas 223
Green Trekking 233
Trekking Tips 237

Get Physical – Sports 247
*Rafting – Bicycle Tours – Mountain Biking
– Mountain Flights*

Daal-Bhaat Country – Cuisine 259
*Daal-Bhaat – Alternative fare – Restaurant
Listing*
   Local Eatables 264

High Altitude Retail – Shopping .....
.... 269
Gift possibilities and restrictions

Path Finders – Suggested Itineraries
.... 277
3– 5– 7– 10 and 15 days trips

BEYOND NEPAL

Beyond The Borders 283
India-Tibet-Bhutan

EASY REFERENCE

Travel Tips 293
Supplement essential for travel planning
Glossary 298
Directory 302
Useful listings
Photo Credits 307
Index 308

Nepali stupas are often painted with the all seeing eyes

The eyes have it...

and the nose, symbolishing unity.

The peoples of Nepal, set in different ethnic and religious cultures, but drawn togethe[r]

in their display of robust features, deep devotions, vigour, resilience and great cheer.

Thrust of the mountains, energy of a trek, pride of a climb,

souvenir of a trip... its all here, mountains, valleys

and watering holes.

Culture and art preserved in stone, wood and bronze — a heritage from the past

— honoured in the present.

It is hard to imagine a more deeply affecting landscape. Freud speaks of places where you can lose yourself, abandon your personal identity and be enveloped in an "oceanic feeling, similar to a spiritual experience". On a clear morning, looking out at the glowing white face of the Himalayas, you may well feel you have found such a place.

There are few countries with a geography as diverse as Nepal's. Within its narrow borders you will find a complete climatic range, from tropical to temperate, alpine to arctic. The high peaks scatter rainshadows and rain basins everywhere, so that virtually each of the hundreds of valleys and gorges has its own unique micro-climate.

No wonder nearly 800 species of birds – about 10 per cent of the world's bird species – are found in Nepal. In the southern sub-tropics of the country, you can stand in thick jungle and hear the grunts of an Asian single-horned rhinoceros or the deep growl of a Royal Bengal tiger. And, in the near horizon, in the

Home of the world's highest mountains, birthplace of the "Enlightened One", Nepal is stirring.

Swagat Chha!

mountainous terrain, a reclusive snow leopard may be stalking a herd of golden-eyed blue sheep.

Within this spectacular geography is also found one of the richest and most diverse cultural landscapes anywhere. The country's population of 19 million is a potpourri of ethnic and sub-groups who speak as many as 30 different languages and dialects. Nepali or *parbate* is the *lingua franca*; the others belong to the Indo-European and Tibeto-Burman families.

Nepal is home to two of the world's great religions, Hinduism and Buddhism, which were superimposed on earlier Shamanistic beliefs and now co-exist harmoniously.

Some of Hinduism's most sacred pilgrimage spots are found here. Nepal is also featured in the two great epics of Hindu literature, the *Ramayana* and the

Mahabharata.

Siddhartha Gautam, the "Buddha" (the "Enlightened One"), was born in Lumbini in Nepal's southern plains, and is believed to have set foot in the Kathmandu Valley. Buddhism remains strong, particularly in the northern Himalayan belt.

Nepalis are justly proud that theirs is one of the few countries in Asia that escaped colonialism. For centuries, (by her own choice), Nepal remained closed to outsiders, with a few exceptions. From 1881 to 1921, only 64 Europeans visited Kathmandu, very few of whom were permitted outside the Valley. Yet times have changed, and over the years Nepal has entertained a diverse spectrum of visitors; religious pilgrims, trekkers, mountain climbers as well as people who came simply to bask in the splendour of the Himalayas!

Many tourists go to Nepal expecting to see the lost city of Shangri-la tucked in the mountains. Hardly a utopia, Nepal is one of the world's poorest

A Shavaite sadhu.

Fast Facts

Area: 145,391 sq km (56,139 sq miles), about the size of Switzerland and Austria combined.

Population: about 19 million, 50 per cent under age 21; growth rate of 2.7 per cent annually.

Capital: Kathmandu, with a metropolitan population 500,000 and one million in the Valley.

Government: Constitutional Monarchy, under His Majesty King Birendra Bir Bikram Shah Dev; with B P. Koirala heading a Nepal Congress cabinet, following his party's victory in 1991 in the country's first elections in 32 years.

Religion: Officially, Hindu 90 per cent, Buddhist 8 per cent, Islam 2 per cent (though more like Hindu 70-75 per cent, Buddhist 20-25 per cent, and many of these two faiths follow Shamanistic and animistic practices)

People: More than 30 different ethnic groupings, among them Gurung, Magar, Tamang, Rai, Limbu, Newar, Sherpa, Loba, Walungwa, Tharu; Indo-Aryan caste groups of Brahman and Chhetri; high profile population of Indians and Tibetans.

Economy: over 90 per cent agrarian, per capita income of about US$175 per year.

Language: Nepali (the official language) 58 per cent, Newari 3 per cent, Tibeto-Burman languages 19 per cent, Indic languages 20 per cent. In all more than 30 languages and numerous dialects spoken.

Currency: Nepali Rupee; US$1 equals Rs34.50 in May 1991, and Indian Rs1 equals Nepali Rs1.68

National Flower: Rhododendron

National Bird: Danphe Pheasant

National Colour: Scarlet Red

Highest Point: Mt. Everest, 8,848m (29,028ft), the highest point on earth.

---

countries, as measured by her per capita income. Life here is difficult, as most Nepalis admit, but in the same breath they will also tell you that they can never live anywhere else.

Meeting Nepalis is one of the distinct pleasures of visiting Nepal. Nepalis are friendly, tolerant, and patient; tolerance of all faiths, languages, and cultures of the pluralistic society they belong to; patient in the face of all the big and little setbacks, and things that do not quite go right but are part of everyday life in Nepal. You may rightly expect that with the deep impact of both Hinduism and Buddhism the Nepalis are also a very philosophical lot!

Likewise tolerance, patience, and a touch of humour are the best equipment you can take with you – as you will soon find out when, things do not happen as planned.

In spite of that, Nepal is a traveller's paradise. For where else could you stare at the world's highest range, trek to the lower slopes where the mountain folk live, ponder and admire the rich culture and artistic achievements of the Kathmandu Valley, raft down a snow-fed river, seek out rhinos from atop an elephant, and even visit a casino, all in one visit? Few would visit Nepal without the Himalayas and the rich culture beckoning one back, again and again.

So to all intrepid travellers to Nepal we bid you – Swagat Chha!

At one time, Kathmandu Valley was thought to be submerged under a primordial lake. Legend goes that the Vipaswi Buddha, a holy man, came and sat on the hill of Nagarjun to meditate. Inspired, he planted a lotus seed in the lake. Six months later, on the full moon, it bloomed. But, it was no ordinary blossom, a blue flame emanated from it and illuminated the image of Swayambhu, "the self-existent one." The luminescence filled the valley and rose to the heavens.

7

Tibetan Buddhists earn merit toward a better future by placing carved "mani" prayer stones in holy places.

Further north the Bodhisattva Manjushri saw the glow and set off to find it. Reaching the hill of Nagarkot he stopped and meditated on the glow of Lord Swayambhu for three days and nights. Then he walked to the southern rim of the valley. Rushing down from Phulchowki, with his sword held high, he cut a gorge at Chobar in one stroke, thus draining the valley of its waters. The lotus rested on the hill of Swayambhu, where Manjushri built a shrine.

The Valley plausibly hosted a lake thousands of years ago, but its early history remains shrouded in legend. However, what is certain is that Kathmandu Valley was definitely inhabited long before the Kiratis arrived from eastern Nepal in the 7 or 8 BC.

The Kirati

The Kirati tribe, believed to be of Mongolian origin, established a powerful kingdom in the valley. They are described as fine warriors, and their greatest king, Yalambar, the first and most remembered king, is said to have participated and died in the climactic battle of the *Mahabharata*.

Many of the Valley's settlements

Reading the mantras.

and monuments were founded during the Kirati period. The inhabitants were mostly Hindu, who primarily worshipped Shiva. There is a high probability that they were great traders as 4th century records note that large quantities of Nepali wool were sold in the great city of Pataliputra (Patna). Trade was conducted with Tibet and as far away as present-day Sri Lanka.

Early visitors to the Valley may have included Buddha and his greatest propagator, Emperor Ashoka, who visited Lumbini, and are believed to have visited the Valley as well. Ashoka erected four *stupas* in Patan and his daughter, Charumati, married a Valley prince, Devapala. Together, they founded the town of Deopatan.

Around 200 AD, the Kirati were driven from the Valley by the Licchavi from northern India. The Kirati resettled in their eastern homeland, the forebearers of today's Rais and Limbus.

The Licchavis

The Licchavis were forced to abandon their kingdom of Pushpapur in North India. Their reign is regarded as one of Nepal's golden ages during which the kingdom prospered from its trade with India and Tibet. Chinese visitors wrote in praise of temples and palaces of this period which were ostentatiously decorated with gilt and sculptures.

One of the great Licchavi kings was Manadev. A stone column dated 467

Statue of Jang Bahadur Rana on the Tundikhel.

AD commemorates his rule at Changu Narayan Temple on a hill above Bhaktapur. He expanded the kingdom to Kali Gandaki in the west, and Kosi in the east.

Licchavi Nepal reached its cultural zenith under Amshuvarma. His seven-storeyed palace in Deopatan (present day Chabil), Kailashkut Bhavan, was legendary. Amshuvarma sponsored poets and wrote a treatise on grammar. He also successfully resisted pressure from both India and Tibet by arranging the marriage of his sister to an Indian prince and marrying off his own daughter to Tibet's powerful King Songtsen Gampo thus successfully forging alliances with India and Tibet.

It was a timely move as Songtsen Gampo (c. 609-649) and his fierce nomadic warriors turned Tibet into a regional power which threatened to cross into the Himalayas.

Amshuvarna's daughter Bhrikuti carried the Buddha's own begging bowl over the high passes as part of her dowry. The Tang princess Wencheng travelled from China to become Gampo's other wife bringing with her an original set of Buddha statues.

Together they converted their ruthless king to Buddhism. Today, he is revered as the first of Tibet's three great "religious" kings. Tibetans worship Bhrikuti as an incarnation of the green Tara, symbolising the benign side of the Tantric forces in Tibetan Buddhism. A beautiful image of revered Bhrikuti re-

13th century temple relics as insights to kingdoms of the past.

sides at Swayambhu.

Licchavi rule ended in the 9th century. The period was followed by three centuries of Nepal's "Dark Ages." Power was then passed to the Thakuri kings of Nuwakot. The Tibetans made an unsuccessful bid for the Valley in 705, followed by a Kashmiri attempt in 782. Though history is sketchy, it seems many institutions of modern Nepal were founded then, including the cult of the *Kumari*, the living goddess.

The only king who stands out in this long period is Gunakamadeva who

The Mallas

Malla rule in Nepal began with Ari Deva in 1200. The Mallas are immortalised in the *Mahabharata* and in Buddhist literature as rulers of small kingdoms in the Terai in 600 BC.

The early Malla period was marked by violence and destruction. An earthquake devasted the Valley in 1245, and invaders from the North Indian kingdom of Mithila plundered the Valley five times between 1244 and 1311. Patan was razed in 1311. Khasa raiders from far western Nepal looted the valley six times between 1287 and 1344. Altogether it was an unsettling time for the Valley.

A significant figure from this period was Raja Harisimha or Hari Singh. According to obscure legends, he conquered Bhaktapur and Patan and ruled from Kathmandu. Whether he actually ruled in the valley is questionable. Ousted from his own kingdom by Moslems, he made his way to Bhaktapur in 1324. From his ancestral home in Karnataka, he brought with him the image of the goddess Taleju Bhawani, (a South Indian deity) who still remains the royal goddess of Nepal.

In 1346, just as the threats from Mithila and Khasa receded, Sultan Shamsuddin of Bengal and his hordes ravaged the Valley for seven days. Most of the population fled to the forests. It took decades before social and political order were restored.

is credited with founding Kathmandu (then called Kantipurat) and building the temple Kasthamandap (House of Wood) from a single tree – from which Kathmandu derives its name. Gunakamadeva is also said to have initiated the festival of *Indra Jatra*.

Shamsuddin's invasion was only one example of the waves of Moslems that were sweeping across India, breaking up the great Hindu kingdoms. Members of the Hindu aristocracy, they fled north to Nepal's hills to form hilltop kingdoms such as the "baaisi rajas" (22 Princes) of west Nepal and the "chaubisi raja" (24 Princes) of central Nepal.

One family, the Shahs, was said to have fled Udaipur in Rajasthan, and set up a small kingdom around its hilltop palace in Gorkha. According to another version, they were survivors of the sacking of Chittogarh in 1303. Whatever their origins, four centuries later, they conquered Kathmandu Valley and their descendents are the present kings of modern Nepal.

Even before the Moslem pillage, the Valley was already divided into the smaller kingdoms of Kathmandu, Patan, and Bhaktapur.

It was a time when bandits roamed the countryside, and kings and princes battled for control of the Valley, each building protective walls around their own towns.

Nepal's renaissance started in 1372 when Jayasthiti Malla ascended the throne. He was responsible for codifying and enforcing the caste system. The Mallas were strict Hindus who although they worshipped Shiva were tolerant of Buddhism. The Malla line were considered the living incarnations of the Hindu god Vishnu, as the present Shah kings are today.

Yaksha Malla (1428-1482) built a kingdom on the foundations laid by Jayasthiti and extended his kingdom's borders. A devout Hindu, he brought priests from Maharashthra to serve in Pashupatinath and built many fine temples. At the same time he also funded many Buddhist monasteries. The Newar traditions of sculpture, woodcarving, and architecture began with him.

Though a strong king, he neglected to make the crucial decision of succession. As a result, following his death, his kingdom was divided among his children. For centuries, these tiny states of Kathmandu, Patan, Bhaktapur, Banepa and Kirtipur bickered, schemed, and fought, not one of them strong enough to dominate the others.

These kingdoms somehow survived and even prospered. Most of the monuments we admire today were built during this period. The politically fragmented Valley was an alluring treasure which was not usurped until the mid-18th century.

The Shahs

Prithvi Narayan Shah, the ninth King of tiny Gorkha, had his sights set on the Valley long before he ascended the throne in 1742. In 1745, after suffering his first defeat, he tasted his first victory, controlling Nuwakot, northwest of the Valley.

More than two decades and several defeats later, he finally made his triumphant entrance into Kathmandu in

1768. It occurred on the main day of the *Indra Jatra* festival, dedicated to the virgin goddess *Kumari*.

Prithvi Narayan Shah was an ardent nationalist, determined to preserve his kingdom and its lucrative trade position. He set down a policy of isolation which lasted until 1951.

"If foreign traders are allowed in, they are sure to impoverish the people," he said, and kept out even Indian entertainers. About the British, he prophetically exclaimed, "Be friendly with the Emperor of the South Seas, but do not let his missionaries and merchants into the country." So although the Malla kings allowed Capuchin monks to establish a mission in the Valley in the 1730s, the new king expelled them.

Prithvi Narayan Shah's successors expanded their kingdom until it reached Kashmir and Tibet and Sikkim to the east. An attempt to gain territory in Tibet led to a disastrous war. Coming to the aid of the Tibetans, a Chinese army reached Nuwakot and forced the Gorkhas to sign a treaty in which they pledged not to attack Tibet as well as agreed to send tribute to Peking every five years, a practice which was only discontinued in 1912.

The Gorkhali system of rewarding soldiers and officers with tracts of land prompted expansion, and the fertile Terai was the only place to go to. Gorkhali movement in the Terai caused conflict with the other expanding power in the area, namely the British East India Company.

The British

In 1810 war broke out. Initially the Nepalis held out, but were forced to sign an agreement when a British army under Ocheterlony threatened to cross from Mukwanpur into Kathmandu. Under the 1816 "Treaty of Friendship" negotiated at Sugauli, Nepal lost all the territory to the east and west of its present borders, including most of the Terai, and Sikkim became a British protectorate.

The British also gained the right to station a resident in Kathmandu, but the Nepalese had the last word: the

Statue of King Malla in Patan.

High Rana officials and the Maharaja Padma Shamsher seated
between Lord and Lady Mountbatten in 1945.

resident was given the worst piece of land and his movements were restricted to the Kathmandu Valley.

The war with the British left Nepal's rulers even more distrustful of foreigners. For the next century and a half, Nepal remained almost completely closed to the world.

The loss of the Terai land weakened Nepal. The aristocracy had derived their income from the region. Suddenly, Nepal found itself with a large idle army and an irritated corp of officers. With no external threat looming, the leaders

A Queen's Revenge

It was an explosive situation. The spark that finally triggered it was not so much lust for power as plain lust. Late on the night of September 14, 1846, the queen's lover was shot and killed in his prayer room. Enraged by grief, the queen ordered the entire court to assemble in the courtyard of the *kot* (fort), next to the Hanuman Dhoka palace. From her second-floor window, her hair dishevelled and tears streaming down her red-rimmed eyes, she ordered the gates locked. The dozen nobles who were present in the courtyard looked around nervously to check where their friends and their foes stood.

No one could leave, commanded the queen, until the murderer confessed. Accusations, heated denials, and counter accusations followed. Then three persons in the court approached the dark stair to talk with the queen. Shots rang out and two of the nobles fell down the stairs, dead.

"...Jang Bahadur had an ugly method of dealing with emergencies."
Percival Landon

Jang Bahadur Rana, a main figure in the palace intrigues, who was surrounded by his brothers and troops, made most of the opportunity when the fighting started. It is not certain how many died that night; some said 200, but 60 is more likely. All accounts, how-

found enemies amongst themselves. The king deliberately kept his chain of command unclear while the queen schemed privately. The court became mired in a tangle of plots and intrigues, whispers and innuendoes. And the restless army, threatened to revolt.

ever, describe the gutters outside the *kot* gates as flowing with blood. The Nepali court with the exception of the ranas and their supporters was toppled.

The Kot Massacre, as historians call it, set the course of Nepal's history for the next century. On the morning following the gruesome event, Jung Bahadur became the Prime Minister and took complete control, by reducing the status of figureheads. The Rana family themselves had their share of internal squabbles and intrigues, but they managed to rule Nepal as their private estate until 1951.

Ranas

The Ranas took to building enormous palaces in a mishmash of European styles, importing marble floors and crystal chandeliers from Europe. Today, they stand as the only reminders of the century of selfish Rana rule (as everything the Ranas did benefitted only themselves). They did everything within their powers to eliminate any opposition, such as the suppression of education. In 1952, only 10 per cent of the population were literate.

One of the first to object were the returning Gurkha soldiers. They did so through the Gurkha League, a semi-political organisation founded in 1921. Their experiences in World War One had opened their eyes to the outside world. The first open protest against the Ranas was a strike at a jute mill in

Biratnagar on March 4, 1947, led by BP Koirala, President of the Nepali National Congress (NNC).

With an independent India, British support for the Ranas crumbled, and opposition mounted. The Ranas tried gaining foreign support. They ended Nepal's diplomatic isolation, drew up a constitution, and signed a treaty with India which recognised Nepal's sovereignty and independence.

The Shahs Again

The NNC continued to press for change in spite of the Ranas' "reforms." The Shah king, Tribhuvan, became the catalyst for the Ranas' downfall. On November 6, 1950, using a family outing as a ruse, he escaped and sought protection at the Indian Embassy, surprising everyone – the Ranas, the NNC, India and Britain. On November 10, the day Tribhuvan was permitted to fly to India, the NNC took control of Birgunj, and by January, 1951 it controlled the Terai.

The Rana rule ended. An interim government, half Rana, half NNC, was formed, and on February 18, 1951, Tribhuvan returned as King.

The democracy promised by King Tribhuvan's 1951 government proved difficult to bring about. He died in 1955, leaving his son, Mahendra, to oversee the first general election in Nepal's history to be held in the spring of 1959.

BP Koirala was appointed Prime Minister and his new party, the Nepal

A young lady of the Rana court, c. 1900.

Congress Party (NCP), controlled a strong majority. The subsequent parliament proved to be tumultuous, given that it was a new democracy. Seeing his policies ignored and his own power slipping, King Mahendra decided to act.

On December 15, 1960, army officers arrested the cabinet. Citing that politics had brought the country to chaos, and that democracy was a foreign idea inappropriate to Nepal, King Mahendra seized direct control. He banned all political parties, and BP Koirala spent the next twenty years in jail and exile.

Mahendra then instituted the *panchayat* system. In accordance with it, the prime minister and his cabinet were appointed and dismissed directly by the king. Freedom of assembly, speech and the press were curtailed. It became illegal to criticise the monarchy.

A Long Time Coming

When Mahendra died in 1972, he was succeeded by his son, Birendra, who declared his intention to retain the *panchayat* system and to ease Nepal's dependence on self-reliance. Over a period of time, with the constant overseas postings of soldiers and returning students, the improvement in communication and education, Nepalis became more politicised and disgruntled about where their country was heading. There was widespread belief that large amounts of money designated for development was going into the pockets of corrupt officials.

In 1979 people took their protest to the streets. Violent demonstrations rocked Kathmandu until King Birendra announced a referendum in which the people would decide whether to allow political parties. The former-NCP leader BP Koirala campaigned, but surprisingly, the vote went to the *panchayat* system.

Even before declaring the vote, the king instituted further reforms. The national parliament would be elected by direct vote, and the Prime Minister elected by parliament. But, following the first election in May 1981, it became apparent that little had changed. The palace still held virtually absolute power. Dissent was suppressed and Nepal remained a persistent concern of Amnesty International reports. Despite the large amounts of foreign aid pouring into the country, the lives of average Nepalis did not improve. When the Trade Treaty between India and Nepal lapsed in March 1989, India placed severe restrictions on the movement of goods across the border, thus effectively crippling Nepal's tottering economy. In the spring of 1990, protests over shortages of basic goods turned into demonstrations against corruption and the absence of rights, including the ban on political parties. Led by the underground NCP and several communist parties, the demonstrations gained widespread support. The political parties, still illegal, formed an alliance to press their demands for democracy. By March 1990,

The Gurkha Legend

The legend of the world famous Gurkha soldiers originated in the war with the British. A British general was so impressed with the Nepalis that he built a monument to them inscribed, "It is a present in honour of our brave enemy Balbhadra and his brave Gorkhali friends."

After the war, the British started recruiting Gurkhas, mainly from the Gurung, Magar, and Thakuri Chhetri groups who formed the core of the Shah army. Incidently, the word Gurkha does not apply to any ethnic group.

During the Indian mutiny of 1857, the British Gurkhas together with 12,000 troops sent by Prime Minister Jung Bahadur Rana played an important role in lifting the sieges on Lucknow and Delhi. The traditional Nepali knife, the *khukuri*, became their emblem.

When India gained independence, the 10 Gurkha regiments broke up. Six regiments became the Indian Gurkha Rifles, which saw action in the wars with Pakistan and in the Sino-Indian war of 1962. The other four regiments remained with the British army, fighting in Cyprus and against communists in Indonesia and Malaysia. Lance Corporal Ram Bahadur Limbu was awarded the Victoria Cross for his heroism in Sarawak in 1965.

More recently, the Gurkhas fought in the Falklands War. Such being their reputation, the Argentine troops were reported (in British papers) to have dropped their weapons and fled when the Gurkhas advanced.

To become a Gurkha soldier is still a respected goal for young men in the middle hills. Their salaries and pensions, more than US$15 million yearly, form the main source of income in the hills.

Recruits are required to pass physical and written exams, then undergo 10 months of arduous training in Hong Kong. It may well be the first time these young men have left their close-knit families and villages. During their enlistment, the Gurkhas can return home to their villages once every three years. They can have their families stay overseas with them for only one three-year term.

The Gurkhas' fate may change. One regiment has been deputed to the Sultan of Brunei. With the status of Hong Kong due for change, the Gurkhas face an uncertain future.

Gurkhas at an army camp in Hile, east Nepal.

the government was in serious trouble when government civil servants also joined the protests.

The palace reverted to the old tactic of repression, but by then demonstrations had broken out in the Valley, the Terai, and the hilltowns. Offices were

King Birendra Bir Bikram Shah and the Queen.

killing about 100 people. Shortly after, the king agreed to the demands for democracy. Krishna Prasad Bhattarai, who had suffered years in prison, was named Prime Minister of a coalition cabinet made up of Congress and communist members.

As a committee drafted a new constitution, the palace issued statements which seemed unclear as to whether the king actually agreed to give up power. Once again in September 1990, thousands of demonstrators took to the capital's streets.

The deadline for the new constitution passed. The palace delayed their response to the draft constitution, then presented a counter draft. It was the murk and manoeuvering of the 19th century all over again. At last, the alliance's draft was accepted by all the parties, and Nepal's first multi-party elections in more than three decades was held in mid-May 1991.

The Nepal Congress won a bare majority to form the new cabinet, with party Secretary-General BP Koirala as the new Prime Minister. Despite its victory, the Nepali Congress was drubbed in the prestigious Kathmandu constituencies. To great disappointment, Prime Minister KP Bhattarai, a Gandhian-styled leader, lost his contest. The real victory went to the Communist Party of Nepal (United Marxist-Leninist), who came in second with a significant 69 seats. Against all predictions, the two former *Panchayat* parties barely won four seats.

boycotted, some set on fire, and Patan declared her "independence." On April 6, a massive demonstration approaching the palace was fired on by police,

Economy

The mountains that cover more than 80 per cent of the country are both its boon and curse, the source of its wealth (spiritual and material) and its extreme poverty. Thousands are lured by the mountains, which help make tourism the country's leading money-maker. Yet, without this natural asset, other economic possibilities might have been developed, and the reliance on tourism might have lessened.

A harvest near Changu Narayan.

With a per capita income of about US$175 per year, Nepal easily qualifies as one of the world's poorest countries. As in many parts of the third world, there is a great disparity in income distribution. According to one study, 47 per cent of the national income goes to the wealthiest 10 per cent of the population, and the poorest 40 per cent get by on 9 per cent of the national income. An estimated 42 per cent of Nepalis live below the government stipulated poverty line!

Agriculture

About 90 per cent of the popu-

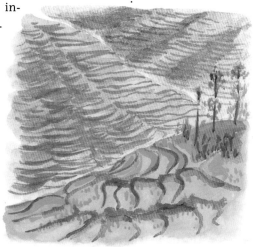

Corn is a significant subsistence and cash crop for many Nepalis.

lation live off the land. For the most part, they are subsistence farmers. Their crop of choice is rice, planted both for the social status it denotes and for its own value. The other crops grown are corn, wheat, millet and barley.

Rice requires warm temperatures and plenty of water. In a mountainous country like Nepal, this eliminates a great deal of the cultivable land. Generally, rice is not grown at elevations above 2,000 m. In the middle hills, it is not uncommon for a farmer to grow rice at the base of a hill beside a river, whereas wheat, corn and millet are sown in the higher terraced fields around his house which are not irrigable.

About 75 per cent of Nepal's rice is grown in the alluvial plains of the Terai, where irrigation and a subtropical climate make multi-cropping and higher yields possible. Terai farmers also use more fertilisers and updated agricultural techniques. Many farmers, having been pushed to adopt these new methods, are finding that any gain in yield is offset by their high capital investment. The green revolution has espoused the use of a strain of high-yield seeds and chemical fertilisers. More recently, the approach has become more balanced, favouring hardier traditional seeds. In the middle hills, corn and wheat remain the main crops.

In recent years, more and more land has come under cultivation. From 1974 to 1985, even though food production increased by 14 per cent, the popu-

Much of the alluvial plains of the Terai are used for rice-fields.

lation increased by 34 per cent. Moreover, the increase in food production was the result of an increase in newly cultivated land rather than a higher yield from existing crops. In many instances, the yield per land unit actually dropped because of the availability of more cultivable land. Farmers also stopped allowing fields to lie fallow.

With their declining yield, many farmers did not grow enough to feed their families. At present, large areas of the country do not have enough food. For example, in 1984, Karnali Zone produced only 31 per cent of the grain it needed, the rest of its requirements came as food aid from donor countries and international agencies which sold their grain holdings at subsidised prices.

Although rural families need cash to buy food, they are typically cash-poor. Consequently, the village men are forced to migrate to India for a few months every year in search of jobs requiring unskilled labour. In their absence, the women and children are left to do all the farming and household chores (in any case, women do an estimated 70 per cent of the farmwork and most of the domestic work).

Trade and Industry

Nepal once controlled a large share of the lucrative trade between India and Tibet. During the Malla rule, Nepal was even contracted to mint silver currency for Tibet. If for nothing else, the architectural wonders of Kathmandu Valley are testimony to Nepal's former prosperity. The Nepalis were able to resist all British and Indian entreaties to allow their traders into the country.

The British invaded Tibet in 1904 and forced Tibetan authorities to allow British access to Tibetan markets via British-controlled Sikkim. Most of Nepal's lucrative trade was drained off by this development. When the communists sealed the border in the 1960s, trade was reduced to a trickle. Today, the northern *Bhotiya* people continue to engage in small trade across the border

Tourism has brought significant earnings.

under terms set down by the Chinese. Nepalese rice, wheat and corn are traded for Chinese wool and salt.

There are still several northern border towns which fit Dr Hooker's 1847 description of Mewa Gola, near Taplejung:

"*Myawa Gola* is a large village frequented by Nepalese and Tibetans, who bring salt, wool, gold, musk, and blankets, to exchange for rice, coral, and other commodities; and a customs officer is stationed there, with a few soldiers. The houses are of wood, and well built: the public ones are large, with verandahs and galleries of carved wood."

Tourism

After centuries of self-imposed isolation, tourism is ironically the largest industry which brings in much needed foreign exchange. Indians are by far the single largest group of tourists. After Indians, the largest source of tourist arrivals are from the United States, followed by Britain, France, Germany, Japan, and Australia.

But the amount of money earned by tourism is deceptive. It is said that as much as 80 per cent of tourism's foreign exchange earnings leave the country in payment for goods and services that must be imported.

Most of the benefits of tourism remain in Kathmandu Valley, except for trekking, which offers seasonal employment for Nepalis who work as porters,

Drying freshly-dyed wool in Patan Industrial Estate.

carrying goods to and through the countryside and villages. This works to inject cash into the rural economy, and stimulates local business.

Carpets

The carpet business is Nepal's only industry, surpassing even tourism as the leading foreign exchange earner contributing US$70 million compared to the US$68 million earned by tourism. Carpets are Nepal's only large-scale export.

In 1960, hardly a single carpet was being made commercially in Nepal. As recently as 1984, carpet manufacture was still considered a cottage industry, but around 1988, it shot up to become Nepal's second largest industry, in terms of hard currency earnings and the employment it generates (the industry employs about 300,000 workers).

The carpet industry owes its success largely to the enterprising community of Tibetan refugees who resettled in Kathmandu after fleeing Tibet in 1959. Most were homeless when they landed at the refugee camps in Dhorpatan, Pokhara, Chialsa and Jawalakhel.

The Swiss, who were assisting the refugees, began searching for a viable livelihood for the Tibetans. The idea of marketing a Tibetan traditional craft appealed. Traditionally, carpets in Tibet had always been a folk past time that people engaged in within their

Women in the Economy

Most women put in 10 hours of work to their husband's six hours. Yet the National Census Bureau report that the woman contributes 20 per cent less than her husband to the national economy.

Women are found to contribute 44 per cent more than men. Seen thus as "unpaid family labourers" rather than "homemakers" or "housewives," the women's role in the national economy is found to be central.

The economic activities that women participate in are largely confined to domestic and family-centred tasks. Of which the most important is work on the family farm, which supplies 80 per cent of the family's needs.

Animal husbandry, fuel and water collection and food processing are also central to women's work. Between these, and their familial tasks, women find little time or energy for economic activities with higher returns.

Outside the home, they most often sell home produce and manufactured goods. Women with an entrepreneurial knack also take to shop-keeping and inn-keeping. Some women, often from the poorest families, leave their villages for short periods for employment as porters or agricultural workers. In these jobs, they are paid less than their male counterparts.

The industrial sector provides a negligible amount of work for women, and the women who are employed in industries work in textile or carpet factories.

Employment in urban, modern areas is also low. Women constitute less than 10 per cent of all private and government employees. Factors that discourage women from formal employment range from their low educational levels, employers' favouring of men, cultural inhibitions and the lack of child-care facilities.

Few women, however, qualify as being formally unemployed, in the sense of not being able to find work for which they are skilled. Even urban women not employed in office work or teaching are involved in kitchen gardening, or in somehow providing for the family. Leisure time is known to only a few women in the upper strata of urban society.

Many development programmes in the past mistakenly assumed that women were unproductive. While these programmes provided practical help to men, such as loans, they saddled women with time-consuming and economically unprofitable tasks. Only recently have such programmes begun focusing on making women's house work more efficient, teaching them skills that may generate income, and providing them with direct loans.

But women are still a long way from being independently secure. Because of their social position as their husbands' inferior, little of what they earn belongs to them. Little wonder that most village men, in choosing a wife, look primarily not for beauty or grace, but for the ability to work hard.

Not an easy time for women.

homes. Among the refugees, only three women were adept at traditional designs and techniques. The Swiss Agency for Technical Assistance got these three women to train others, and gradually to increase production quantities for both domestic and foreign markets.

A decade later, carpets became Nepal's largest handicraft. A Tibetan carpet became a favourite memento for tourists to take back home. In time the Swiss moved out of the venture, and the Tibetans proceeded to make carpets highly profitable.

In the mid-80's, the carpet industry took off. Exports, not significant until then, began to grow tremendously, particularly in Germany and France. In

Cottage industries still thrive to service the domestic and regional markets.

homes across the valley, new abstract designs were being woven side-by-side with traditional ones. New colours and a special washing resulted in a product people could not have even begun to imagine a few years before.

Tibetans still control a major share of the business, though most of the weavers are hillfolk, particularly the Tamangs, who come from deprived village economies situated around the Valley. The labour intensive nature of the carpet industry is a boon to villagers hardpressed for cash. Without carpet-weaving, these people might be unemployed.

Meanwhile, true to their roots, Tibetans have used their hardwon affluence to build schools and monasteries to preserve their cultural identity. They do so while integrating themselves into their new home. Many Tibetans have opted for Nepali citizenship, others retain refugee identification cards, as a painful reminder of their plight.

The garment industry is also a significant export industry, having contributed US$30 million in 1990. Unfortunately, this business, like the carpet industry, is almost wholly based in Kathmandu Valley.

A hefty source of hard currency in the hills still remains the salaries and pensions of Gurkha soldiers (see p.19).

Imports and Exports

Nepal's export earnings have grown steadily, as has its demand for con-

School's out but no fun is to be had ... child labour is a common sight.

sumer goods, which it must import. The imbalance in income distribution is a contributing factor; urban centres like Kathmandu, Pokhara and towns in the Terai bristle with television antennas while over 50 per cent of the country lives without electricity. Local businessmen have begun carrying televisions, video cassette recorders, generators and gasoline to show Hindi movies in cramped rooms to villagers and charging Rs5-10 per head.

More than half of Nepal's trade is with India. In the days of the British East India Company, this trade was conducted in Nepal's favour. That changed a long time ago and the trade balance now leans heavily in India's favour. The Nepali government realises the importance of diversifying its trading partners as well as developing its own industries.

In March 1989, the Trade and Transit Treaty between the two countries lapsed before a new agreement could be reached. India closed 11 of the 13 transit points along the border and imposed transit and trade restrictions that crippled Nepal's economy. One such move reduced the supply of petroleum products. The dispute was finally settled in May 1990 by the interim government that was swept into power.

Foreign Aid

Foreign Aid contributes a significant portion towards Nepal's total national budget. In the 1984/85 budget, foreign aid grants paid for 11 per cent of expenditure while foreign aid loans paid for 21 per cent. In the same year, one-third of Nepal's total budget came from foreign sources, and the proportion of foreign aid keeps rising. According to the National Planning Commission, 45 per cent of the budget in 1989/90 was expected to come from foreign aid grants and loans. Donors to Nepal include the World Bank, the Asian Development Bank, and various United Nations agencies such as, UNICEF, FAO, UNDP and WHO. Aid also comes from donor countries such as Japan, USA, Germany, Australia, Holland, Britain, France, China, and India. In addition, more than 50 international non-governmental organisations (NGOs) engage in development activities in Nepal.

Children and Work

Sit down in any teashop in urban Nepal and a pre-teen child will take your order. In villages you are bound to see small children (usually girls) carrying wood, fodder or water. Child labour is a significant component of the workforce in Nepal. Official figures in 1981 revealed that 57 per cent of children between the age of 10 and 14 work. The percentage was about the same for boys and girls. These figures may be low as the census discounts childcare or the collection of fuel, water, and fodder, chores which are are usually performed by children, preferably girls.

Nepal is about 900km from east to west and averages 180km from north to south. Its north and south borders parallel the curve of the great Himalayan range.

Nepal is wedged between the two colossi of Asia, China to the north and India to the west, south and east. Or, as Prithvi Narayan Shah, Nepal's first king of the modern era, succinctly described this landlocked position: "Nepal is a yam between two boulders."

Apparently neither India nor China found Nepal a particularly tasty yam since neither has attempted to "swallow" it, content to leave Nepal alone. At any rate, Nepal has always needed a fine touch to balance its relations with its neighbours.

It is remarkable that a country of Nepal's size has a range of landscape and vegetation including sub-tropical jungle, mountain tundra and desert. Also remarkable are its rivers which flow from the Himalayas and cut across mountainous terrain to end in the

Waterfalls abound in the mountains.

Geography

33

Sagarmatha, the supreme at 8,848 m.

lowlands, leaving behind deep valley corridors in their wake.

Nepal can be divided into three east-to-west geographical zones. Going from north to south, these zones are the Himalayas, the Siwalik and Maha-bharat middle hills, and the lush plains of the Terai. These zones also find corre-spondence in the cultural dimension, with Mongoloid in the north, Aryan in the south and elements of both in the middle, as best illustrated by Kath-mandu.

The Himalayas

The word "Himalaya" comes from San-

skrit: hima – snow, laya – dwelling place. About one-third of the Himalayas' long sweep across Asia runs along northern Nepal. Eight of the world's 14 peaks over 8,000m are situated within Nepal, including Mount Everest (which is known as Sagarmatha in the Nepali language).

The suddenness with which the Himalayas throw themselves up is as remarkable as their height. The dis-

tance between Raajbiraj, near the Indian border, and Mount Everest, almost directly due north, is only about 180km. Raajbiraj stands at an altitude of 200m, whereas Everest soars to 8,848m.

The Himalayas form a divide between the monsoon-wet lands to the south and the Tibetan trans-Himalayan desert. Most of the major rivers of the subcontinent as well as China have their

Kathmandu Valley

source in Tibet before cutting through the range, indicating a wetter plateau before the upliftment of the Himalayas.

Over 3,000m in elevation, the Himalayan zone takes up about a quarter of Nepal's total land area. About 10 per cent of Nepal's population ekes out a living in a harsh climate ranging from alpine to arctic. The land is poor and people depend on trade and animal husbandry to make ends meet. The main crops are potatoes, buck-wheat and barley. Among the tree species are maple, birch, pines, highland scrub and brush.

The mountains are great rain-catchers or great rain blocks, depending on where you live. Lumle, in front of the Annapurna massif, receives 565cm of

rain per year. Manangbhot, only about 30km north, but on the other side of the

Hydropower Rescue

Since 1951, when Nepal entered the modern age, the country has been contemplating the goose that may lay the golden egg. It is not tourism or carpets, but hydropower.

The source of this hydropower are the 6,000 rivers and streams that flow down from the Himalayas, cutting deep gorges through one of the most mountainous terrains in the world. The potential of some 45,000 megawatts of hydro-electricity (the oft-quoted 83,000 MW may be theoretical, according to some experts) is an awesome power for a country of Nepal's size, and the only hope for one often billed as the world's third poorest.

The key to economic development lies in developing and selling this immense hydropower. It has the capacity to transform the lives of a majority of Nepal's 19 million who presently eke out a precarious subsistence livelihood. But difficult hurdles need to be crossed before the day of the Nepali water sheiks.

At present, only half a dozen rivers have been harnessed to produce a meagre 220 megawatts of hydropower, less than one per cent of Nepal's touted potential.

In a way, that says much about the complexity and challenge of following this path to

becoming "the Switzerland of the East," as some may like to put it.

The golden egg lies in the export of this hydropower to Nepal's southern neighbour, India. The main problem, as Nepalis view it, is that Nepal finds itself in a "monopsony," – a situation of having only one buyer. This creates a dependency for both countries, as seller and buyer, for whom a solution has been elusive.

Aside from securing financing from donor countries and international agencies, Nepal and India need to thrash out vital issues including that of power pricing and of control over mantainence and management of the plant. Unfortunately, these issues cannot be solved by technocrats as they are inherently political. Both sides recognise that they must negotiate, albeit with the vital ingredient of trust.

Thus, it could be some time before Nepal can use its water resources to rescue itself from perennial poverty, a while before the 85 per cent of Nepalis who presently use wood fuel can cook their *daal-bhaat* on electric stoves.

Also, though Nepal may one day become a seller of hydropower, it, ironically, faces power shortage in the immediate future.

According to recent reports, the country is already using all of its installed capacity of 220 megawatts and the demand for power is estimated to be growing by 10 per cent every year. But the next project to come on line will be the 403-megawatt Arun III, expected to be completed only by 2005 or so. There are no other smaller power projects to tide the country over in the interim period. Experts place full blame on the *Panchayat* system's lack of vision and motivation, and the inefficiencies and corruptness of its three-decade rule.

Besides Arun II, the project most talked about – with no conclusion as yet – is the Karnali Chisapani Project, a behemoth of a project the likes of which has never been seen in the Himalayas. Its envisioned capacity of 10,800 megawatt is 50 times Nepal's present capacity. And the cost is an estimated US$5 billion, which is the country's budget for two years. Given the problems ahead, Nepal's colossal power potential at present remains just that: a potential.

As mountains are thrown up, their waters bless the valleys with scenic lakes such as Pokhara.

Annapurnas (and about 1,000m higher), receives only 38cm of rain per year. The farmers living around Lumle are prosperous by Nepali standards, whereas Manangis became traders who travelled far because their land was poor.

The Mahabharat

South of the Himalayas is the Mahabharat range. Reaching heights of up to 3,000m, they would be considered mountains anywhere else in the world. The Mahabharat form a wide belt across the country's "middle," and hence they are known as the middle hills. The heartland takes about 50 per cent of Nepal's land area and is home to almost 50 per cent of its people. Nepal's two major cities, Kathmandu and Pokhara, are situated in valleys sheltered between the Mahabharat's tall ridges. These *pahar* (hill regions) are inhabited by diverse ethnic groups who were self-sufficient until their population grew beyond the land's capacity to sustain them.

This belt was originally covered with thick deciduous forests of chilaune, mock chestnut, rhododendron, oak and alder but the land has been subject to the pressures of overpopulation and deforestation. The character of the middle hills changes as you travel from east to west across the country. In the east, because the hills are bunched closer together, travel means walking to the

A yak trail on the way to Tibet.

top of a hill, down the other side, then crossing a river to start up again.

Farther west, the hills open up. Settlements are farther apart, and there are longer traverses between climbs and drops. Rainfall decreases as you move from east to west. Farms in the east are more prosperous, whereas the west's rural population cannot sustain themselves from their land and rely on trading and herding to get by.

The Terai

The southern lowlands – 60 to 280m in elevation – bordering India is called the Terai. The only large flat area in the country, the belt is a continuation of the Indo-Gangetic plain in India. The Terai is sub-divided into three east-to-west bands; an inner and outer Terai of hardly 200m height, separated by the Siwalik Hills, which go up to about 1,500m high. Composed of sandstone, shale, and marine limestone, the Siwalik are heavily eroded, barren and sparsely populated.

The inner Terai between the Siwalik and the Mahabharat is a series of long valleys also known as the "doon". In the past, its malaria-filled jungles were considered the only line of defense Nepal needed. The outer Terai is only 25 to 40km wide, a seamless extension of the Ganges plain to the south.

The Terai has always been vital to Nepal, originally because of its thick

Stony, rocky and gushy in the central Nepal area.

jungle which served as a natural barrier. Today, it has only 10 per cent of the country's total forest-cover. Prime Minister Bhimsen Thapa considered its possession important enough to wage a two-year war with the British in the early 19th century. But until recently, large parts of the Terai were uninhabitable. The tigers, elephants, rhinoceros, leopards, cobras and kraits that lived in its thick jungles were a sufficient deterrent, but the real menace was the virulent malaria (called "aul") which saturated the mosquito-infested jungle. A trip through the Terai then was virtually suicidal . A WHO mosquito eradication programme (using DDT) almost totally eliminated malaria in the 1950's.

Today, the Terai is home to about 50 per cent of Nepal's population. It has become Nepal's breadbasket, yielding more than 70 per cent of the rice, and most of its oil seed, sugar beet and tobacco. Most of Nepal's industries are located in the Terai and most of Nepal's migration is from the hills to the Terai.

Pleasant in winter, the Terai turns into a furnace during the dry months of May and June. Temperatures hover around 38°C. The monsoon arrives in late June, providing a reprieve from the heat and water for the rice crops.

Oceans and Mountains

Nepal and the Himalayas owe everything they are to the break-up of Gondwanaland millions of years ago.

8,000m peaks in Nepal

Name	Height	World Rank
Everest	8,848m	1
Kanchenjunga	8,593m	3
Lhotse	8,511m	4
Makalu	8,481m	5
Cho Oyu	8,153m	6
Dhaulagiri	8,167m	7
Manaslu	8,156m	8
Annapurna	8,091m	9

At that time Nepal was underwater, part of a vast ocean called the Tethys Sea, of which the Mediterranean is a remnant.

If you went fishing for trilobites in the Tethys Sea and anchored your boat where Kathmandu is, looking south you could see the Indian subcontinent on the horizon, coming closer slowly but relentlessly. To the north, you would be able to see the Asian continent moving closer. Great rivers dumped enormous amounts of sediment rock. As it moved closer, Asia folded this sedimentary rock into the Tibetan Marginal Range of today's Tibet-Nepal border, which includes Mount Everest.

When that happened, the sea got shallower. One day, 10 to 15 million years ago, it turned into dry land. The Indian subcontinent collided with Asia, pushing itself over and against Asia in what is now called the Main Central Thrust, forming the main Himalayan chain and lifting the Tibetan Marginal Chain higher. These huge forces formed the Tibetan plateau.

Clouds bumping into the new barrier of mountains pour increasing rain. The south-flowing rivers, such as the Kali Gandaki and Arun, with a steeper gradient from the uplifting and an increased volume from the heavier rain, carved steep gorges through the mountains. About 600,000 years ago, more thrusting raised the main Himalayan range even higher, blocking some rivers. Rara Lake, Nepal's largest natural lake, was formed at this time.

A short time later, a vast major geological commotion formed the Mahabharat Lekh and the Siwaliks. The rivers had difficulty forcing their course through this new barrier. Running east to west, only three managed to incise the Mahabharat; the Karnali (at Chisopani) in the west, the Kali Gandaki (at Deoghat) in the centre, and the Kosi (at Barahchhetra) in the east.

More lakes were formed, including one filling the Kathmandu Valley which dried up 200,000 years ago.

Today, Asia and India are still colliding. Beneath the earth's crust, two currents of magma, one from the north and one from the south, join and plunge towards the earth's core along the line of the Himalayas. The magma currents push the earth's crust to twice its normal thickness of 35km and pull and tug on the plates. The Himalayas are constantly shifting, resettling, and being pushed higher.

Shifting below means earthquakes, and Nepal is one of the most seismically active places on the planet. Most of the earthquakes pass unnoticed, but larger

ones regularly devastate Nepal. In 1988, an earthquake in the east killed a thousand and left thousands homeless. A decade earlier, another quake in the west had similar results. In 1934, large areas of Kathmandu were destroyed and thousands were killed. In 1833, a large quake devastated the entire valley. The worst quake on record occurred in 1255, killing more than a third of the Valley.

Hot springs, a pleasant result of tectonic faultlines at Lattamarang.

Hot Water

While trekking in the middle hills, you will hear of places called *taatopaani* (hot springs). Hot springs are found in the vicinity of the main central thrust, indicating tectonic faultlines or rupture lines in the earth's crust.

Rest assured, magma will not well up any second; instead you may be able to take a hot bath or shower. Ask the local people if it is used for bathing; few experiences can top a hot soak while on a trek. One of the most famous hot water springs is Taatopaani on the Jomosom trail. Several more are spread over the Annapurna Circuit trek.

To the naturalist, Nepal, with its wonderful variety of climate and vegetation, is one of the most interesting countries in the world, for not only does its fauna vary with the wide range of altitude of its mountains, but it also varies strikingly as one proceeds from east to west.

Percival Landon in **Nepal**, 1928.

Mountains and Rain

Its astounding geography and the monsoons give Nepal its wide variety of flora and fauna. The monsoon is lighter the further west you go, as it breaks on the barrier of mountains. The disparate profiles and heights of the mountains create rain breaks which vary in size, shape and in the amount of rain they catch. Temperatures vary with altitude and all these factors combine to give Nepal its diversity of microclimates.

Hardy yaks in east Nepal.

Jungles and Beasts of the Terai

The Terai, with its semitropical climate, was once covered in forests. Although much of the land has come under cultivation,

Flora and Fauna

45

there remain impressive forest areas. The primary tree is a hardwood called *sal* which, like mahogany, is used in furniture-making and is an important cash crop.

The thick Terai jungles, in particular the valleys of the inner Terai, have always supported a rich variety of wildlife. Today, their most famous inhabitants, the Royal Bengal Tiger and the Great Asian One-horned Rhinoceros, are almost exclusively found in the national parks and forest reserves, of which the most famous is the Royal Chitwan National Park.

Much effort is being made to preserve such endangered species as the tiger and rhino.

Spy a tiger at Royal Chitwan National Park.

Other species of wildlife include wild buffalo (gaur), leopard, sloth bear, barking deer, hog deer (a favorite prey for tiger), wild boar, monkey, otter and a number of small jungle and civet cats. There are also two kinds of crocodiles; the needle-nosed fish-only eating Gharial, which has not been known to attack man, and the marsh mugger, blunt-snouted and dangerous.

King cobras, kraits, and pythons slither through the undergrowth in Chitwan. The park is particularly rich in birdlife, with about 300 species identified in Chitwan alone.

Wild Elephants

Wild elephants roamed the Terai for many years. In the 1850s, a Dr Olfield's **Sketches of Nepal** described an elephant "roundup" which dispatched tame elephants into a wild herd to trap them:

"This elephantine mass kept swaying backwards and forward till they came close on the edge of the river, where... it was very deep. In rushed the wild ones closely pursued... by the tame ones, as well as their own young ones. The water was soon over their heads, but still the scrimmaging went on; the mahouts clung, like leeches, with wonderful tenacity to their elephants, as the water deepened each mahout raising himself into a standing position on the elephant's back; so that as the elephant swam along you could see the tip of his trunk only above the water, and about

Another inmate at Chitwan.

a yard behind it the black head and shoulders of the mahout...

There must have been altogether about twenty elephants in the water together, all pushing, wallowing, fighting, trumpeting, rolling like a party of hippopotami having a frolic, and the little mahouts popping up and down here and there among them, busy in taking advantage of the confusion to secure the ropes round the wild ones' necks....

During the melee the mahouts had managed to secure the lasso round the neck of every one of the wild elephants, seven in all..."

Today the wild elephants are gone – though sightings are reported in Western Nepal – but the back of an elephant is still the main means of sightseeing in Chitwan.

The Middle Hills: Just Surviving

The situation is different in the middle hills area because of the decrease in rain from east to west. In the west there are oaks and chir pine, fir and birch. At higher elevations blue pine, hemlock, and some juniper are found. In the far north-west, tall stands of blue pine on south-facing slopes and spruce on the north and west make for an enjoyable walk. Apricot, walnut and apple are also found.

In central Nepal, vegetation is in an

Environment & Conservation

The ecological fragility of the Himalayas is often disguised by their serenity and majesty. The Himalayas and their foothills are, in fact, dynamic.

As the world's youngest mountains continue their slow collision against the Tibetan Plateau, the lands below are besieged by recurring earthquakes, flashfloods, landslides and natural dams.

In order for human and wildlife habitations to survive in these conditions, human beings must strike a delicate balance with the environment, taking great care not to add new pressures. Nepali villagers, intimately familiar with the volatility of these mountains, understand that their long-term survival hinges on their ability to live with nature.

But of late, this balance has been impossible to maintain.

The country's population is growing at the rate of 2.7 per cent a year, and its demands from the land are increasing. The scarcity of arable land has led villagers to clear forests for fields and settlements, and to plunder them for firewood.

Deforestation, once unknown in Nepal, is now occurring at an alarming rate – 3 per cent of the country's forests are disappearing each year. With that has come the increased erosion of precious fertile topsoil, and the increased incidence of landslides.

One of the most serious consequences of deforestation, is the devastation of the natural habitat of Nepal's wildlife. The tremendous genetic diversity of Nepal's plant and animal species is diminishing. Several rare animals, such as the legendary Snow Leopard and the Himalayan Musk Deer are under threat of extinction.

Others, like the Wild Asiatic Elephant, and Gharyal, a rare species of crocodile, which are now classified as vulnerable or rare, will meet the same fate if the present trend continues unchecked.

Some measures have been taken to remedy the situation. In recognition of the importance of providing sanctuary to endangered animals, wildlife reserves have been established in Shukla

Conferred with the right to survive, these rhinos at times annoy the farmers.

east-west transition as well as a north-south one. Trees common to the west are usually found on south faces and eastern species are found in the north. Rhododendron forests are common in this region. Even more common are whole forests of rhododendron which, in spring, turn whole hillsides red, white, and pink. In the east, the middle hills have subtropical forests at lower elevations. These give way to broadleaf forests which, higher up, give way to evergreens.

Phanta, Bardia, Parsa and Kosi Tapu. National parks , which aim to preserve unique ecologies, have been established in Khaptad, Rara, Shey-Phoksumdo, Chitwan, Langtang, Sagarmatha and Barun-Makalu.

A Conservation Area, which differs from the others in its attempt to integrate human settlements into conservation efforts, has been established at the base of the Annapurnas. In addition, a hunting reserve has been established in Dhorpatan. All together, close to 15,000 square km are protected from environmental damage.

While parks and reserves obviously play a central role in conservation, they do not relieve the larger problem of the population's increasing demand.

The destruction of forests continues unabated in unprotected parts of the country. At this rate, warn environmentalists, Nepal may lose its forests in the next thirty years.

Perhaps the only way to solve this nationwide crisis is through the effective utilisation of natural resources. For instance, agricultural income, which sustains 90 per cent of the population, could be supplemented or replaced by alternate, non-agricultural sources of income. This would entail the establishment of small-scale cottage and rural industries, animal rais-

Trees are often decorated by parasitic beauties.

ing, and tourism-related trade. Firewood, now used by most for cooking, could be replaced by electricity generated by small hydropower projects, or by kerosene. Current farming practices could be replaced by more productive techniques, so as to reduce the pressure to turn more forests into farmland. In these various ways, the demands on the land could be fulfilled more efficiently and the serious threat of deforestation slowly curtailed.

Responding to these challenges is no easy task, but a failure to do so would not only lead to a devastating loss of Nepal's wealth, but also threaten the very survival of the Nepalese people.

The red rhododendron blossom *laliguras* is Nepal's national flower.

Wildlife in the middle hills tries to survive in areas which have not yet been cultivated, but these areas are becoming increasingly scarce. Leopard, several types of deer, goat, goat-antelope, and Himalayan black bear are some of the larger inhabitants. There are also wild boar, *langur* and *rhesus* monkey and the rarely-seen *red panda*.

At night the eerie human-like cries of jackals can be heard. Mongoose, weasels, porcupines and several types of wild cats are also found.

The Himalayas

The vegetation in the Himalayan belt, above the tree line, is similar to that found in other mountainous areas.

Plants can be found up to about 6,100m. Plants blossom between April and October, making the most of the monsoon. Watch for primulas, polygonums, edelweiss, gentians, and larkspurs.

Wildlife in this high Himalayan zone is mostly found in the rainshadow area north of the Himalaya. Musk deer, protected by law, are prized by poachers for the supposed medicinal properties of their musk glands. Blue sheep – short-legged, broadbacked, golden-eyed and usually brown and not blue, may sometimes be spotted at dawn and dusk. Also found are wolves, brown bears and lynx.

The natural habitat of Nepal's national bird, the *Danphe* (Impeyan Pheasant), is at altitudes of between 2,600m and 4,575m. You will be struck by the beauty of its iridescent nine-coloured coat.

Laliguras, the national flower.

The Snow Leopard

Recent research has revealed that the existence of the snow leopard may not be as precarious as it once seemed to be. Solitary and shy, the habitat of this beautiful creature happens to be one of the earth's most remote, inhospitable environments, and perhaps that is why the creature invokes such universal sympathy in all of us. Until quite recently, the snow leopard was so rarely seen it was beginning to attain a semi-mythical status. It was his personal journey during his search for the snow leopard that became the subject of Peter Matthiessen's book **The Snow Leopard**.

Several years ago, Rodney Jackson successfully tracked the snow leopard, using radio-telemetry. Since then, much more has become known about the snow leopard's habits and social system, but sighting it is still a cause for celebration. Snow leopards are not particularly big, weighing about 45kg and are not more than 2m long, about half of which is composed of its splendid thick tail. Pale frosty gray with black rosettes, icy gray eyes set wide in a classic leopard face, huge paws used in walking on snow or launching its powerful leaps, it is indeed a sight anybody would be fortunate to catch.

The Snow Leopards are cunning hunters, who are capable of killing prey more than twice their own weight although they sometimes kill livestock, including young yak. The Tibetan hero, Milarepa, is said to have assumed the form of a snow leopard to defeat the demons at Mount Everest. The creature

He Is Or He Isn't

The Sherpas call him *Yeh-tch*, or "monkey of rocky places." But the rest of the world knows him as the *Yeti*, the "abominable snowman."

The enigma of the creature's existence remains one of the intriguing quetions of the Himalayas. According to most accounts, the *Yeti* is about the size of a man with longer arms, large out-sized feet, a body covered with red, black or blond hair, and a bullet-shaped head. Granted, not the picture of handsomeness!

At first Westerners dismissed early accounts of the *Yeti* as local superstition. Then in 1899, Major LA Waddell, a British expert on Tibet, came across what looked like *Yeti* footprints in the snow. In 1921, Colonel CK Howard-Bury, leading a reconnaissance party to the north side of Everest, reported seeing dark figures and later found huge footprints in the snow. In later years, similar footprints were reported by experienced and credible mountaineers such as HW Tilman and John Hunt.

In November 1951, noted climber Eric

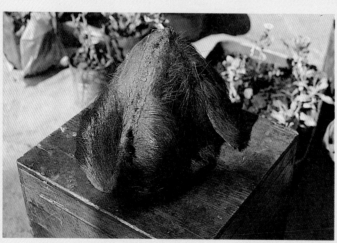

Monkeys of the rocky places ... one scalped and on display at Pangboche monastery in the Everest area.

Shipton took photos of mysterious footprints conjectured to be the *Yeti's*. The tide in the *Yeti* legend suddenly surged to prompt several search expeditions for the creature. None of them returned with conclusive evidence.

In 1960, Sir Edmund Hillary led an expedition to the region around Gauri Shanker where Shipton had taken his photos. The expedition returned with several furs, the famous *Yeti* scalp of Khumjung, and photos of many possible footprints. Tests conducted in foreign labs determined the "scalp" to be a serow, a type of Himalayan goat; the other furs belonged to the Tibetan blue bear, and the footprints, it was concluded, were of ordinary animals melted into strange shapes by the sun.

The doubters snorted and declared the proof conclusive that the *Yeti* was a hoax, but belevers refused to dissapear.

Then in 1974, a Sherpa woman grazing her yaks near Machhermo was attacked by a creature that bounded from behind a rock, injuring her shoulder. The "thing" then attacked and killed several of her yaks. The woman, (unfortunately for science), passed out just then, but the horns lay on the ground as if they had been snapped off the yaks. Police inspected the carcasses and concluded the handiwork could not have been any human being's. The event revived the speculation in the Himalayan phantom.

In 1974 and 1980, climbing expeditions found strange footprints around their camps. Screams rented the air when they started to follow the tracks.

In 1983, the late writer Bruce Chatwin came across a set of mysterious footprints in the snow near Gokyo at 15,000ft. In any case, the evidence is not in yet to dismiss the *Yeti*. Remember that until recently, we knew next to nothing about the snow leopard. The *Yeti* may well be a creature of greater cunning in successfully avoiding human contact.

is often hunted, however, by humans for the commercial value of their skin.

Parks and People

There are few large tracts of wilderness left in the country. Population pressure has pushed people ever in search of land to live wherever possible. When a tract of land is turned into a park, the protected area, however, claims the homes of people who have lived there for generations.

When Nepal's first park – The **Rara National Park** was established in 1956, the inhabitants of two villages were displaced. Forced to leave homes and land that had been theirs for more than a century, they became "refugees," to be resettled on newly cleared land in the Terai. Within a few years, only about half the population of one village had survived.

Generally, even after a park has been established, conflicts rise between the park and the villages surrounding it. Rhinos from Chitwan regularly cross the Rapti River boundary to ruin crops nearby. The loss can be devastating to most of Nepal's subsistence farmers.

Likewise, the monkeys that prove an entertaining distraction on the trails, are in fact one of the worst enemies of farmers. A troop of monkeys can denude a field of crops in no time. The food the monkeys eat deprives the farmer and his family of sustenance.

Once an area is established as a

Birding In Nepal

Over 840 different birds have been recorded in Nepal. An unusually high number for a relatively small country. This is not because Nepal is a centre for endemism, in fact only one species, the *Spiny Babbler*, is found; rather Nepal is at an ornithological cross-road; bird populations from the northern Palearctic region and the Oriental region to the southeast meet and overlap here, 122 eastern species extend no further west than Nepal and 22 western species extend no further east! There are important corridors for trans-Himalayan and East/West migratory birds, and Nepal has a wide variety of habitats allowing many different birds and animals to settle, from low wetlands to montane forests and high alpine regions.

The tropical lowland regions in the south offer the best avian diversity, 589 species are regarded as lowland birds occurring mainly below the 300m contour. The large Chitwan National Park is a popular site where 450 different birds have been recorded. Originally gazetted to protect the Indian Rhinoceros and other large mammals by preserving the habitat of riverine grasslands and forests the park also preserves the birdlife! The Park is the ideal location for spotting open country birds like bee-eaters, crakes, bitterns as well as numerous birds of prey such as the woodlands pigeons, woodpeckers, sunbirds and babblers; remember to look out for the majestic Great Hornbill near Tiger Tops.

Further east, about 10-11 hours' bus ride from Kathmandu, is the important wetland Kosi Barrage which is perhaps the best place in Nepal to see migratory and local resident marshland birds. The period February to May is regarded as the peak season where practically all the ducks, herons, waders, storks, gulls on the Nepalese checklist can be spotted, in the tens of thousends!

Other good birding sites in the south include Kosi Tapu and Dharan in the east where many Oriental species are seen and in the far west the little visited Bardia Wildlife Reserve which is the best place to see western lowland birds.

This zone between 1,000 and 2,700m above sea level is perhaps the most rewarding for

birdwatching in Nepal because there is still a lot of vegetation cover at this elevation and a correspondingly high species diversity, and this is also where you will see most of the unique Himalayan montane birds.

The Kathmandu Valley area with the surrounding hills is the main location here, heavily populated of course and the environment somewhat degraded but there are still places to go. The Bagmati and Manora Rivers are close by and good for open country birds like waders, pipits, warblers and other passage migrants. Just 12km north of Kathmandu lies the Sheopuri Wildlife Reserve with many forest birds like barbets, thrushes, and flycatchers. A little further to the south past Godevari where the Botanical Gardens is well worth visiting lies Phulchowki, peaking at 2760m and probably the best location for montane birds, including Oriental specialities like leafbirds, minivets, forktails and many babbler species typical of this upper montane habitat.

Birdwatching in the Himalayas is like any other trip into the mountains: you go trekking and look around! The Jomosom Trek is one of the most popular and the keen birdwatcher can see 200 species here over a couple of weeks, including the Danphe Pheasant, the national bird of Nepal, and several other spectacular pheasant species as well as anything from tiny finches and buntings in the bushes to giant vultures soaring overhead.

Closer to Kathmandu in the mountains just to the north Gosainkund and Langtang are other popular treks where high altitude birds

Clockwise from left: Mountain Bulbul, Great Hornbill, Silver-eared Mesia, Cattle Egret.

can be spotted. The west is less explored and the bird-life here is not as well known, treks north of Jumla however have got a lot of potential. But for scenery and alpine avifauna there is no grander place than the Sagarmatha National Park at Mount Everest in the Khumbu region. As you ascend the habitat becomes more barren and the number of bird species decline, "only" 77 species have been recorded in Nepal in the high alpine zone above 4,270m where no trees can grow – they include some rare Himalayan specialists that you are unlikely to ever see again anyplace else!.

For full enjoyment of Nepalese birds bring a pair of lightweight binoculars and a field guide so you can identify and recognise the many different species. Robert L. Flemming's **Birds of Nepal**, Avalok 1976, is the book to carry with you. For the latest scientific details get Carol & Tim Inskipp's **A Guide to the Birds of Nepal**, Tanager Books 1985, and for practical advise Carol Inskipp's **A Birdwatcher's Guide to Nepal**, 1988.

The rhododendron, a tree at mid-levels, a shrub as the altitude changes.

national park, farmers lose their traditional use of the forest resources and must search for alternative sources of firewood and animal fodder. This often entails walking longer distances to other sources, extra time and work performed usually by women and girls.

Little wonder that farmers often resent the national parks that have been imposed on them, especially if they are

the poorer for it. Obviously parks must be created, but not at the expense of people trying to eke out a threadbare living from their environment.

The Nepali government is making efforts in conservation. The Annapurna Conservation Area Project (ACAP), be-

gun a few years ago, represents an enlightened approach. The ACAP seeks to protect the environment by educating and training villagers on their role in this undertaking in a way which accrues material and educational benefits to them in the process.

People

Over the centuries wave after wave of immigrants have found safe haven in Nepal. People of Mongoloid stock struggled over the high mountains from the north, and Aryan groups somehow made it through the Terai's deadly jungle.

They met in the hills and valleys of Nepal. What is so remarkable, is that these very disparate groups of people somehow managed to live in peace next to one another. Nepal did not become a "melting pot". Each group has retained its own language and culture through the generations.

A dark-skinned Nepalese beauty.

Today there are more than 30 languages and dialects and as many distinct ethnic groups. The rugged terrain keeps the regions isolated so that often people in adjacent valleys speak dialects which are unintelligible to each other.

Caste Hindus

The Moghul invasion and conquests forced a major migration of caste Hindus from the plains of India between the 12th and the 15th centuries. The vast majority of the Hindus in the hills today

A saddhu reads holy scriptures in the grounds of Pashupatinath Temple.

are their descendants.

Hinduism, a way of life as much as a religion, structures society with its hierarchical caste system. The majority of the settlers were from the *brahman* (priestly) and *chhetri* (warrior) castes. Leaders in India, they dominated the political and social structure in their new home as well.

Coming from the plains, they settled in the lower elevations of Nepal's hills and mountains, where they can be found to this day. The Nepali language was born from them and caste Hindus are one of the few groups for whom Nepali is a native tongue.

They are still a very dominant group in hill society. They marry strictly within their caste and marriages are arranged by their parents. *Brahmans* tend to marry

young. Marrying off a daughter is a great obligation for her parents, who will usually want to discharge it quickly. Though outlawed, child marriages still continue.

Although some of the restrictions regarding diet (no liquor, onions, garlic, and some kinds of meat) are less strictly observed in Kathmandu and urban centres, these prohibitions are rarely broken in the villages.

Chhetris observe many of the same customs as *brahmans*. Their marriages are arranged within their caste and they are subject to the same dietary restrictions. Nepal's royalty are Thakuri *chhetris* who are said to have come from Rajasthan. There is one group of *chhetris* in the west called *matwali* (liquor drinkers) who have lost the right to wear the

Ladies' day during the Teej Festival.

janai (sacred thread of their divine birth).

Among both these groups divorce is almost non-existent. Traditionally, men often took a second or third wife if no son was born from present marriages. Although outlawed, this practice still occurs.

These castes were the only educated groups and so they monopolised jobs which required a formal education. They are still dominant in the civil service, teaching, money-lending and many are also farmers and shopkeepers.

Only in the far northwest do *brahmans* and *chhetris* live at the same high elevations as *bhotiyas*. It is also the only place where high-caste Hindus make their living off the trade between Nepal and Tibet, as their Buddhist neighbours.

As ready-made clothes, shoes, tools, and other consumer goods are increasingly available in Nepal's hills, the lower-caste Hindus designated to produce these items are finding fewer takers for their products and services. As a result, many now work as tenant farmers, porters and day labourers.

The lower castes continue to suffer the brunt of traditional prejudices. Their entry into homes is restricted, and often, instead of going into a tea-shop, they will squat on the door-sill. After drinking their tea, they will wash their own glasses and leave them by the door. Of course, the tea-shop owner will wash the glass again. When receiving anything, they cup their hands so that the item can be dropped in. Many of these restrictions are not enforced but tacitly

body into pieces to be fed to vultures.

The Hill Tribes

Over time, numerous Mongoloid groups crossed the Himalayas to settle in Nepal. Each has re-

The Sherpas, a robust and resilient people.

understood as "correct behavior."

Rituals over death vary with different groups. All Hindus cremate their dead on river banks, then scatter the ashes into rivers which eventually flow into the sacred Ganga. Some hill tribes cremate their dead, others such as the Rais and Limbus bury their dead. Bhotiyas, living where the ground is hard and rocky and where there is little firewood, often follow the Tibetan practice of chopping the

mained separate, proud and culturally self-sufficient. These groups are usually Buddhist, though Sanskritised over centuries, and they sharply differ from the Indo-Aryan groups.

Inter-ethnic marriage is still rare, but within their own tribe young people often have a say in their "arranged" marriages. Several groups observe marriage by ritual kidnapping. The boy kid-

Tibetan women setting up prayer flags.

naps a potential bride, with or without her consent, and takes her home and courts her, chaperoned by his family. If by the end of three days he has failed to win her, she is entitled to leave. Some ethnic groups believe in cross-cousin marriages.

The hill groups live at higher elevations than caste Hindus. Too high for rice, millet, corn, or wheat, they grow potatoes and buckwheat. They lead a pastoral lifestyle, spending months in high mountain pastures with large sheep and goat herds. Many of the men carry a *khukuri*, the Nepali curved-blade knife, handily tucked in their waist sash.

The hill-folk are generally less inhibited and tend to be more open with

Rais and Limbus are famed for their service as Gurkha soldiers.

strangers than most caste Hindus. Their women are more likely to interact with you, and even crack jokes at your expense.

In the east live Rais and Limbus, descendants of the Kirati tribe which once ruled the Kathmandu Valley. Many of the men carry large *khukuris* tucked in their belts. Limbus have a reputation for being quick-tempered and ready to use their *khukuris* at the drop of a *topi*.

Both groups are

Nepalis of Tibetan origin are steeped in Buddhist practices, such as their yearly dedication to monkhood.

famed for their service as Gurkha soldiers (see p.19). They also work in the tea plantations of Ilam and Darjeeling and travel all over India for work. You are likely to meet Rais and Limbus while trekking in the Solu Khumbu area and eastward. Look for them at Namche's weekly bazaar.

The middle-hill people are thought of as caste-less, but that is not quite true. Limbus, for example, have over 20 different *thars* (clans), and Gurungs have a group of four upper and sixteen lower *thars*, between which marriage is not encouraged.

Tamangs are one of Nepal's largest ethnic groups. They mainly live in the area surrounding Kathmandu. *Tamang* means "horse soldier" in Tibetan, suggesting an earlier incarnation as Tibetan cavalrymen. They are Buddhists with their own *lamas* (priests), though they also have their own *jhankris* too. They are mainly farmers, but many are found in Kathmandu driving taxis, three-wheelers and *rickshaws*, and often working as porters.

Gurungs, another Mongoloid group, live mainly in the hills of Lamjung and Kaski. They live in larger villages; Ghandruk, the largest, has more than 700 homes. Among the Gurungs many are Gurkha soldiers, and it is a rare house that does not have a military connection. The *rodi* is a noteworthy Gurung invention. Boys and girls in their adolescence form a club with an elderly man or woman as adviser. The chaperone's house is turned into a dor-

Village Life

Life in rural Nepal is simple, revolving around daily necessities. Far from idyllic, it is marked by a struggle for food, fuel, animal fodder, water and a cash-income for other needs.

A village family comes to life with the proverbial crow of a rooster, as early as 4 am. The family consists of Bhim Bahadur and his wife, grandmother, Bhim's married son and his daughter-in-law, Bhim's younger son and daughter. Typically, Bhim's wife is first out of bed, a straw mat on the floor. She sweeps the house with a broom made out of little branches.

The daughter-in-law is up next. She lights the wood fire and begins cooking breakfast while her 18-month boy cries and crawls after her. The baby's crying wakes up the gnarled grandmother, (a tough woman who has lived in these harsh conditions longer than anybody else), then the man of the house and his elder son. After grandmother finishes her chanting, she yells at the dozing younger members that the day is half-gone! Sleepy-eyed, the girl wakes up and heads (with a brass or aluminium vessel) to the stream or "tap" to fetchwater.

The deaf-mute servant, who sleeps in a shack nearby, arrives with a half-filled pail of milk, fresh from the family's cows. Breakfast cooking, the wife, with smoke in her eyes, picks up her baby, admonishing and cooing in turn.

Everyone gathers to eat breakfast – millet bread, potatoes, and fresh milk. Then they disperse to do the day's chores.

Bhim and his son leave for the fields to plough, plant, fertilise, or harvest their crop – maize, millet, rice, or wheat, depending on the slope of their plot, how close the water is, and the elevation of the terrain. The son, 19, married two years ago, stopped going to the village school after he turned 13 and could help his father. Three years of casual attendance in the two-room windowless stone house taught him to read and write, but today this knowledge is of no use.

With the infant strapped on her back, the daughter-in-law goes to the stream to wash some grain and clothes. Bhim's wife heads out to fetch wood and fodder for the cattle. She calls out to her childhood friend, who, it turns out, is on the same chore today. The deaf-mute takes the four heads of cattle to graze on a slope with scraggly grass. The two younger ones alternate play with work; as casual students, they have not been at *i-skool* for 10 days.

The afternoon sun beating strongly, Bhim and his son break for lunch beneath a *pipal* tree. Lunch is millet bread, curd, and some roasted corn. Bhim's wife and her friend also stop for a rest and something to eat, their bamboo *dokos* piled high with branches and grass.

Back at the house, the daughter-in-law is trying to quieten her screaming baby, but the day is not far off when he will get less attention. Realising that it is feed time, she warms up some cow's milk and millet porridge. That and her own milk make up the infant's diet.

The day wanes; one by one, everyone returns home. Bhim and his son are perspiring, their faces flushed. The wife dumps the *doko*-full of greens and some wood near the shed. The wood she gathered will be used for fuel instead of cowdung or "cooking bread," which can be used to fertilise the field.

The sun has set. Before long, everyone sits to eat the evening meal which the daughter-in-law has somehow managed to cook. It is millet or wheat porridge, or *dhido*, with radish leaves as garnish. The wood fire and the lone oil lamp cast shadows on the room and the yard; the elders squat with visiting neighbors, some of them spilling out onto the front porch, puffing filterless cigarettes as they discuss crops and politics.

The sky is lit with stars. One by one, family members head to their hard floor beds. Talk fades into murmur. From his bed, Bhim continues talking while his wife and the daughter-in-law wash pots, then put out the fire, and are finally done. Fortunately, there is not much in the way of entertainment to keep sleep away from these tired bodies.

Siklis village in the Annapurna region.

mitory called the *rodi*, where members work together and mix socially.

Later, visits are exchanged between boy and girl *rodis* when the host *rodi* provides food and entertainment and the visiting *rodi* leaves presents; often romances begin and subsequently end in marriages. In essence, the *rodi* is an indigenous "modern" institution that helps young Gurungs in their coming of age.

The Thakalis living in the valley of the Kali Gandaki have a reputation far beyond their deep wind-swept valleys. They are skilled hoteliers and savvy businessmen and women.

Magars, a Mongoloid group known to have had a long military tradition, once had a powerful kingdom called Barh-Mangrant (12 Principalities) in their homeland in central Nepal. They remain one of the core group of the Gurkhas. Long exposed to Hinduism, they are the most Hinduised of the ethnic groups and have largely lost their own language, *Magar Kura*.

All across the northern edge of Nepal are the Bhotiya, a collective term for several distinct ethnic groups inhabiting the trans-Himalayan region. Their languages and cultures are basically Tibetan. Most are Buddhist, some are *Bonpo*, practicing the pre-Buddhist sha-

manistic religion of *Bon*. These high-landers grow barley, potatoes, and buck-wheat and they typically combine farming with the herding of sheep, goat, and yak, which are used to carry goods for trade. Among them, one woman may be married to two or more brothers, a custom brought on more by economic consideration than anything else. The best known Bhotiya group are the Sherpas, who live mainly in the Solu Khumbu area.

Before its eradication, malaria made the Terai largely uninhabitable except for the Tharus group, who somehow seemed naturally immune to it. The Tharus cleared the jungles for farming and worshipped their own animistic deities. The opening of the Terai to accommodate migrating hill people is putting pressure on this region.

Marriages are arranged and there is also the custom of a boy working for a girl's family for two to three years to earn the right to marry her. The Chitwan is one of the areas that has a high concentration of Tharu people.

The Kathmandu Valley owes most of its cultural achievements and great vitality to the Newars, the Valley's indigenous people. The matter of their origins is still debated, but it is quite probable that the Newars have been

A Newari in
Bhaktapur.

here since prehistory.

The Newars are of mixed Mongoloid and Aryan blood. One result of this mix is the Newari language which belongs to the Tibeto-Burman family. Another is a people with great creativity. The great temples and palaces may have been ordered by the Mallas and Shahs, but it is the artistry and skill of Newari craftsmen we admire when we look at them.

Newars are found in all the major towns of Nepal. Outside the Valley they are almost exclusively traders and shopkeepers. Inside the Valley they are a microcosm of Nepal, a parallel society of their own.

In his seminal work, **People of Nepal**, Dor Bahadur Bista writes:

"Sub-divisions within Newar society are...unique and involved. One's religion is either Hindu or Buddhist or both; and furthermore, one belongs to a particular sub-group which is ranked in order by the rules of the caste hierarchy."

Newar society has its own caste system, with the intricate subdivisions of the Indo-Aryans. You can identify a man's caste from his name. For example, *Shresthas* are merchants, and *Sakyas* are silver and goldsmiths. The women wearing black saris with a red stripe border belong to the *Jyapu* farmer caste, which in turn is subdivided.

The Newars are a townspeople. Even their farmers live in multi-storey brick homes pressed tight around a courtyard or against the street curb. Inside these houses are large joint families of up to three generations.

Outside the family the most important social unit is the *guthi*, an organisation which can be social, religious, or economic. A *guthi* often denotes a person's socio-economic status, and membership of the *guthis* can be bought like the membership of a country club.

Marriages are usually arranged by parents. Marriages outside one's caste are still rare. Divorce is frowned upon, but a unique ceremony makes allowance for it. At the age of 7 or 8, girls are married to the god Narayan in the form of a *bel* (fruit) which means they will never be widows and they cannot be divorced.

Religion

On the north side of Kasthamandap sits the small temple of Ashok Binayak, more commonly called Maru Ganesh. Dwarfed by its neighbours in size and reputation, this small plain temple is one of the most dynamic corners of Kathmandu.

From dawn to dusk worshippers arrive. Men in *topis* and suit coats, faces wrapped in mufflers, pause and bow on their way. Women carrying their shopping in nylon bags walk clockwise around the temple, throwing a small coin into the shrine before moving on.

Siren-red Ganesh at Pashupatinath Temple, Kathmandu.

People wait in line to do *puja* in the cramped interior. Each person carries a small tray with water, a small lit oil lamp, flower petals, *sindoor* (red powder), and sweets. A little of each is offered as *bheti* to the image of Ganesh; then the worshipper sprinkles a little *prasad* (blessing) from the gods on his or her own head.

Meanwhile, all around the temple is the whirl of daily life. A flower-seller sprinkles water on garlands of glowing marigolds; a customer haggles with a vegetable vendor; a cow makes a sudden reach for an alluring pile of spinach but is waved off. Children play with coins while men squat holding glasses of steaming milky tea beside the tea-maker's roaring kerosene stove. Behind them a black stone Buddha sits in meditation. And a tourist contemplates how to photograph it all.

Here the different threads of human life seem to belong to one fabric. No clear line seems to separate the sacred from the mundane, the religious from the social activities; rather, they occur side-by-side, without intruding on each other.

A Tibetan Gelugpa (yellow hat) Lama in ceremonial robes.

Mutual Tolerance

Under the monarchy, Nepal proclaimed itself "the only Hindu Kingdom in the world." It was illegal to change the religion one was born into as it was to proselytise.

Nepal's interim government in 1990, declaring religious freedom as a right, released more than 30 persons who had been imprisoned for infractions to do with religion.

According to the 1981 census data, Nepal is 89 per cent Hindu, 5 per cent Buddhist, and 3 per cent Moslem, with the remainder Jain, Christian, or "other," but these figures may not be quite so accurate. Many ethnic groups in the hills are Shamanists more than they are either Hindus or Buddhists, or they are a little of all three, though many are likely to call themselves Hindu.

Hindus and Buddhists have lived together peacefully for centuries, often reinterpreting the other's beliefs to fit their own or worshipping deities common to them, the "commingling" that Nepal is rightly known for. Indeed, Nepal may be proud of its religious tolerance.

Buddhists see the Hindu trinity of Brahma, Shiva and Vishnu as manifestations of the original, primeaval Buddha. Hindus, far from rejecting the Buddha, have added his teachings to their great tradition of philosophies and beliefs, holding the Buddha to be an incarnation of the god Vishnu.

Hindu Gods and Goddesses

The various aspects of the single "Om" are represented by Hinduism's myriad gods and goddesses. The Hindu trinity consists of Brahma the creator, Vishnu the preserver and Shiva the destroyer.

Brahma created the cosmos and the other gods and goddesses. However, he is less actively worshipped.

Vishnu, often called Narayan in Nepal, is the protector and preserver. He takes on many *avatars* (incarnations), including that of the man-lion Narsingha. Hindus consider Ram, hero of the *Ramayana*, and the Buddha, as *avatars* of Vishnu. His vehicle is Garuda, the man-eagle. Vishnu's consort is Lakshmi, goddess of wealth, to whom lamps are lit at the *Tihar Festival*.

Shiva, the most popular god in Nepal, is a complex personality. Shiva is represented by the icon *lingam*, a phallic-shaped symbol of fertility. Shiva temples often carry a *trisul* (trident) and his mount Nandi the bull is itself a fertility symbol. Another popular image of Shiva is the loving husband with his consort Parvati.

Shiva is both destroyer and recreator. He is *Nataraj* (King of Dance), as well as Bhairav in his

Brahma alcoved at
Changu Narayan.

tantric form who revels in the dance of destruction. Shiva sometimes prowls graveyards and cavorts with ghosts and spirits, and is most often depicted as an ash-smeared *Yogi* with the third, vertical eye of complete knowledge.

Ganesh, Shiva's son, with his elephant head and potbelly, perched on his vehicle – a mouse – is everybody's favourite. Sri Ganesh is prayed to before any activity or journey is undertaken. The belief is Shiva accidentally chopped off his son's head and replaced it with the head of the first creature he saw. Ganesh shrines are often found at the entrance of other temples.

The most important of the goddesses is Mahadevi, the great goddess. As Shiva's *Shakti*, she is the active element in the tantric *Shakti* cult of the cosmic mother goddess, which predates the Vedas. Among the many forms she takes is that of Kali, the Black Goddess and Durga, The Terrible of Many Names, who are both offered animal sacrifices.

Saraswati is the goddess of learning, often depicted playing a *veena* and riding a swan.

Hanuman is the popular monkey god who Ram, in the *Ramayana* epic, befriends. His statues are usually draped in or painted red, symbolising power and vigor.

Indra, the god of rain and heavens, is often depicted riding an elephant. The *Indra Jatra Festival* is dedicated to him.

Deity honoured in wood.

The sale of garlands of brilliant saffron and red adds colour to street life.

Hinduism

Hinduism is a term that embraces numerous sects, cults, dogmas, the worship of countless deities and choice of many paths, a prescribed social order, and a profound and sophisticated philosophy. There is no one founder of Hinduism. Its oldest scriptures, the *Vedas* (Books of Wisdom), were written down about 3,000 years ago. The portion called the *Upanishads* lays out the tenets of Hindu philosophy – the "knowledge that destroys the bonds of ignorance and leads to the supreme goal of freedom."

The complex amalgam that is Hinduism makes it difficult to define categorically what it is. In essence, it holds that the goal of the soul or *atman* of any sentient being is to become one with Ultimate Reality, or the Brahman, of which it is a particle. An individual can attain this by closely following the prescribed Hindu behaviour in his or her soul's successive reincarnations.

Peoples' Epics

While the philosophical discourses of the *Upanishads* may pass over the heads of many devotees, the spirit of Hinduism may be better accessible through the *Mahabharata* and the *Ramayana*, two epics about heroes and villains, virtue and evil, high adventure and tender romance. Like the West's *Iliad* and *Odyssey*, they are based on stories, embellished with miraculous deeds and the intervention of gods and goddesses.

Completed about 2,000 years ago, the *Mahabharata* and *Ramayana* remain meaningful archetypal stories, evident in their highly popular televised adaptations shown in India and then imported to Nepal. Many children are named after the heroes and heroines of the stories, and many children can relate dozens of anecdotes from them containing an instructive moral.

In the *Mahabharata*, the heroes are the Pandavas, five brothers who fight for their kingdom against their one-hundred evil cousins. But the pivotal character is Krishna, one of the most popular of Hindu gods. His *Bhagavad Gita* (Song of God) is one of the most important passages of the *Mahabharata*.

The *Ramayana* recounts the adventures of Ram, the proto-typical Hindu hero. He is wrongly banished to exile; his wife Sita and his brother accompany him in his wanderings. In exile he befriends Hanuman, king of a race of monkey people. Rawana, who is Ram's nemesis, kidnaps Sita and takes her to his home in Lanka.

Hanuman finds her and leads Ram to her rescue, reaching Lanka by crossing a bridge constructed by Hanuman and his men. Ram defeats Ravana and eventually returns in triumph to rule his own country.

Nepal features in both the *Mahabharata* and the *Ramayana*. King Yalambar, the first king of the Kirati kingdom, is said to have met his end in the *Mahabharata's* climatic battle. Muktinath, the pilgrimage destination north of Jomsom, finds mention as a holy place.

Janakpur, in the Terai, is believed to be the traditional home of Sita.

The Merit and Self

The vast pantheon of gods and goddesses worshipped by Hindus are really different aspects of the one true God, Brahman, the "Self," who is represented as "Om," the sound with no form.

The Self, whose symbol is Om, is the omniscient Lord. He is not born; he does not die. He is neither cause nor effect.

Saddhus or holy men are often seen in or around temples.

This Ancient One is unborn, imperishable, eternal; the body may be destroyed, but he is not killed.

Smaller than the smallest, greater than the greatest, this Self dwells within the hearts of all. When a man is free from desire, his mind and senses purified, he beholds the glory of the Self.

The Upanishads

The Soul is found everywhere in animals, rocks, trees, people. Hinduism's deities are manifestations of this one omnipresent reality.

Hindus believe in *samsara*, a cycle of life, death, and rebirth from which one tries to obtain *moksha* (release). Your actions, or *karma*, in this life affect your rebirth just as your present life is the result of the action of your previous life. The emphasis is on good acts that will bring you higher successive reincarnations, bringing you closer to *moksha*.

Dharma, (righteous living), is the set of principles for maintaining and enriching social, ethical and spiritual harmony in life.

The merit earned (or discarded) in this life by following (or rejecting) *dharma* determines your birth in the next life.

A Social System

Hinduism sets out four major hierarchal social divisions called castes. At the top are *brahmans*, the priestly caste. They are the only group who can conduct the complex rites and rituals as prescribed in the Vedas. Next are *chhetris*, the warrior caste. Nepal's royal family, the Thakuris, come from this caste. Traditionally members of these two castes monopolised the most powerful and lucrative positions both in and out of government.

Both these castes have dietary restrictions, particularly the *brahmans*. As a symbol of their high caste, *brahmans* and *chhetris* wear the *janai* (sacred thread).

The *janai* is worn over the left shoulder and under the right arm. It is three cotton cords symbolising body, speech and mind. Wearing the *janai* signifies the wearer has gained control over them. Boys receive these threads at their *bratbandh* ceremony during adolescence as a reminder of both their status and obligations.

Below these two "high" castes is the

vaisya, the caste of merchants and farmers. Below them is the *sudra*, artisans and menials, among them the lowest "occupational" sub-castes, whom Gandhi called *harijans* (Children of God): *damais* (tailors), *sarkis* (leatherworkers) and *kaamis* (blacksmiths) are some of these so-called lower castes.

In Nepal the Hindus came originally from India, with the non-Hindu ethnic groups, mainly in the hill regions, becoming Hindu over centuries. Here, often, a distinction is made between the *janai* castes and the *matwali* groups, literally meaning the "alcohol-drinking castes."

Caste In Nepal

In many ways the caste system is an institutionalisation of the divisions that exist in many societies. Under it there is no escaping or changing your caste or the various restrictions of job, diet, marriage and social interaction.

The caste system has been used as a system of political and social control. The Mallas established 64 categories of occupational castes, with divisions as specific as the finger-and-toe nail cutters' caste!

The kings mandated almost all aspects of a person's social life based on caste; such as where they could live, what they could wear, how they should be addressed and how they must address others.

The caste system was finally abol-

ished by King Mahendra's National Civil Code in 1960. But the caste system was woven into Nepal's social fabric over a thousand years. As governments often find, it is one thing to proclaim social change and quite another to get people to accept it. Things are changing slowly.

In the hills, where traditional conservative values are still maintained, occupational castes would not think of entering a Brahman home, nor would a Brahman think of accepting a meal or a glass of water from the hand of a *sarki* or *damai*.

Buddhism

The Four Truths

The basic tenets of Buddhism are embodied in the Four Noble Truths:

• In this world there is suffering or *dukkha*. Suffering is physical and mental. This does not deny that one can experience temporary happiness or *sukkha* in the world of *samsara*, the endless cycle of existence of which suffering is a fundamental condition.

• There is a cause of all suffering. Suffering is caused by desire, or thirsts, which are rooted in ignorance. Desire is not confined to the desire for material wealth and sensual pleasure. Even the wish to do good deeds expresses desire. Desires keep us in the cycle of *samsaric* life, taking us from one moment and from one life to the next.

• This cause of suffering can be ended. There is a way we can free ourselves

The Buddha's Life

Lumbini, in the central Terai, is little more than a small pond bordered with brick. On its north side is a plain temple sheltered by a huge tree. This is the unpretentious birthplace of Siddhartha Gautam, better known by his appellation, the Buddha, the Enlightened One. It is the example of his life and his teachings on which Buddhism is based.

Maya Devi gave birth to him on the spot where the temple stands today in 563 BC. She died shortly afterwards.

Suddhodana, Siddhartha's father, was a member of the royal family of Kapilvastu. A holy man who saw the baby immediately prophesied his future. To thwart the prophecy, the king isolated his son in a palace where all the boy's wishes were met and everyone was young and healthy. He was afraid the sight of suffering would turn the young prince to his spiritual search.

Nonetheless Siddharta was unspoiled by his comfortable life and was intelligent, kind and sensitive, athletic and a skilled warrior. At the age of 16, he married beautiful Yashodhara after overcoming her other suitors in a series of contests.

Curious about life outside his beautiful palaces, Siddharta secretly made three trips out with his groom, Channa. For the first time, Siddhartha saw for himself the fate of every human being. On his wanderings, he encountered an old man, a sick man, and, finally, a corpse, the "signs" that would change his life, according to the prophecy.

These experiences made him ask the fundamental questions of the nature of life. Instead of retreating to his palace, he ventured beyond its gates again.

There he and Channa met a *sadhu*. In rags, and with no possessions, home, or family, the *sadhu* however radiated contentment. How could a man without a single possession find such peace in a world full of suffering? he asked himself.

He realised there was no course but to follow the *sadhu's* path if he was to find an answer. Though he loved his father and his wife – and wanted to be with his soon-to-be-born child – the quest for the truth was stronger. On the midnight of the very day his son was born, Siddhartha left the palace to begin his search.

Exchanging his silken robe with a *sadhu* for his rags and leaving his jewellery and house to Channa, he started off on his spiritual quest. He deprived himself of every comfort believing that only extreme suffering would yield the answers he sought.

Suffer as he did, the truth seemed to elude him. Then the realisation struck him that he would starve before he found his answer. He began to eat again.

His experience of total sensual indulgence and extreme self-mortification told him the answer lay in a middle way that did not embrace or reject the world and was truly detached of either.

At Bodh Gaya in north India, he sat under a Bodhi tree, resolved to find his answers or die trying. Mara, the temptress, tried everything to lead him astray. Or perhaps it was just his own fears, doubts, and desires that assailed Siddharta.

Buddha statues at Swayambhunath.

Through *vipassana* meditation, he gained increasing awareness until his perception of his own being and the world around him underwent a radical transformation. He had gone beyond the habitual perception of ego, or the illusion of self, which we consign due to ignorance, according to Buddhism.

He emerged from his meditation to see the world with a new clarity. He was no longer Siddhartha but the Buddha, the Enlightened One.

For the next 45 years, he walked all over northern India, perhaps even reaching Kathmandu, giving teachings. During this time, the Buddha converted hundreds to be *bhikkhus* (monks) and *bhikkunis* (nuns), members of the sangha, a community of renunciates.

At age eighty, the Buddha died in Kushinagar, just south of Nepal's border. His last words were:

"Impermanent are all created things. Walk On!"

from our desires, a path that would extricate us from the cycle of rebirth and deliver us to *nirvana* (Buddhahood).

• There is a way for ending suffering. There are practical steps to overcome our desires and set us on the path of the *dharma*, namely, the eightfold path through right.

- Understanding
- Thought
- Speech
- Action
- Livelihood
- Effort
- Mindfulness
- Concentration

Hinduism and Buddhism both believe in *karma*, which can be defined as a sort of moral cause-and-effect. *Karma* refers to the willed actions of mind, body, and speech – and their effect. Actions have consequences, both for the actor and to whomever or whatever the action is directed. Good or bad actions sow good or bad consequences. As the *Dhammapada* states:

"...if a person speaks or acts with unwholesome mind, pain pursues him, even as the wheel follows the hoof of the ox that draws the cart."

Buddhist Schools

After the Buddha's death, his words were subject to various interpretations, resulting in splinter schools over the centuries.

The Theravada School or "Way of

the Elders" (or Hinayana, The Lesser Vehicle, as it is disparagingly called) professes to adhere most closely to the Buddha's actual utterances. This form of Buddhism is today predominant in Southeast Asia and Sri Lanka.

According to Hinayana, the goal of each individual is to attain self-realisation or *arhat-hood*, or release from *samsara*, the otherwise unending cycle of births. After attaining this goal of *arhat-hood*, the *arhat* dedicates himself or herself to working for the others.

In Mahayana (Great Vehicle), which spread north and east into Nepal, Tibet, China and Japan, individuals forego *nirvana* until all other sentient beings are similarly released from *samsara*. Such a person is called a *bodhisattva*.

Mahayana considers enlightenment to be a state of the union of perfect compassion and wisdom. Avalokiteshvara or Chenrezi, the patron saint of Tibet, is the *bodhisattva* of Compassion, of whom the *Dalai Lamas* are considered incarnations.

Of the four major sects of Tibetan Buddhism, the presently dominant one is the *Gelugpa* (yellow hat sect), to which the Dalai Lama belongs. The *Kagyupa* (red hat sect) outside Tibet, is centred in Rumtek, Sikkim while there is also the *Nyingmapa* (old ones), and the Sakyapa, (those of the earth).

Vajrayana (Way of The Thunderbolt), is practiced both by Newars and Tibetans. It is the esoteric path of *tantra*, the quick but powerful path meant for only those with the capacity. In *Vajrayana*, the thunderbolt sceptre, held by deities, represents the male principle of skilfull means, and the bell, or *ghanta* (the female principle of wisdom).

Tantra

Tantra has become an important component of both Hinduism and Buddhism in Nepal. The practice of tantrism originated in India in the Hindu *Vedas* and the *Upanishads* .

Tantrism holds that the cosmic forces, the energies of an individual, all things and action, are intertwined and can be put to use. Sex, too, is regarded as a potent metaphor for spiritual enlightenment, as evident in both Buddhist and Hindu iconography. *Tantra* is rich in esoterica – *mantras* to be recited, *mandalas* to aid in medication, all of which can be used by those properly initiated. Stories of monks levitating or flying are examples of harnessing this tantric power.

But tantric practice is intended for a person properly initiated and guided by a *guru* (teacher). Different people have varying capacities and different degrees of receptiveness, and only the *guru* can judge how far his student can go.

There are two main tools the tantric uses. One is his *mandala*, a drawing symbolising both the cosmos and a human being, a map of the tantric's spiritual journey and psychic potential.

The second main tool is the *mantra*,

of which there are two types. The *bija mantra*, the seed mantra, is a single sound which incorporates the essence of a specific tantric deity.

The tantric's *mantra* is a passage, usually of Sanskrit origin. To the properly trained user, his *mantra* crackles with potential energy.

Tantrism stresses action, ritual and true experience. One of its beliefs is that sex can be used to unleash tantric power. In Hinduism this is often represented by the union of Shiva with his *shakti* (power), his female counterpart.

Tantric or *Vajrayana* Buddhism is still observed by Newars, despite the process of Hinduisation of the Valley brought on by the 18th century unification of Nepal. Their monasteries remain, though with only a small number of monks, who marry and form the *Vajracharya* caste, not unlike the *brahman* priests.

Long exposed to both faiths, the Newars follow both, worshipping Avalokiteshvara as well as Macchendranath and Gorakhnath, all of whom are believed to be manifestations of the other; *Kumari* the living goddess, an incarnation of Durga but picked from a Buddhist family; *Manjushri*, the *bodhisattva* of Wisdom, and *Tara*, the embodiment of the female principle in *Vajrayana*.

Muslims, the minority, worship at their mosque in Durbar Marg, Kathmandu.

Then there are the deities and spirits who must be appeased.

Shamanism

Shamanism is the term for a wide range of religious customs and beliefs predating Hinduism and Buddhism, both of which absorbed many shamanistic elements.

For most of the ethnic groups, who fall between the two organised religions, shamanism remains a significant part of their religious practice.

Mediums, the intermediaries to gods or the spirit world, most commonly called *jhankris*, carry out (through the use of magical incantations and spirit possession) the responsibility of addressing all manner of ills that befall human beings.

I t sometimes seems as if every second day brings a festival in some part of Nepal. Almost all festivals have their basis in Hindu, Buddhist or Shamanist belief. Another example of the intertwining of religion and everyday life, they affirm the relationship between man and his gods, man and nature, or the bonds within the family.

For the nation, the most important festival is the ten days of Dasain in late September. It is a household festival, and Nepalis will do everything to get home for the critical final days. Dasain celebrates the victory of the goddess Durga over the demon Mahashashura. Each house prepares a shrine to welcome her, and Nepalis take ritual baths at sacred *ghats*.

On the first day, a *brahman* priest blesses the planting of rice seeds, and a vessel of holy water is especially placed to receive her. The blessed water is worshipped throughout the duration of the festival. Kite competitions mark the fifth day. On the seventh day, *phulpati* (flowers and leaves), are offered to Durga. On the eighth day, there are military parades at

Pine boughs are burnt, offerings are made and prayer flags fly during Loshar (New Year).

Young women selecting tika, the mark of blessing worn on the forehead, during Kumbeshwar Mela in Patan.

Tundikhel. On the ninth, every household makes an animal sacrifice to the goddess. In addition, animals are sacrificed and their blood smeared on every vehicle, from motorcycles to Royal Nepal Airline jets, to ask for Durga's protection for the next year.

On the final day, known as *Vijaya Dashami* (Day of Victory),the Royal Palace is opened, and anyone can receive *tika* (caste mark dotted on the forehead) from the King. Runners from Gorkha, the ancestral home of the Shah kings, arrive with a *phulpati* for the King.

Tihar, or The Festival of Lights, is celebrated by Nepalis for five days in late October. On each day a different animal is worshipped; crows, dogs, cows, bulls and man. During the day, a path is painted and at night most of Nepal is splendorously lit with lamps and candles to welcome Lakshmi, the goddess of wealth, who visits at night. No one wants her to miss their house in the dark. Groups of singers go from house to house, and firecrackers welcome the goddess.

Bhai Tika is on the last day of Tihar On this day boys and men receive a special *tika* from their sisters. The sisters are thanked with presents of fruit, clothes and money. If a man has no sisters, a female relative or a friend will "adopt" him as a brother. This is an exciting time as it is also the Newar New Year.

Usually celebrated in September, *Indra Jatra* is a spectacular eight-day festival of Kathmandu Valley. Indra, Lord of Heaven and God of Rain, as the

Kumari, the living goddess is lifted into her chariot before her procession.

story goes, came down to the Valley to steal some beautiful flowers. But he was caught and kept captive – obviously unrecognised. His mother grew worried when she saw Indra's mount, the elephant, wandering the streets in search of its master.

Descending from heaven, she agreed to two demands for his freedom, to take the souls of all the people who had died in the past year to heaven and to send heavy wet dew and morning fog to help Kathmandu's farmers in the rainless winter. The people rejoiced, and a festival was born. Dancers representing Indra and the demons he fights walk through the street. His elephant, now frantic, rushes through the streets (two men in a bamboo and cloth), bumping

through the holiday crowds. But the highlight is the third day, when the entire Valley, including the King, pays homage to the *Kumari* (the living goddess) and her chariot is accompanied by her attendants, Ganesh and Bhairav, in the form of little boys. The narrow streets are jammed with people, her chariot often careens into buildings and occasionally a person is hurt.

Besides Indra and the *Kumari*, Bhairav (God of Destruction) is also honoured as seen in the numerous Bhairav masks displayed everywhere. The huge mask at Indrachowk is especially compelling. The grille is taken off the four-metre tall Seto Bhairav. At night young men vie for the alcoholic drink pouring through a spout from his mouth. Who-

Folk Beliefs and Superstitions

Despite recent claims to modernity, Nepalis remain a deeply superstitious people. Even Kathmandu's most cosmopolitan urban professionals hesitate to break the numerous taboos that mark traditional life. After all, the inconveniences they cause are nowhere as great as those possibly incurred by ignoring them. In fact, to the many Nepalis living with little protection, these superstitions are a means of obtaining some insurance, and reassurance.

To a visitor, guidelines offered by sympathisers appear arbitrary: do not snuff out a candle with your breath, do not step over others, do not leave your shoes with their soles turned up, do not eat alone in the presence of other people, do not comb your hair at night. One may well wonder, is there nothing one can do without invoking the wrath of Nepal's myriad gods and demons?

When in doubt, consult the stars. Most Nepalis are given personalised astrological charts upon birth, which they consult throughout their life and particularly before embarking on important ventures. In the charts, there is a time to travel, a time to marry, a time to stay put, and a time to begin new endeavours. Should the charts be unfavourable, marriage plans are called off, jobs quit, and people and places avoided so as not to ruffle the powers that be.

Some superstitions appeal to common sense. The ritual impurity of sharing food is sensible particularly in rural areas where medicine is scarce and infections are hard to cure. Similarly, the rule barring eating with the left hand is sensible, given that the left hand is used to clean up after going to the toilet. The inauspicious reading attributed to a sneeze while taking leave of home is also easily explained as a sign of ill health, which can hamper the journey.

Some superstitions are more outrageous. Eating stolen elephant ears causes headaches, stealing pumpkins or touching the neck causes goitre. Earaches are cured by wearing a copper ring, and backaches by rubbing against a staircase. To cure an eye infection, one must knock at a door until somebody inside asks, "Who is it?" – to which one must reply, "An eye infection."

To complicate matters, Nepal's different ethnic groups subscribe to varying beliefs. Un-

ever gets the occasional small fish in the "beer" is counted specially blessed.

One of Patan's most important festival is *Rato* (red) *Machhendranath* in April/May. After constructing the chariot and its towering spire of pine-covered bamboo, the image of Rato Machhendra is placed inside. He is the god of compassion and of harvests and is equally venerated by Hindus and Buddhists alike. The chariot is pulled through the streets for a month. When the spire sways and threatens to collapse, people pull the ropes to reposition it while worshippers swirl around the base (see Patan p.139).

The festival culminates at Jawalakhel, where a *bhoto* (bejewelled waistcoat), believed to belong to the serpent king, is displayed in front of the King. The deity spends three months a year at the nearby village of Bungamati, which shares the ownership of this waistcoat with Patan.

The *Biskhet Festival* of Bhaktapur commemorates the slaying of the two serpent demons, and it falls around the Nepalese New Year in April.

A long time ago, there was a beautiful princess who took a new lover each night; come the morning, he was found dead. A visiting prince heard the story and resolved to break this curse. He met the princess and after a passionate night, the princess fell asleep. The prince,

like farmers in the rest of the country, Kathmandu's Newars will not harness bulls to plough their fields because they consider them to be the vehicle of Shiva. The Sherpas will not sell ghee or curds on Mondays. They consider their hearths to be sacred, and no refuse may be burnt there. The Gurungs cannot refuse the requests of old women they consider to be village witches and so they avoid them as much as possible. People of all ethnic groups spend a great deal of energy appeasing the various deities of the wood, the water, air and land, usually through sacrifices of food, grain, flowers and animals.

In any case, should one unsuspectingly break these taboos, help is available. Nearly every ethnic group seeks the aid of shamans to remove curses by angry gods, or possession by witches and demons. These diviners of spirits, called *jhankri* and *dhami* by some, or *gubaju* by dwellers of Kathmandu, may participate in ritual sacrifice, blowing, exorcising, chanting – and sometimes, western medicine – to help cure the person.

Nailing down that toothache at the Vaisha Dev shrine at Asan Tole, Kathmandu.

crouched in a corner of the dark chamber, watched in horror as two snakes emerged from her nostril to become two huge serpents in search of the night's victim.

The prince slew the serpents and married the princess, who was now free of her curse. It is theirs and the city's joy that is celebrated. In Taumadhi hundreds of men pull ropes to erect a 24 m tall pole. Two long banners representing the vanquished snakes are unfurled from the top. The deities Bhairav and Bhadrakali are brought to the pole in their chariots. Thousands come to worship the chariots and to touch the base of the pole.

Tucked away in west-central Terai where the Narayani River meanders into India is a sleepy village called Tribeni. For 364 days of the year, it is in the middle of nowhere, but on the night of the new moon in Magh, thousands of Hindu devotees come for a ritual dawn bath and bring Tribeni into festive focus. The festival is celebrated in January and is called *Tribeni Mela*. Across the river are the ruins of Balmiki Ashram,

Tribeni Mela at dawn, an awesome atmosphere of riverside devotions.

where millenia ago, Sita lived and studied with her *guru* (teacher) Balmiki. It is her presence that draws the bathers. Now circuses pop up, hokey magicians amaze and wandering thespians entertain you. All through the night, people laugh and rejoice; then at dawn, 100,000 people scramble for a freezing bath. By 10 am, everyone has packed up, and by evening, Tribeni returns to being a quiet nowhere place until another year comes.

Festival Calendar

April/May

Baisaakh is the Nepali New Year. The month includes *Bisket* in Bhaktapur. In

This is also the month for *Rato Machhendranath*. Buddhajayanti celebrates the Buddha's birthday on the full moon.

Swayambhunath is packed in the morning and blazes with lit butter lamps at night; other celebrations take place at Boudhnath.

May/Jun

Jeth. The great Sherpa Mani Rimbu dances are held at the Thami Monastery near Namche Bazaar; the same festival is held in November at Tengpoche, also in the Khumbu region.

June/July

Asadh Tribhuvan Jayanti honours the king who overthrew the Ranas.

July/August

Srawan Naga Panchami placates the powerful *naga* (serpent) gods who control the monsoon rains. A picture of the *nagas* is fixed above each door with a daub of cow dung.

It also the time of *Janai Purnima*, *Braksha Bandhan*, and the *Kumbeshwar Mela* (see Patan p.139).

The birth of Krishna, the most adored deity, is celebrated at *Krishna Jayanti*, when images are displayed and his life story is narrated. Worshippers throng the Krishna Mandir Temple in Patan's Durbar Square.

August/September

Bhadra Dasain and *Indra Jatra* both occur at this time. *Gai Jatra* is best enjoyed in Bhaktapur, where elaborate palanquins topped by a cow's image are carried through the streets.

Fastened to the palanquin is a photo

nearby Thimi is *Balkumari Jatra*. Each neighbourhood carries their local deity in a palanquin (32 in all) to worship at the temple of Balkumari. Red powder flies everywhere, and the whole town takes part. Thousands of Tamangs gather to carry lamps around the Boudhnath stupa. The 22 dragon-spouts of Balaju bathe thousands for *Balaju Jatra*.

Monks in procession carrying a picture of the Dalai Lama.

of a family member who has died in the last year. On this day, the soul of the dead can enter heaven by hanging onto a cow's tail as it enters heaven's gates. In front of the cow palanquin, dozens of boys thrash sticks to scare interfering demons away.

Lord Krishna's birthday is celebrated on *Krishnastami*. The King comes to worship at the Krishna Temple of Patan's Durbar Square. *Gorkarna Aunsi* is the Nepali version of Father's Day.

Teej is the only festival strictly for women. Women walk to Pashupatinath to take a ceremonial bath in the Bagmati in honour of their husbands.

The unmarried sing and dance to Shiva and his consort Parvati, the married are bedecked in gold saris and jewels. Women also undertake to go on a fast.

September/October
Dasain falls in this month. *Ganesh Jatra* celebrates the elephant-headed god who after an argument with the moon goddess, placed a curse that whoever looked at the moon on this night will become a thief.

October/November
Kaartik Tihar leaves everyone in a good mood.

November/December
Ashwin. During **Bala Chaturadasi**, recently deceased family members are worshipped in a pilgrimage starting at dawn from Pashupatinath.

In Janakpur, a procession – everything from bullock carts to elephants – recreates the wedding of Ram and Sita during *Sita Bibaha Panchami*.

December-January
Poush is an inauspicious month. The

Jhankris, witch doctors in a trance – state dance at the Festival of Khumbeshwar in Patan.

birthday of His Majesty King Birendra is celebrated on December 28th.

January/February

Maagh, an auspicious month, is a favourite for weddings. *Basant Panchami* celebrates the coming of spring and Saraswati, goddess of learning, is also worshipped. On the final day of *Maagh*, thousands bathe in the Bagmati and the Sali Nadi near Sankhu.

February/March

Phaagun. Democracy Day celebrates the Ranas' overthrow. The springtime festival of *Holi* douses everyone, prudently wearing old clothes, with coloured powder. *Holi* celebrates the onset of spring, a variation of the annual water festivals held in Thailand.

Thousands of pilgrims from the subcontinent and numerous *saddhus* (holy men) gather at Pashupatinath to bathe at dawn during *Shaiva Raatri* (See Pashupatinath, p.136), the most important festival of the year, dedicated to Shiva in his form as Lord Pashupati, the guardian of Kathmandu Valley and protector of animals.

Tibetans celebrate their New Year during *Loshar*, best enjoyed at Boudhnath.

March/April

Chaitra. The image of *Seto Machhendranath* is drawn through Kathmandu's streets in a chariot for four days. On the last day, Machhendra is taken back to his temple on a small palanquin. *Ghaora Jatra* brings a day of horseracing and gymnastics on *Tundikhel*.

In Patan a crowd urges on a drunken rider and his equally drunken horse. The following day, two goddesses have a cosmic meeting in *Asan Tole*.

Nepali art is public art, around which daily life takes place. Masterpieces in wood, stone, metal, and brick are treated with intimate familiarity, as befits an old friend. Sometimes it is hard for some of us, used to hushed fluorescent-lit museums, to realise the finesse of what is all around us in Nepal.

Most of Nepali art is created as devotional activity by adherants of the two great religious traditions that shape so much of life in the country. What little non-religious art there is is contemporary. And Nepali art is anonymous art. We know the names of the patrons but not the artists and craftsmen who executed their commissions.

Thangkas – although originally temple and religious artefacts, they have become a continuing art expression in Nepal.

The earliest examples date back to the Licchavi era and they are in stone. They are religious in nature, and bear a distinct Indian influence. These include the huge *Sleeping Vishnu* of Buddanilkantha, the 6th century *Dhum Varahi*, and the beautiful 4th century *Vishnu* at Changu Narayan.

The name of only one Nepali artist is relatively known. Arniko, a 13th century master Newari

89

Art

Details of the Turana at Uku Bahal reflect gorgeous
details from religious epics.

builder, travelled to Tibet and China. He was also invited to the imperial court by the Emperor of China, where he became a high court official. He is credited with Nepal's characteristic pagoda-style, bequeathed to the rest of east Asia. For the earliest examples of woodcarving, view the 12th and 13th century struts at Uku Bahal in Patan and the carvings on the Basantapur Tower of Hanuman Dhoka.

Newar Renaissance

The story of Nepali art is really the story of the Newars. The only group in which the cultures of the north (Tibet) and

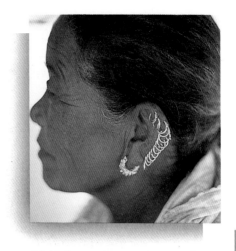

Multiple earrings – a personal
ornamentation as well as wearing
of one's wealth

were locked in a fierce battle to outdo the other. Like everyone else, artists and craftsmen became subject to caste restrictions. One was born an artist, literally, a member of the *chitrakar* caste. The *sakyas*, the caste of gold and silversmiths, created the fine masterpieces in metal. Art was a craft, an occupation, and the craftsmen depended on commissions from wealthy patrons to live and work.

The period of greatest prosperity and creativity was from the late 14th century to the Gorkha conquest in the late 18th century. During this time, works in wood and metal were the finest ever produced. Bhaktapur became the centre of woodcarving. You need look no further than the *Pujari Math* in Dattatraya Square for evidence of their genius. When looking at the courtyard, remember to step back from the magnificent details for the effect of the whole

south (India) melted and combined numerous traditions to create a unique style.

The Newars supplied the skill, talent, and energy. Their Malla rulers provided the most crucial ingredient, that is, moneyed patronage. They lavishly embellished their city squares with monument after monument. After visiting the different *durbars*, you cannot help but suspect that each of the rulers

Details of artful woodcarving on Pujari Math, the house of a priest.

architectural conception.

Patan became "The City of the Golden Roofs," famous for its metal workers. For a *tour-de-force* in metal, go to Kwa Bahal in Patan. The Golden Temple has elaborate metal work stretching from its base to the very tip of its elaborate *gajur* (pinnacle). Although a Buddhist temple, it carries features of Hindu edifices. Kwa Bahal is almost 600 years old, and it is as beautiful and vital as ever.

For a different and more serene example, see the lovely brass repoussé statues of the goddesses Ganga and Jamuna in Mul Chowk at Patan's Durbar Square. Repoussé techniques use hammer and chisel to fashion a design in a sheet of metal, as seen in the brilliant example of Bhaktapur's Sun Dhoka (see Bhaktapur). Repoussé is very much a living art in Patan. Just walk around the Mahaboudha Temple in Patan and you will hear the sound of metal-workers working as they did a thousand years ago. You will also see craftsmen using the "lost wax" method to make Hindu and Buddhist iconographical sculptures which gave the Newari artisans their much-deserved reputation.

The end of the Malla rule brought a halt to the Newars' tremendous artistic works. The Ranas seemed to have preferred European neo-classicism and kitsch. Today, several projects such as the UNESCO-funded restoration of Hanuman Dhoka and the Bhaktapur Development Project have been helpful in revitalising these crafts. Addition-

Elaborate window woodcarving in Tukche.

ally, works of high quality are in greater demand owing to the recent spurt of new monasteries in the Valley.

During the Malla period, artists were painting manuscripts in a style influenced by Indian and Tibetan *thangka* painting. These Newar paintings, called *paubha*, are rarely displayed in public. Samples exist in the National Museum in Bhaktapur.

Thangkas

Thangka paintings, on the other hand, are found everywhere. Tourists may snap them up as souvenirs, but *thangkas* are religious objects that grace private altars, used by certain practitioners for visualisation purposes. Newaris were producing them two hundred years ago.

As the original purpose of *thangkas* (spiritual diagrammes) is not observed by tourists, *thangkas* are being pro-

Erotic Art

Images of rapturous lovers are depicted in every kind of traditional Nepali art – in wooden sculpture, lost-wax and repoussé metal statues, stone carvings, frescos, *thangkas* and gouache paintings. They are found in the architecture and on the walls of temples, the pages of religious manuscripts, and in the numerous way-side shrines. Except for contemporary work made for the tourism-based market, these works are invariably religious in intent.

Puritanical Nepali society accepts these depictions as part of its rich storehouse of religious iconography. Some explain their significance through superstitions – they ward off the virgin goddess of lightning, they separate the human realm of temples from the spiritual realm, they encourage procreation, so that the number of worshippers is increased. But many look to erotic art forms for spiritual guidance.

The origin of most erotic art in Nepal is related specifically to *tantra*, the much misunderstood doctrine that infused Hindu and Buddhist practice as early as AD 300. In India, *tantra's* influence on art was subdued by later Islamic art and thought. In Nepal, it continued to shape the art work well into the 18th century. Strains of *tantric* thought are still found in contemporary cultural practices.

Though *tantra* is a vast and sophisticated body of literature, and though its contributions to Hindu and Buddhist practices have included key elements such as *mudra* (symbolic gestures), *asana* (yogic postures), *mantra* (verbal formulae), *yantra* (mystic diagrammes), *tantra* has of late become most famous for condoning the path of the *pancamakara*: "Wine, meat, fish, parched rice and sexual union."

Tantra rejects spiritual paths that require renunciation, asceticism and withdrawal from worldly concerns. Instead, it preaches the fullest acceptance of human desires and conflicts. Through the union of the spiritual and the material, the *tantrika* seeks to attain higher levels of consciousness.

In the Hindu erotic art that stems from *tantra*, woman symbolises the active, dynamic aspect of the material world. She is *Shakti* (cosmic energy), or *Prakriti* (cosmic nature). Man symbolises the passive, contemplative aspect, the realm of the spiritual. He is *Siva*, or *Purusha*, cosmic consciousness. *Siva* without *Shakti* remains dormant, unrealised. From their union springs true knowledge.

This union is depicted in many styles – sometimes figurative, and at other times symbolic. A 13th century example is found in Panauti, at the Indresvara Mahadeva Temple, where a seated couple is shown in loving embrace. A 17th century example of similar erotic work is found at the Taleju Temple in Hanuman Dhoka. At Pashupatinath and Guhjeswari, as at Dakshinkali, male and female are symbolised by stylised phallic and gynic shapes. Some more recent figurative gouache paintings are on exhibition in Bhaktapur's National Art Gallery.

Buddhist erotic art, produced under the school of *Vajrayana* (Way of the Thunderbolt), depicts the union of *Upaya* (Means or Method), with *Prajna* (Pure Wisdom). In Buddhist iconography, the active principle, *Upaya*, is male. *Prajna*, the female, remains passive without his activity. Often, the figures, called *yidams* (tutelary deities), are of a fantastic, horrendous nature. Their frenzy is found more in Nepali art work than in the ancient Indian images on which they are modelled.

These images were once secret. They were shown only to those who were capable of grasping the depth of their meaning. Today, they are available for anyone who seeks them, and their significance resides in the eye, and mind, of the beholder.

A fabulous bathing pool, Tusha Hiti, Sundari Chowk in Patan.

duced *en masse* for the tourist market. Many paintings are slovenly produced, sometimes ignoring or violating tradi-tional prescriptions and then stuck over a smoky fire to give them an instant "antique" look.

A few Newari and Tamang artists continue to make good *thangkas*.

Verbal Arts

Poetry is a dominant oral form in Nepali literature. There are yearly competitions which are closely followed, and even broadcast on television. Pratap Malla, who sits atop his pillar in Durbar Marg called himself the King of Poets. In a society that was largely illiterate, it was natural that verbal artistry was prized. To this day, Nepalis love a clever, witty speaker. "*Kati mitho bolchha!*" literally means "What a tasty speaker!"

A common feature of any fair or festival in the hills is a repartee singing competition. Two teams of boys and girls gather by a *pipal* tree, and try to outdo the other with verses composed on the spot and sung to a simple tune. The most skillful of these can last for hours. These days the best singers are recorded on portable cassettes for those unable to attend. Until recently, *gainis* or wandering troubadours travelled from village to village, literally singing for their supper. To the accompaniment of their four-stringed violin-like *saringhi*, they sang age-old songs of Hindu gods and heroes and of the latest palace gossip. Genuine *gainis* come from a single village in Pokhara Valley; they claim their descendence from Rajasthan. Today, they are a vanishing breed, replaced by young boys screeching out the french folk song *Frere Jacques*.

There are, however, a number of individuals maintaining traditional methods, prescription, and standards in Boudhnath, Swayambhu and the Solu Khumbu area.

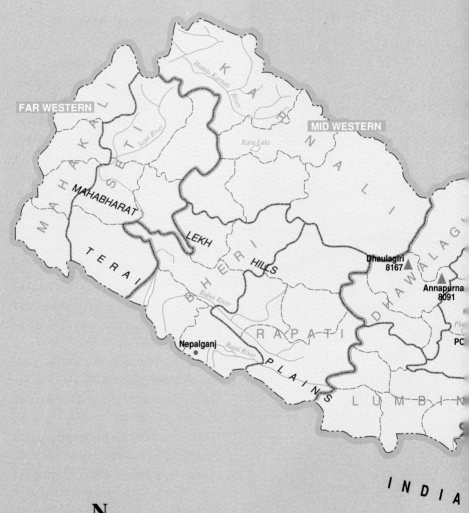

MAHABHARAT

LEKH

HILLS

TERAI

Babai River

Nepalganj

Rapti River

RAPATI

PLAINS

LUMBIN

Humla Karnali River

Septi River

Rara Lake

Dhaulagiri
8167

Annapurna
8091

Phe

PC

INDIA

NEPAL

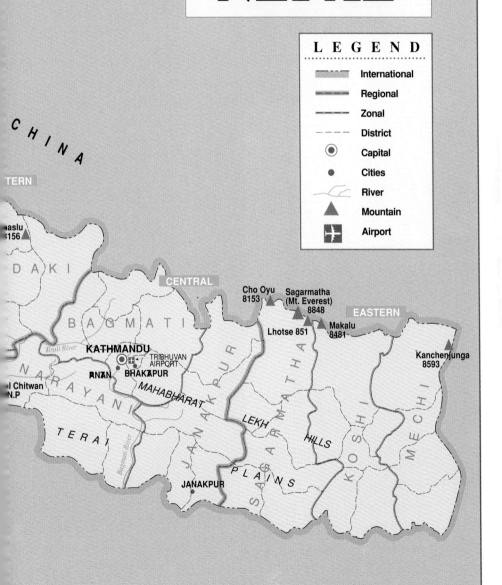

LEGEND

░░░░	International
▬▬▬	Regional
───	Zonal
-----	District
◉	Capital
●	Cities
～	River
▲	Mountain
✈	Airport

CHINA

TERN

aslu
156 ▲

DA KI

CENTRAL

Cho Oyu
8153 ▲

Sagarmatha
(Mt. Everest)
8848 ▲

EASTERN

BAGMATI

Lhotse 851 ▲

Makalu
8481 ▲

Kanchenjunga
8593 ▲

Tisuli River

KATHMANDU

TRIBHUVAN
AIRPORT

NARAYANI

ANAN   BHAKTAPUR

l Chitwan
N.P

MAHABHARAT

JANAKPUR

NARAYANI

TERAI

Bagmati River

SAGARMATHA

LEKH

HILLS

KOSHI

MECHI

JANAKPUR

PLAINS

Kathmandu

Rudyard Kipling knew that the "wildest dreams of Kew" were as common as potatoes in Kathmandu. A hundred years later Bob Seeger sang that he could not wait to get to the mountains and the peace of "Ca-ca-ca-Cat-man-duu."

Well, the people of Kathmandu now watch the latest wildest dreams of Kew on video cassette recorders and via satellite dishes and young Kathmanduites can sing Seeger's song with him karaoke-style and perhaps even pound it out on their electric guitars.

The clocktower, a landmark in the city.

Kathmandu was completely shut off from the outside world until 1951; it did not have a motor road to the outside world until 1958. The city is certainly making up for lost time – tearing down rich brown brick and throwing up grey concrete in their place. Mini-supermarkets, boutiques, Toyotas and Honda motorcycles, ice-cream parlours and pre-packed noodles have taken over.

But old aspects of Kathmandu stubbornly remain; and the city still retains the atmosphere that is derived from its warm and friendly population. Away from the main commercial and shopping areas, you will see lots of

BALAJU

American Embassy ●
Japanese Embassy ●

Indian Embassy ●

British Embassy ●

● Shanker Hotel

Swayambhunath
Stupa

THAMEL

Central
Immigration ●

Kaiser
Mahal ●

Royal Palace ●

International
Clinic ●

Nepal-Arab
Bank ●

Annapurna
Hotel ●

Everest Cultural
Centre ●

Varja Hotel ●

Vishnumati

British
Council ●

Yak and Yeti
Hotel ●

KIMDOL

National
Theatre ●

Royal Nepal
Academy ●

13

14

15

Rani
Pokharl

● Clock Tower

17

16

12

11

Bir
Hospital ●

19

Ratna
Park ●

● Bhaktapur
Bus Stop

18

9

10

20

7

5

8

● Central Bus Station

CHHAUNI

Durbar Square

New Road
Gate ●

6

RNAL

● City Hall

National Musuem
●

4

Nepal
Bank Ltd ●

TAHACHEL

3

2

Lalupate Cultural Group
●

1

Genaral
Post Office ●

KALIMATI

● Hotel Soaltee

Central Telegraph
Office ●

National
Stadium

TEKU

Trolley Bus
Stand ●

TRIPURESWAR

THAPA

Bagamati River

● Thai
Emassy

To Patan ↓

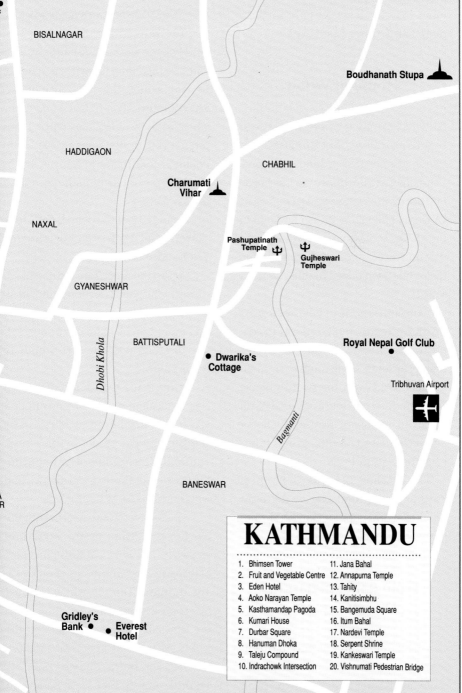

BISALNAGAR

Boudhanath Stupa

HADDIGAON

CHABHIL

Charumati Vihar

NAXAL

Pashupatinath Temple

Gujheswari Temple

GYANESHWAR

BATTISPUTALI

Dhobi Khola

Royal Nepal Golf Club

Dwarika's Cottage

Tribhuvan Airport

Bagmanti

BANESWAR

Gridley's Bank

Everest Hotel

KATHMANDU

1. Bhimsen Tower
2. Fruit and Vegetable Centre
3. Eden Hotel
4. Aoko Narayan Temple
5. Kasthamandap Pagoda
6. Kumari House
7. Durbar Square
8. Hanuman Dhoka
9. Taleju Compound
10. Indrachowk Intersection
11. Jana Bahal
12. Annapurna Temple
13. Tahity
14. Kanitisimbhu
15. Bangemuda Square
16. Itum Bahal
17. Nardevi Temple
18. Serpent Shrine
19. Kankeswari Temple
20. Vishnumati Pedestrian Bridge

fine brick neighbourhoods in narrow lanes. So you will have to go down these alleys, walk around and explore.

House of Wood

Early records say that Kathmandu was shaped like the sword of Manjushri. The sword disappeared a long time ago. "The streets do not appear to have been laid out in any particular system," wrote Dr Henry Oldfield, a British Resident in the 1870s. Today's visitors can verify to that and more, since a new contributing factor has been added to those streets – traffic.

The jewel in the hilt of the sword is **Kasthamandap**, built in the 12th century where an east-west route intersected the north-south trade route from India to Tibet which was the sword's blade. Kasthamandap ("House of Wood") still stands, a temple, a travellers' shelter and a community centre, just as it has been for centuries.

Tiny **Ashok Binayak** is north of Kasthamandap and one of the most important and popular Ganesh shrines in the valley (see Religion, p.67).

From Rani Pokhari to Durbar Square

The street from **Rani Pokhari** to **Hanuman Dhoka** was an important trade route and bazaar long before the reign of the Mallas. Though rapidly chan-

ging, the **Kamlachi-Asan-Indrachowk** area is still one of Asia's great bazaars.

The 16th century small temple in Rani Pokhari was built by Pratap Malla's wife as a memorial to their son. It had to be rebuilt after the 1934 earthquake. The **Pokhari** (Pond) was supposedly where trials by ordeal took place. It has often been a site for suicides. Rani Pokhari looks pretty to tourists but its troubled history gives many Nepalis a queasy feeling.

To the east of the pond is the **Clock Tower**, built by the Ranas, marking **Trichandra College**.

Across the street from the northwest corner of the pond is Kathmandu's bicycle centre, where you can rent Indian and mountain bikes for a pittance. Follow the road past the bike stands to **Asan Tole**.

Asan is the real centre of the old city. A bustling and crowded fruit and vegetable market, every available space is taken up by a vendor of some kind. The front of the **Temple of Annapurna**, the Goddess of Grain, is always waylaid with burlap bags of rice for sale.

The more westerly street eventually reaches the **Bishnumathi River** and crosses it. This is an old-fashioned part of the city, lined with shops of all kinds. The **Ugratara Temple**, which is visited by people with eyesores, is a little up on the left (look for the eyeglasses on the wall!). At the next major intersection, turn left for **Indra Chowk**, right for **Thahiti**, and straight on to go toward the river and **Swayambhu**.

The temple at Seto Machhendranath.

Turning left, you will see a mass of nails around an image of Vaisha Dev, the Toothache God. The nails pin down the evil spirits causing the trouble. To help the God there are local dentists, with dentures showcased in their windows, on both sides.

Towards Thahiti on your left are stone lions guarding the entrance to **Srigha Chaitya** (also called Kathe Shimbu), supposedly a miniature replica of Swayambhunath stupa.

Starting from Asan Tole, you should follow the main traffic. Jutting into the road on your right is an octagonal Temple of Krishna with fine wood-carved windows, though the entire temple seems a little wobbly. On the left stands a 19th century house, among the first – not counting the palace – to be allowed glass windows. Look for the carving of gun-toting soldiers.

Where the street opens up a little, past the unusual sounding **Lunchun Lun Bun Temple**, look for a doorway guarded by two snarling beasts. This is the entrance to the **Seto Machhendra**. In the passage on the right is a *bhajan* (hymnal) where men gather in the evening to sing hymns.

A jumble of *chaityas* and statues are in front of this tall Buddhist temple dedicated to **Avalokiteshvara**. One large statue-lamp of a woman in flowing gown could have come from a Victorian parlor. It is always busy here with worshippers, family celebrations and the daily life of courtyard residents.

Day labourers waiting for assignments at a gathering spot at Indra Chowk.

In March/April the image of *Seto Machhendra* is taken through the streets for four days in his huge chariot.

A small passage at the back takes you out to the main pottery market. Clay pots, vessels and animals are stacked high at the back of a temple. Go to the top of the temple to watch the bustle of the morning bazaar.

Exit the way you entered and continue to **Indra Chowk**. Directly in front is the **Temple of Akash Bhairav**, with the altar on the second floor. During the *Indra Jatra* festival, the huge mask of

Akash Bhairav is placed on a platform in front and lavishly decorated with flowers. The *kumari* (living goddess) also visits in her chariot.

Behind and to the left of Akash Bhairav, is the market for *potes*, (necklaces made from glass beads worn by married women). There are hundreds of styles and the beads can be customstrung to your liking. Many of the potemakers are Moslems originally from Kashmir. *Pote* necklaces make beautiful wearable and inexpensive gifts.

Turn left for shops and the "supermarket," the nearest place for foreign goods for Indian tourists and the Nepali middle-class. Inside the "supermarket" you can find Nepal's first escalator. The supermarket opens out to New Road on one side. Leave the way you entered, and turn right to reach the potters' market. Go to the left of the Akash Bhairav shrine to reach **Makhan Tole** and **Hanuman Dhoka**.

New Road

New Road was built by Prime Minister Juddha Shumsher Rana following the 1934 earthquake, which devastated the whole area. He still supervises it from his pedestal at the west end of the street. It has become the city's main commercial and shopping area. The large pipal tree is one of the main newsstands and meeting places of the city. Men on their way from work will linger here to read the news, gauge the political pulse of the city, meet with friends for a walk and a snack.

South of New Road, near **Khichapokhari**, is one of the main areas for butchers in the city, and in a large courtyard another fruit and vegetable bazaar. There are also many provision-cum-cold-storage stores here.

Near the Central Post Office is **Bhimsen Tower**, nothing architecturally magnificent but interesting for its history. It commemorates Bhimsen Thapa (1775-1839), one Nepal's greatest prime ministers, who was able to get back most of the Terai from the British. His rivals accused him of poisoning a prince and had him arrested. On hearing that his wife had been paraded naked through the streets, he hacked his throat with a *khukuri*, but its blade was dull and he had to suffer nine days before dying.

Walk west from Buddha's statue to **Basantapur**, a large open square filled with trinket sellers, and the royal elephant stables that were destroyed by the earthquake. **Freak Street** runs south on the east end.

Here and Gone

In the late 1960s, hippies and flower-children found a beautiful valley where you could get by on a dollar a day with a little leftover for marijuana and hashish which were sold over-the-counter – positively Shangrila. They came from all over the world to linger in darkened

Pigeons, pagoda fringes and temple wind chimes flutter at the towers
of Hanuman Dokha Palace.

restaurants, nodding to Hendrix and the "Dead" in-between sipping lemon teas and bites of hash brownies. They walked the streets wrapped in velvet and satin, rings in their ears, barefooted or sporting "thongs." Streets that had never seen westerners suddenly became theirs – "Freak Street" and "Pie Alley".

Then long past its days in the west, the hippies were gone. Some say it started with the clean-up effort made for King Birendra's coronation. Visas were refused, new regulations were introduced such as no visible means of support. There was no ruckus nor protests, the hippies just vanished. Then the next wave of westerners returned reincarnated as trail-nuts-munching trekkers in designer T-shirts, expensive sneakers,

catching up on the best deals in the restaurants of the new mecca – **Thamel**.

Freak Street is Basantapur again. The super-cheap lodges, the pie shops, and the displays of tie-dyed fashions are giving way to smart new concrete. One can still see the occasional die-hard hippie, and some cafés, with their sixties' songs, have remained.

North of Basantapur Square is **Hanuman Dhoka**, the old royal palace. High up on the east is **Lalitpur Tower**, to the west is the nine-storeyed **Basantapur Tower** with its exquisite wood-carving.

At the west end of the square is the **Kumari Bahal**, residence of the *living goddess*, built in the mid-18th century. The wooden windows and doors are well-carved (look at the skulls on the door lintels); the carving around the interior court is even more splendid.

The Living Goddess

Stories vary on the origin of the *kumari* cult. According to one version, a king spent his evenings gambling with the royal goddess *Taleju*, who visited in human form. One evening (perhaps there were new wicks in the lamps), the king suddenly realised how beautiful his gambling partner was and lust raised its ugly head. Sensing his thoughts she became enraged. She would only return, she said, in the form of a young undefilable virgin.

The *kumari* is worshipped as *Kanya*

Kumari, a form of Parvati; some believe she is Durga. She is chosen, at the age of 4 or 5, from the Newar Sakya clan of gold and silversmiths. She undergoes a series of tantric rites and tests. As a final test, she must remain unperturbed in a darkened room littered with severed buffalo heads while men in demon masks jump from the shadows to scare her. She must also select the proper objects from those laid before her.

Once chosen she lives in the *bahal*, away from her family. Her most famous public appearance is during the yearly *Indra Jatra Festival* when she rides in her chariot through the streets and gives a *tika* to the king. She remains the *kumari* until she loses blood, either through injury or the onset of her menstruation.

After life as a goddess, many *kumaris* face difficulty adjusting to ordinary human life. In addition, marrying an ex-goddess is said to bring bad luck and an early death to her husband. There are several *kumaris* throughout the Valley, but the one here is recognized as the royal *kumari*.

Walk out of the *kumari's bahal* and into the largest of the three *durbar* (squares) in the Valley. Because of its large scale, it does not have the same sense of enchantment and intimacy of the other two, particularly Patan's, but it certainly projects the sense of power and authority appropriate to the greatest city in the kingdom.

To your left on leaving the *kumari's bahal* is a temple of Narayan built in 1670. On its west side is a stately statue

A fearsome mask of Bhairav displayed during the Indra Jatra Festival.

of Garuda kneeling in homage.

Kasthamandap is further to the west. To the northwest of Garuda is a small Shiva temple with some interesting shops, including an old coin shop. North of that is the large temple of **Maju Deval** with rickshaws waiting at the base and tourists resting at the top. At the north end of the square, Shiva and Parvati have been at their balcony window for about 200 years.

The white *durbar* with classical fea-

tures was built by the Ranas. The king stands on its balcony during the Indra Jatra festivities. Walking down the street, past Shiva and Parvati, are the huge 19th century drums and the great bell of Taleju. A little ahead is a Krishna Temple built by **Pratap Malla**, king between 1641-74, who sits atop the column on your right. He is responsible for much of the architecture around him.

In front of him is the **Seto Bhairav**, a terrifying four-metre high mask. Its

sexual positions and combinations imaginable. Explanations offered suggest that the kings ordered them as entertainment for the public and a subliminal suggestion to have more children to increase the strength of the kingdom. Another idea is that these erotica were to shame the lightning goddess, a chaste virgin, from striking the building.

Hanuman Dhoka

From Jagannath, proceed to **Hanuman Dhoka**, the entrance to the old palace.

The oldest building standing dates from the Mallas. The Mallas claimed descent from Ram, so it is natural that Hanuman, Ram's devoted companion, guards the entrance to their palace. Hanuman's features are concealed by a thick layer of red *tikas*. The statue was erected by Pratap Malla, who also erected the statue of Narsingha, the half-man, half-lion *avatar* of Vishnu just inside the entrance and to the left.

In **Nasal Chowk**, the largest courtyard in the complex, the long verandah on the left is the old audience hall of the kings. This area was also used as the royal theatre. The Shah kings hold their coronations rites here using the platform in the centre. **Nasal Chowk** takes its name from the small white shrine dedicated to *Nasaleswar* (the dancing Shiva). Above the verandah is the five-tiered round tower of **Pancha Mukhi Hanuman** (five faced Hanuman). Visit the **Tribhuvan Museum**, and go

screen is opened only during Indra Jatra, when young men push to drink a little *thon* (liquor) pouring from his mouth.

On Pratap's left is the handsome **Jagannath Temple** (16th century), famous for its erotic carvings.

No One Knows

On the struts of many temples below the main deity, you will see the strangest

The temple of Kasthamandap (meaning house of wood) from which
Kathmandu takes its name.

through the passage on the southeast to **Lohan Chowk**, former residence of the Shah kings. Their three-storeyed building around the courtyard is **Vilas Mandir**. In each corner is a tower, the largest is **Basantapur** (spring) **Tower**, north of it **Kirtipur Tower**, east of Kirtipur is **Bhaktapur Tower**, and **Lalitpur Tower** is to the southeast.

The towers were built by Prithvi Narayan Shah after his conquest. The names given to them refer to the city that had the "honour" of paying for its construction.

This whole area was extensively repaired under a UNESCO programme in the 1970's. Walk up as high as you can. From the **Vilas Mandir**, look into the Malla's royal court, **Mul Chowk**, which is closed to visitors.

Back outside **Hanuman Dhoka**, look for the huge statue of Kal (black) Bhairav, who is Shiva at his most destructive. This huge statue was supposedly found in a field north of the city and brought here in the latter 18th century. There are an estimated 5,000,000 Bhairav images in Nepal. With his necklace and crown of skulls, bulging eyes and a bloodlusting leer, not to mention three pairs of arms holding weapons and skulls, this statue is certainly one of the most impressive in existence.

According to traditional belief, anyone who tells a lie in front of this Bhairav will immediately die vomiting blood. Until recently, criminals and government officers were required to take an

Drying grain in the quieter side streets of Kathmandu.

oath in front of the statue.

The massive **Taleju Temple** towers above its high wall in the northeast corner of the square. Built in 1563, the goddess of the royal house sits in this beautiful temple. The woodcarving is exquisite, and the temple is among the best proportioned in the Valley.

The north side of Taleju faces **Makhan Tole**, with its line of *thangka* shops and a Garuda half buried in brick. The road continues on to **Indra Chowk**.

Across the street from Kal Bhairav is the police headquarters. An alley leads around the headquarters and west of the large temple with its fringe of carom boards. This area, or perhaps the open court nearby, is the site of the *Kot* Massacre (see history). The courtyard is also the site of the yearly *Dasain* sacrifice of hundreds of water buffalo. During the sacrifice soldiers attempt to chop off the heads of water buffaloes with a single stroke.

Other Points of Interest

The Ranas built dozens of palaces all over the city.

Singha Durbar, built in 1901, was proclaimed the largest private building in Asia, with its more than 1,000 rooms and numerous courtyards. It became the seat of government following the overthrow of the Ranas. In 1973, a fire severely damaged it (not to mention the records that were lost!). Its front eleva-

Education – an investment into the future.

tion has been restored.

One of the most accessible and interesting Rana palaces is the **Kaiser Mahal** near Thamel. Field Marshall Kaiser Shumsher JB Rana filled his palace with more than 35,000 books. Today, his palace houses the **Education Ministry** and a public non-lending library. Go in to see the palace, the eclectic collection of books and the overgrown palace grounds.

The **Yak and Yeti** and the **Shanker Hotels** were also Rana palaces. Kathmandu underwent a total facelift for the South Asian Area Regional Council in 1987. One place that was transformed was **Nag Pokhari**, the pond to the east of the palace. We suggest a bicycle trip around the pond.

The centre of sightseeing may be the **Durbar Square** area, but the place to hang out in is Thamel. Restaurants, budget hotels, trekking equipment and bicycle rentals, even fax and telex services are all found here. This is a great place to stroll, shop, dine, stay, and collect all your traveller information.

Kathmandu was once enclosed by a wall. Only caste Hindus were allowed to build inside. The "lower castes" – sweepers, blacksmiths and cobblers, were forced to live in slums outside.

There are still neighbourhoods made up largely of people whose name identifies them as traditionally having "unclean" occupations. From **Ashok Binayak**, head east down to the **Bisnumati** to see the life of this ignored section of the populace.

I n 1984 seven sites in Kathmandu Valley were included in UNESCO's World Heritage List. This more or less gives you an idea of the richness of the culture and the monuments in the valley.

To really enjoy your visit to Nepal, take some walks out of your hotel entrance without a guide or your guidebook. You are bound to see fascinating temples and monuments.

Getting "there" is just as important as the destination. Kathmandu Valley is a compact area almost entirely accessible by foot or bicycle. Buses are crowded but they reach every corner of the Valley, and they will bring you into close contact with common Nepalis.

Kathmandu is one of the least threatening of travel destinations. It is easy to feel comfortable here. Many travellers have come and stayed on and many never failed to return.

Start at the rim of the Valley and work inward.

Valley activities are often related to the subsistence of its people.

Around the Valley

117

Around the Valley Rim

Nagarkot (2,066m or 6,778ft) is on the northeastern rim

The land is farmed in terraces all around the valley rim.

of the Valley. Famous for its mountain views, you can pick **Mount Everest** out on a clear day as there is an observation tower at the very top.

Nagarkot makes for a good short hike and you walk on the ridge. It has also become a popular stop for mountain bikers. You can catch a bus for the one-hour ride to Nagarkot from the bus-stop in **Bhaktapur**. A taxi will cost about a hundred times more. Some visitors drive up, spend the night at one of the moderately-priced lodges and walk down by any number of routes.

From Nagarkot it takes 2½ hours down a well-worn trail through several villages to Bhaktapur. Or, walk for 3 hours down to **Changu Narayan**, one of the most magnificent temples in the Valley. Start at the same trail for Bhaktapur. After about an hour, follow a wide trail on your right that leads down to the temple. From the temple, follow the trail to the **Manohara River**

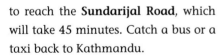
Mustard plant blossoms line
the road to Godavari.

statues from the Licchavi era, as well as several from the more recent Malla period, including that of King Bupatindra and his queen in a gilded enclosure from the 17th century.

Changu Narayan is also patronised by the Valley's Buddhists who worship *Lokeswar* (another name for Vishnu).

Before starting down from the temple, take a moment to enjoy the panorama of the Valley. Imagine it as the lake it once was: the ridge on which you stand was a peninsula jutting out to the lake.

to reach the **Sundarijal Road**, which will take 45 minutes. Catch a bus or a taxi back to Kathmandu.

Changu Narayan is one of the most beautiful Hindu temples in the Valley. The present structure was built in the early 1700's, but at the entrance of the main shrine are stone tablets with the inscriptions dating to 400 AD.

Facing the entrance is a 5th century statue of a human-faced Garuda, the mount of Vishnu (who is also called Narayan). There are many other fine

On the southern rim of the Valley is **Phulchowki** (2,782m or 9,155ft), or "flower hill," its tip is a pilgrimage site, now with a telecommunications station and a broadcast antennae for Nepal Television. There is a rough gravel road to the top; you can hire a car/taxi to go up there, but there are no buses. Frequent buses ply from **Lagankhel**,

A view of Kathmandu city from Swayambhu Hill.

Patan's main bus-park, to **Godavari**, where the walk begins. The bus journey will take up to an hour. You will take about 3 to 3½ hours to walk up the steep trail from Godavari and 2 to 2½ hours for the descent.

When the bus stops, ask for directions to the temple of **Phulchowki Mai**, the forest's guardian deity. It is an uphill journey all the way, past **St Xavier's School**, a few hundred metres on the left. Enter the temple compound, and take the uphill trail in the back.

To your west as you start climbing, you will see the **Godavari Marble Quarry**, one of the Valley's environmental problems. The marble is not of top quality and some of it is burned – with wood from Phulchowki's forests –

to make lime.

The quarry itself is an eyesore but even worse is the drastic loss of trees. Some environmentalists have tied the loss of the watershed with the drying up of the holy Godavari Springs in 1983. Local residents did more damage when they turned the slopes of Phulchowki into charcoal to sell in Kathmandu. Godavari's forest is an example of the pressures Nepal's forests have come under.

The climb is steep, but you will be in a bird watcher's haven as about 300 species have been identified here. Also, keep an eye out for orchids. In spring, bright red rhododendrons splatter the forest. Carry your own drinking water and snacks. Be warned that the air is rare and one can get out of breath rather easily at this altitude. The views along the way and on the summit are stupendous, the entire Valley and a breathtaking panorama of the *himals* lies before you. From the left, view **Dhaulagiri**, the **Annapurnas**, **Manaslu**, **Ganesh Himal**, **Langtang**, the **Jugals** and **Gauri Shanker**. To the south are the Terai plains bordering India.

Godavari, the starting point for the hike up Phulchowki, is itself worth a trip. Take a bike out as it is only 13km away, much of it uphill, but there are numerous places to stop at along the way that you can practically coast the whole way back.

At Godavari, the place to visit is **St**

Namaste by a winged stone sculpture of Vishnu in the Valley.

Xavier's, a Jesuit-run elementary school, the **Royal Botanical Garden**, a medicinal plant farm and **Godavari Kunda**. The *kunda*, a clear spring flowing from a cave, is a special pilgrimage spot for Hindus. A bath in the spring's waters earns special merit for the bather. Once every twelve years (the latest being 1992), this is the site of a special bathing festival.

On Saturdays, the Botanical Garden is usually crowded with Nepali families on picnics. There is always a strong possibility that you could be invited to join a family for a meal.

If you are bicycling, try to make your return journey along another road. Ask in **Bandegaun** or **Thaibo** for the trail to **Lubhu** and **Sanagaun**.

Another important *kunda* on the south side of the Valley is at **Lele**. Lele makes for a good bike trip. Near the village is the **Saraswati Kunda** set in a grove of trees beside a 17th century shrine. The Lele Kunda is beside a temple with a 12th century stone panel of Shiva and Parvati.

Farther west on the **Ring Road**, a road leads to the town of **Bungamati**. Established by the King of Patan in the 16th century, this is the second home of Patan's Raato Machhendra. As in many of the Valley towns, life here is communal, taking place in the temple square with Buddhist *chaityas*. In these tucked-away corners of the Valley, even Kathmandu itself and the 20th century seem far away.

Ask for the trail to nearby **Khokana**.

Sadhu, sadhus everywhere.

The fertile fields here make it one of the Valley's prettiest areas. Look for the statue of Manjushri, who drained the Valley with a single stroke of his sword. You can take the road to Kathmandu from here. If you are in Nepal for a short stay and cannot explore the countryside, places like Khokana and Bungamati will be the best substitutes.

A Single Stroke

When Manjushri strode around the rim of the Valley, he chose **Chobar** from which to wield his sword. With a single stroke he bled the valley wall, thereby draining the lake. The **Bagmati River** still crashes through this narrow gorge,

An apple orchard at harvest time.

but now a modern cement factory spews smoke, its fine powder coating everything in the area.

The best place to view the gorge is from the small suspension bridge, one of several prefabricated bridges shipped from Scotland in 1903 (look for the plaque on the bridge). At the base of the gorge, the river widens again beside the **Jai Binayak Temple**. On top of **Chobar Hill** stands the Buddhist temple of **Adinath Lokeswar**, one of the homes of the Raato Machhendra.

The same paved road continues to **Dakshinkali** from Chobar and the cement factory.

In Nepal you will sometimes feel you are back in an earlier era, as when you visit **Dakshinkali**. Many shrines here give the impression of having grown organically from the surrounding landscape. You will sense a special empathy between man, god and nature.

Though only 20km from Kathmandu, there is enough to see and do on the way to make it an all-day bike trip. There are crowded buses, but bicycling will be more pleasurable and you can stop where you want.

South of Chobar, the Bagmati River widens into **Taudaha Lake**, formed, according to legend, by Manjushri after draining the valley lake as a compensation to the *nagas* (serpents) who had become homeless. People still respect the *nagas*' privacy, though it is a great spot for bird-watching.

Before reaching **Pharping**, on your left is the first hydro-station in Nepal,

Little hamlets appear as if strewn all over the valley.

which was built by the Ranas at the turn of the century.

On the right-hand side is the **Sesha Narayan Temple** with its four bathing pools. Look for the half-submerged 13th century statue of Surjya, the Sun God, in one of them. A stone stairway leads up to the temple. Sheltered by an overhanging cliff, the pilgrimage site is at least 500 years old.

Climb further up the hill to the cave of **Gorakhnath**. Although Gorakhnath was an 11th century yogi who is believed to have been an incarnation of Shiva, the cave has today become a centre for Tibetan Buddhism. Guru Padmasambhava, who established Buddhism in Tibet, is believed to have meditated here. There is also a Tibetan mon-

astery nearby.

A path leads down to the 17th century temple of the Goddess *Bajra Jogini*, who is said to have persuaded Manjushri to action.

The road ends at Dakshinkali. Set in a narrow gorge between two mountains, the temple like many in Nepal is built at the confluence of two streams. The steep hillsides, tumbling streams, and thick forests make it a pleasant spot and popular with Nepali picnickers.

The temple is dedicated to *Dakshin* (black Kali), another incarnation of the mother goddess Mahadevi. Every Tuesday and Saturday, the tile floors of the temple are red with the blood of chickens, ducks, goats and even buffaloes, whose throats are slit and their blood

The Himals form the picture postcard backdrop for the Valley.

used to bathe the goddess. Snakes converge from the four corners of the canopy covering the open temple. Inside is a black stone Kali, six-armed and trampling a man. To worship Kali, devotees offer an animal sacrifice.

The sacrifices are then cleaned on the banks of the nearby streams and become part of the picnic meal that follows.

In the southwest corner of the Valley, perched on a hilltop surrounded by a vista of emerald green rice fields, is the medieval town of **Kirtipur**. Established in the 12th century by the King of Patan, it grew to be an independent city-state, the fourth power of the Valley. When Prithvi Narayan Shah descended on the Valley, he first set his sights on Kirtipur.

His first attack was a disaster. The king had a narrow escape, spared, some say, by the mercy of two Kirtipur soldiers. His most trusted aide, Kalu Pande, was killed, and his troops were routed. In 1764 he tried again, and was again repelled. This time his younger brother lost an eye in the fight.

In December 1767, Prithvi Narayan Shah was finally successful, and Kirtipur was forced to surrender. The conqueror was determined to punish Kirtipur and make it serve as an example to the rest of the Valley. He ordered that the lips and noses of every male should be cut off except for those of musicians and suckling babies. It is said that the noses and lips of the 865 men who suffered this punishment weighed 80 pounds.

Kirtipur became *Nakkatta*, the city of cut-noses.

It sometimes seems as if Kirtipur's grim fate brought it a curse. In spite of the **Tribhuvan University** campus, the **Cottage Industry Centre** and the new **Horticulture Centre** built by Japanese aid nearby, Kirtipur remains neglected. There is none of the energy and the rapid change one instantly feels in the Valley's other towns.

The town is actually spread over two hills with a large pond in the saddle in-between. The southern hill is topped by the **Buddhist Chilanchu Vihar**, a *stupa* surrounded by **Jagat Pal Vihara** (built in 1514) and other monasteries. The northern hill has **Bagh Bhairav Temple**, its famous picture of Bhairav as a *bagh* (tiger). On the upper balconies hang shields and swords used by the city's soldiers against the Gorkhalis.

Kirtipur's indigenous architecture and daily life is best enjoyed by a stroll through the town. Survey the steep hillsides and the rich fields below, and you will see why Kirtipur was once a power in its own right.

You will have a good day's walk if you take a bus or a taxi to Kirtipur, then descend on the west side and head for Chobar. From Chobar, continue on to Patan.

Another idea would be to bus it to Pharping, walk north, climb the ridge to the top of the popular pilgrimage spot of **Champadevi** (2,278m or 7,497ft), then descend to Kirtipur. This would take the better part of a day. Bring a packed lunch and drinking water.

Nagarjun is situated northwest of the Valley. Also called the **Jamacho Forest Reserve**, it is protected by a brick wall and guards. There is a small entry fee. A paved road goes to the top. A pleasant 2-hour walk from the entrance, and you will reach the top where you can enjoy a great view of the Himalayas. It is also a popular picnic spot. Tibetans come up on special days to pray, make offerings and hang prayer-flags. The lush forest contains a vast variety of wildlife and birds.

On the east slope are two caves about a km apart containing Buddha images and a statue of the first century South Indian philosopher Nagarjuna, after whom the forest is named. Ask about the trail at the gate. A winding motor road goes to the top.

When Prithvi Narayan Shah invaded the Valley, he entered over its low shoulder near **Kakani** (2073m; 6822ft). In the 19th century, the British Resident built a summer cottage on the ridge of Kakani when he was forbidden to travel beyond the Valley.

The British Resident's cottage still stands, next to a hotel. The views remain the same ones he saw – Manaslu, Ganesh, Langtang and eastward. Sunsets and sunrises here are especially spectacular. The buses for **Trisuli** stop at Kakani; it is about a 2-hour ride from Kathmandu or a pleasant half-day walk. There are some rudimentary hotels in the bazaar, and a better one next to the British Resident's cottage.

All trails start from the agricultural farm. To walk straight down to **Balaju** (4 hours), do not enter the farm itself. The trail should be fairly well-marked. Stay high in rhododendron and oak until the trail drops steeply. Head toward the village you can see, then walk on to Balaju.

A second trail (about 5 hours) leads into the farm; then walk past a school, and continue up. The forest is thick, but Kathmandu Valley should be visible on your right. After 1½ hours, the trail drops. Look for a wide trail below you, and head south on it and keep right until you drop to Balaju.

Shivapuri (2,732m; 8,991ft) is only a little lower than Phulchowki but with

Kathesimbhu Stupa.

equally excellent views. From **Nagi Gompa**, some ways above **Budhanilkantha**, it takes 3½ to 4 hours to reach the campsite at the summit. There is water near the top, but it is best to carry your own water. Instead of going up to Nagi Gompa, you can also take the main trail from Budhanilkantha, to which there are frequent buses from Rani Pokhari; or take a short taxi ride. Near the grassy top are large boulders and the ruins of an old fort.

You can also get to the top via Kathmandu's reservoir at **Sundarijal**. Take a bus (or taxi) to Sundarijal. Buses ply from the east side of the Tundikhel ground. The walk up from Sundarijal via **Okreni** is about 4 to 6 hours via **Chaubas**. You will hit the **Helambu Trail** part of the way.

Shivapuri means Shiva's place and there may well be a *sadhu* in a cave near the summit. Bring your own food, stove, sleeping bag and tent if you plan on staying overnight. It can get cold at night and it snows in winter.

Budhanilkantha lies at the foot of Shivapuri about 9 km north of Kathmandu. Budhanilkantha comes from one of the thousand-plus names for Vishnu.

Here he is Narayan (Reclining Vishnu), floating on the primeval ocean, (in fact a pond). He is reclining on a bed formed by the coils of the eleven-headed cobra Ananta. A loose robe draped over his crossed legs, each of Vishnu's four arms hold a symbol of his powers; conch shell, *chakra*, mace and a lotus seed.

The valley hosts interesting
species of birds.

Vishnu is often depicted in black and thus the black stone of this sculptured statue.

Only Hindus may enter the pond's compound. The King of Nepal, as an incarnation of Vishnu, is not permited to set eyes on this powerful image. At least three of these massive, almost identical images of Vishnu were carved during the Licchavi period. One of them lies inside the **Mul Chowk Durbar Square**, another in the **Balaju Gardens**. Replicas of the original at Budhanilkantha they are considered quite safe for the king to look at.

The stone – 5m (16ft) long – is believed to have been brought from outside the valley about 1,400 years ago!

During the festival of *Baikuntha Chaturadasi* in November, the compound and roads are crowded with pilgrims from all over the Valley and beyond.

Take a bus or a taxi to Budhanil-kantha in the morning, then walk back. Head for the village of **Tupek**, then **Lasuntar** (literally meaning garlic field!), cross the **Dhobi Khola**, and head toward the Ring Road. Cross the road to visit one of the most beautiful statues in the Valley at **Dhum Varahi**. Continue on to **Harigau** where you can get a taxi or keep walking from there.

Generous rivers supply the fields in the valley while serving as bath places for people and buffaloes.

A Discreet Treasure

Dhum Varahi is one of the Valley's "discreet" treasures. On an open bluff overlooking the Dhobi Khola is a large *pipal* tree.

Wrapped in the twisted grasp of the tree's roots is a small brick shrine with a beautiful 6th century life-size image of Vishnu incarnated as a boar, the form he took to defeat the demon Hiranyaksha, who was trying to tug the world underwater. The sculpture is considered

Encircling the stupa at Boudhnath during Loshar.

one of the masterpieces of the Valley.

Boudhnath

Probably the first foreigner to visit Boudhnath was Ekai Kawaguchi, a Japanese Buddhist who, posing as a Chinese monk, spent time here in 1899 on his journey to Tibet. In his account, *Three Years in Tibet*, he writes that in winter Boudhnath was crowded with pilgrims who "come to this place to pay their respects to the great temple. .... By far the greatest number of visitors are Tibetans...who eke out their existence by a sort of nomadic life, passing their winter in the neighborhood of the tower and going back to Tibet in summer."

Things have not changed much in the 90-plus years since Kawaguchi made his observations. Boudhnath's wintertime population from the farthest corners of Nepal and Tibet have made it a popular spot with those more recent transients, western tourists. You can pick up pieces of turquoise, Chinese goods, bricks of tea leaves for Tibetan tea, and watch (and be watched by) some fascinating characters.

A few kilometres northeast of Kathmandu, the huge *stupa* of Boudhnath is one of the dominant and most distinctive structures in the Valley. It was supposedly built by a woman who made her fortune as a gooseherder! For stealing two flowers from Indra's heaven, she was condemned to be born to a

A Tibetan Buddhist woman.

swineherd. She married, bore four children, and somehow made a fortune raising geese. She then petitioned the king to let her build a temple on land the size of a buffalo skin.

When the king agreed, she proceeded to cut the skin into thin strips, which she tied together to enclose a large area. Some court officials protested, but the king said, "Kings must not eat their words," and she was given the land to build the huge *stupa*.

Her cleverness is our good fortune. The *stupa*'s mystical eyes, glittering spire and umbrella, and hundreds of colored flags sending prayers in all directions, makes it one of the most memorable sights in the Valley.

Boudhnath has always been of spe-

cial importance to Tibetans. Jewellers used to occupy the shops around the *stupa*, the only other shops catered to the needs of the jewellers, but today, these shops are stocked with tourist paraphernalia.

Some Newar goldsmiths are still working here. Traders from Tibet spread all manner of wares on the pavement, from trinkets, ritual objects, to Chinese cloth shoes and mounds of butter and brick-tea.

With the influx of Tibetan refugees in the 1960's, Boudhnath has grown rapidly, even more so in recent years as Tibetans become more prosperous. Today, the fields are disappearing fast – and in their place are many monasteries and Tibetan houses.

Trekking the valley brings one at close range with farms.

There are a number of new *gompas* near the *stupa* belonging to different Buddhist sects. When you visit leave your shoes at the entrance and step into the clerestory-lit chapel.

The chief deities will be on the altar, bedecked with tiny butter-lamps, in-cense, rice, food and money. Elaborate murals of Buddhist gods and Buddhist themes cover the walls.

When you walk around the main *stupa* (in a clockwise direction), try to identify the different pilgrims you see. There will be Tibeto-Nepalis from far off

Dolpa and Mugu, the upper Buri Gandaki, or east from Sankhuwasaba and upper Taplejung.

Of course, there will be many Tibetans, sometimes some Sikkimese, Bhutanese or Ladakhis in their distinctive *chubas*.

The *Stupa*

The *stupa* form is a dominant Buddhist motif, and Boudhnath is one of the finest examples. Large or small, they consist of a large hemisphere of earth topped with a usually brick square called a *chaku*, which faces the four cardinal points. Above the *chaku*, a thirteen-level spire represents the thirteen levels of knowledge, which rises to a crescent moon and a sun, above it a *bindu* (dot) symbolising the perfect union of compassion and wisdom that defines enlightenment.

The distinctly Nepali features are the eyes and nose; the eyes of the all-seeing Buddha and the nose symbolises unity.

The whitewashed base may have a pattern of yellow representing a lotus blossom. The *stupa* of Boudhnath gains height and power from the concentric, stepped terraces in the *mandala* design it rests on. Encircling the *stupa*'s base are 108 inches, each containing a statue of Buddha Amitabha.

On *Loshar*, (Tibetan New Year) celebrated in February or March, depending on the lunar calendar, the *stupa* is cleaned and painted and lines of new coloured prayer flags tied to the spire. Tibetans in their best clothes gather at the *stupa* and mark the new year by throwing a bit of *tsampa* flour into the air, shouting "*Lha Gya-lo,*" or The Gods are Victorious. Yellow-hat monks carry a framed picture of the Dalai Lama around the *stupa* and blow on 3m long horns. On the night of the full moon, devotees and pilgrims circumambulate the *stupa* and offer butterlamps at the altars.

Sankhu is 19km past Boudhnath. Hidden behind the ridge of Changu Narayan, it is a corner of the Valley untouched by the rapid development of Kathmandu. There are some interesting temples and sculptures, but the town looks worn. Above the town is the **Bajra Jogini Temple**, near which is **Gunivihar Temple**. There is a festival here on the full moon of March-April.

Sankhu has an exciting *Bathing Festival* during the month of *Magh* (Jan-Feb).

Swayambhunath had its origins in the lotus planted by *Vipaswi* Buddha. When Manjushri drained the Valley, the lotus settled on a hill formed by its roots, and this hill is now Swayambhu.

The hilltop of Swayambhu has been a sacred place for eons. The Emperor Ashoka from India may have visited it, and while the gothic age was getting underway in Europe, Swayambhu was already an important Buddhist centre, with close ties to **Lhasa**, capital of Tibet.

In 1346, Moslems destroyed the shrine. It was restored and renovated over the centuries. The most recent major undertaking was the construction of a large viewing platform on the southeast corner of the hilltop, following landslides caused by heavy rains in 1979. The platform provides some of the best views of Kathmandu Valley.

It is possible to drive almost the entire way to the top, but one can walk up the 300 stone steps constructed by the Mallas in the mid-17th century. At the base of the stairs, there are three larger-than-life Buddhas in classic postures. Small statues and shrines flank the steps on the way up. The long stairway is guarded by pairs of animals, including elephants, peacocks, lions, and *garudas*. At the top of the stairs is a massive 1.5m (5ft) *dorje* (thunderbolt), placed there by King Pratap Malla in the mid-17th century.

The monkeys that teem the hillside are anything but guardians; they will pilfer anything they can. One story says they originated from the lice on Manjushri's head. The National Geographic Magazine once ran a feature, on "The Sacred Monkeys of Swayambhu."

The *stupa*, built on a *mandala* base, is much smaller than the *stupa* of Boudhnath visible across the Valley. Five Buddhas rest behind iron curtains in niches around the base. Four are *dhyani* Buddhas, in meditative poses with an animal sacred to Buddha depicted below them. The fifth faces the main stairs flanked by stone monks. Between the Buddhas are four *Taras* completing the symmetry.

There are numerous *chaityas* (small *stupas*) at the top, some dating back to the Licchavi period. On the northwest side of the *stupa* is the **Temple of Harati Ajima**, covered with ornately detailed gilded copper, much of it hidden by grime. Its goddess, Bhagbati, protects children from disease, especially small-pox. There are always mothers worshipping here.

There are a few *gompas* at the top. With the greater Tibetan presence, other monasteries have shot up all around the Swayambhu hill area.

Swayambhu is the main centre for Newar Buddhism. There is more of a Nepali-Hindu influence here than at Boudhnath. Women in *saris*, men in *daura-surwal* and *topis* are common. Devotees return with *red tika* on their foreheads.

On the morning of Buddha *Jayanti*, the celebration of Buddha's birthday on the full moon of mid-May, there is an almost continuous line of worshippers

Boudhnath, a landmark of the Valley.

from the Bagmati River to the top of Swayambhu's hill. The *stupa* is crowded with worshippers, *puja* (prayer) trays held high above the throng. The *stupa* blazes with lights that night.

First Letters

On the hill below the main *stupa* is a small shrine to Saraswati, goddess of wisdom. She visits the Valley and this shrine on *Basant Panchami*; the first day of spring (usually in mid-February). The shrine area is packed with families worshiping Saraswati, petitioning her to make their children intelligent. To please the goddess, young children in their best clothes, with looks of extreme concentration, scrawl just-learned alphabets over every inch of wall. Proud parents stand beside them, ready to guide a wayward hand.

Shiva is an extremely complex personality. In the Hindu trinity, he is the "Destroyer" whereas Brahma is the "Creator" and Vishnu the "Preserver". He is also Natraj, Lord of Dance; Bhairav, the wrathful Mahadev, the Great God, and Bhuteswara, Lord of Goblins.

Shiva is most often depicted as an ascetic, his body smeared with ash, his matted hair piled high (with perhaps the river Ganges flowing from it), covered with a leopard skin, and carrying his trademark trident. He has the third vertical eye of complete wisdom in his forehead. In this form, Shiva is the patron of thousands of *sadhus* who re-

Devotees often make a pilgrimage to the Reclining Vishnu.

nounce this world and search for the meditative perfection that Shiva found.

Pashupati is the name Shiva assumes as "Lord and Protector of Animals." Shiva spent a night meditating in the forest here and placed it under his protection. Once a year, on *Shiva Raatri* (Shiva's Night), usually in mid or late-February, he returns for a night. Thousands of Shiva followers from all over India and Nepal come to pray in the temple and bathe in the Bagmati River.

Worship of Shiva usually centres around supplications to a *lingam* (stone phallic symbol). The **Pashupatinath Temple** is one of the four most important sites for Shiva worshippers in the Hindu world. The present two-tiered main temple with its gilded copper roofs was built in 1696 by Birpalendra Malla. Entrance to the temple is strictly prohibited to non-Hindus. Non-Hindus can

view at the rear end a huge statue of the bull *Nandi* (Shiva's celestial vehicle) from the western entrance.

Across the river from the main temple, one can look into the temple courtyard from the hill-top platform above a row of *chaityas*, each containing a *lingam*. The two stone platforms projecting into the river at the base of the temple are cremation *ghats* used only for royalty and prime ministers.

On the south side of the two stone bridges are the public *ghats*. Because of its special significance, Pashupatinath is considered an auspicious place to die. Mother Theresa retains a house for the dying here.

On the south side of the bridge, on both sides of the river are several temples and shelters for pilgrims.

Two major festivals can be observed at Pashupatinath; *Shiva Raatri* in mid-

In the grounds of Pashupatinath Temple.

February and *Teej*, the festival for women, in mid-September.

After crossing the river and climbing up for a view into Pashupatinath, continue through the woods up the hill to **Gorakhnath**, then down to the **Guhjeswari Temple** on the banks of the Bagmati River. Though the temple is forbidden to non-Hindus, the setting is dramatic and there are views across the river to the Boudhnath *Stupa*.

On the southeast edge of Pashupati is one of Nepal's two golf courses. There is an unusual hazard – grazing cows! Over eager small boys may try to help you by fetching your ball. The clubhouse is easy to mistake for a toll-booth.

North of Pashupatinath on the Ring Road is the **Chahabil** area. It is not significant now, but its history is. The small *stupa* on the western road is one of the earliest in the Valley, possibly from the 3rd century BC. The **Chabahil Bahal** was supposedly founded by Charumati, daughter of Ashoka. The area was then known as **Deopatan**, and it was a centre of Licchavi rule. Ask for directions to **Kuti Bahal**.

A New Problem

One of the outstanding sculptures of the Valley, a 9th century standing Buddha, was recently stolen from the Chahabil area. Art theft has become more frequent as Nepali sculpture becomes better known and sought after by collectors. One estimate is that half the art created over 2,000 years has been lost in the last thirty years. Do not be surprised to find a beautiful statue behind heavy bars or wrapped in chains; be happy that it is still there.

Patan

Sitting on a plateau south of the Bagmati River from Kathmandu, with over 130 *bahals* (monastery court-yards), Patan is probably one of the oldest Buddhist centres anywhere. Until recently the limits of the city were marked by four earth and brick *stupas* said to be built by Emperor Ashoka in the 3rd century BC. The two most visible ones are near the Narayani Hotel and south of the Lagankhel bus-stop.

A call to meditation and worship at the Golden Temple in Patan.

Patan has a very different ambience from its sister cities in the Valley. The city grew outwards from Durbar Square. The main streets leading to it are wide and the buildings lining them a jumble of old brick Rana-era pseudo-European columns and plaster nymphs and, unfortunately, ugly modern concrete.

Every morning and evening, rush-hour traffic crosses the Bagmati Bridge between Patan and Kathmandu. Today, Patan is more like an extension of the capital, but for centuries it rivalled Kathmandu for control of the

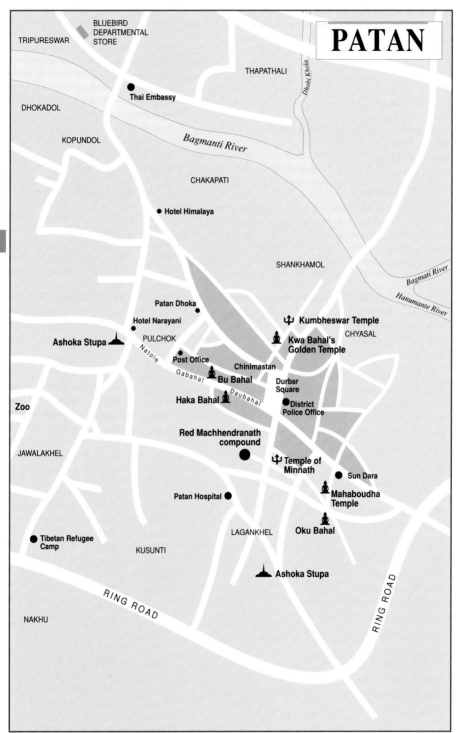

Valley. Its close proximity to Kathmandu has drawn some of the capital's wealth and industry to it. The **Patan Industrial Estate** and several cottage industries are located within the city.

Patan does not have the frozen-in-time feel of Bhaktapur. Commuters, factory workers and students all have one foot in the modern age and the other firmly set in tradition.

In recent years, television antennas and satellite dishes have begun to appear on the roofs of the "City of Golden Roofs." Patan's architectural gems are increasingly elbowed by modern concrete buildings.

A bike or a good pair of walking shoes are all you need to tour Patan. After passing Nepal's engineering campus on both sides of the road, you'll come to **Patan Dhoka** (Patan's Gate), with the Newari Calendar Year written on it.

Follow the road past a well where women haul up buckets to wash clothes and bathe, and pass the **Ashoka Cinema Hall**. All kinds of shops line the street, which is sometimes wide and sometimes narrow. Duck into one of the doorways through which you can see daylight and you will find yourself in a courtyard that may be a *bahal* or a cluster of farmers' homes. It may consist of a few houses or a good-sized park with large trees, a bathing tank and even a temple.

The people here have been living and working together for generations, and there is a strong bond of community and common history. On Saturdays, neighbourhood folk sit on grass, listening to a Buddhist priest espouse teachings on a platform sheltered by a *pipal* tree. Visit the community of **Nag Bahal** to see an example of this.

Further down the street, look for the entrance to **Kwa Bahal**, the "Golden Temple," which can also be entered from the street leading to Kumbeshwar. This is one of the most beautiful and vibrant *bahals* in the Valley. Take off your shoes to enter the inner courtyard. The entire front of the main shrine is covered with detailed metal work, including panels of the Gautama Buddha. Do not overlook the small shrine situated in the courtyard.

Kwa Bahal is still active and well supported by the community. Maintenance of the monastery is rotated among various groups who belong to the *guthi*. It was founded in 1409, thus having more than 500 years of monastic study and community support! It is a pity that other *bahals* are not as well cared for. Visit Kwa Bahal in the early morning or late in the afternoon, when there are fewer tour groups visiting. The young monks will willingly show you around.

Just beyond Kwa Bahal, a side street dips down and north to **Kumbeshwar**, a walled-in compound of temples, resthouses and a large bathing tank. The five-storeyed temple, the oldest in Patan, was first built in 1392. Inside stands a large silver *lingam*. Some of the shrines in the compound date back from Licchavi times.

Durbar Square, Patan's grand central meeting place.

Sacred Threads and Song

During the monsoon, the pool fills up with water. Its source is said to be the holy **Gosaikund Lake**, several walking days north at 2860m (9412ft) elevation. On the full moon of August, the day of the *Kumbeshwar Mela*, devotees of Shiva come to bathe in the pond and to worship the Shiva *lingam* of serpents coiled in the centre of the tank.

Jhankris or *shamans* gather, beating drums, twirling rhythmically in skirts, perspiration trickling under their peacock feather headdresses as they move from shrine to shrine. It is a chance to see a bit of Nepali culture the casual visitor normally misses.

It is also on the full moon of *Jana Purnima*, when *brahman* and *chhetri* men change their sacred thread. Everyone, Hindus and Buddhists alike, can tie the *rakhsa bandhan* or "protective bond" around their right wrist. This thread is thought to bring good fortune and is worn for three months until *Lakshmi Puja*. The wearer removes it and reties it on the tail of a cow. After the person dies, it is hoped a cow will be waiting to offer her tail to the soul for a pull across the river of death.

Later in the day, crowds gather to listen to repartee singers *ad-lib*. Men and women try to outdo each other with wit, humour and poetry. They go on for hours and often have the crowd in stitches. Even if you cannot understand,

The Krishna Temple on a festival evening.

t is fun to watch this cultural "sport." When a truce is finally declared, singers agree to meet in the same spot the following year, and they often do.

Patan's **Durbar Square**, also known as **Mangal Bazaar**, is the smallest but the most complete and accessible of the palace complexes. Most of it was constructed in what must have been a very busy 17th century under the rule of Siddhi Narasingha Malla and Shrinivasa Malla. The palace courtyards are not connected and seem to have been built with no consideration for the style

Tusha Hiti, Sundari Chowk, the royal bathing pool.

of their neighbours, (an oft-heard complaint about modern architecture).

The southernmost building, **Sundari Chowk**, built in 1627, contains *Tusha Hiti*, the royal bathing tank lined with dozens of stone deities. Two stone *nagas* coil its perimeters. At the head of the tank's stairs is a massive stone meditation platform that was used by the king. The king's living quarters surrounded the courtyard – beautiful woodcarved windows fit for royalty.

The Sundari Chowk is guarded by Hanuman (red as always), a white Ganesh and farthest down, Narsingha, the lion incarnation of Vishnu. Above the entrance, a gilded metal window is flanked by windows of carved ivory. A policeman is usually on guard to the right of Hanuman; the door leads to the local police headquarters. During the 1990 democracy movement, the citizens of Patan held the police captive at their own headquarters for several days

To the left of Sundari Chowk is **Mul Chowk**, built in 1640. Palace priests lived in the buildings lining this court, the royal **Taleju Temple**, built in 1671 rises above the roof in the northeast corner. In the courtyard is the small **Bidya Temple**. On the south wall, Ganga and Yamuna guard the shrine of the family's personal secret goddess.

Next comes the large **Degu Talle Temple**, built twice in the 17th century – first in 1640, then in 1662 after fire destroyed it. Tantric rites to a personal deity were performed here. Today, it is

Details in gilt reveal the rich decorative art of the past.

A consultation in progress – oracles, astrologers and soothsayers play their part in Nepali life.

also the entrance to the Mahaguthi Shop, a handicrafts co-op well worth a visit.

Further north is **Keshab Narayan Chowk**, built between 1670 and 1734. It has been renovated into a museum. The main entrance, Patan's Sun Dhoka, contains Shiva and Parvati in its *torana*. Also, take note of the central gilded window. The kings sat here while contemplating a new site for probably yet another temple.

Past the palace and behind two *pathis*, a steep staircase leads four metres down to **Manga Hiti**, first built in the 10th century and still an important source of water for the locale.

Facing the palace are a group of temples, almost all dating to the 17th century. At their southern end is the newest temple, built in 1723, to Krishna. It seems to have become a resting station for porters. To its west is **Bhai Dega**. The water fountain has a bust of a Rana lady who once spouted water from her index finger, as if that was all she could spare!

North of the **Krishna Temple** is the huge **Taleju Bell**, and the **Hari Shanker Temple**, built by Siddhi Narasingha, who kneels atop a column facing Degu Talle. Behind him is a *shikhara*, and to his north, **Char Narayan Temple**, built in 1566.

Then there is the outstanding **Krishna Temple** of black stone, built by Narasingha in 1637. This was said to be his favourite building, which says much, considering his building activities. Scenes

Mane wheels, monkeys and jackfruit in a meditation courtyard.

from the Hindu epics flow like a long cartoon on a frieze. The temple has some Mughal-like touches. Garuda kneels atop his stone column, seemingly in awe of this unusual and finely-proportioned temple.

Narasingha built the earlier temple of **Bishwanath** in 1627. It falls in the shadow of its more famous neighbour to the south, but is not without its own merits.

At the northern end of the square is **Bhimsen Temple**, built in 1681 by Shrinivasa Malla, a favourite temple of local businessmen. The deity is on the second-floor, lit by the large balcony above the entrance.

Northeast of Durbar Square are blocks of traditional homes which re-flect the socio-economic status of their inhabitants. Mainly *jyapu* farmers with some lower-caste members occupy the lower areas. You may stumble on a factory that burns water buffalo bones to make fertiliser. Ask for the Water Taps of **Chyasal**, with Saraswati clad in green and yellow riding her trademark swan. There are also Licchavi era statues nearby.

If you walk east from the Durbar Square for 5 minutes, you will come to **Sundara**, named after its fine gilded waterspout. It is still in regular use as indoor plumbing remains unaffordable for many Nepalis.

Sundara is an important stop during the *Raato Machhendranath* Festival when the god's huge chariot is pulled

Temples are not just about religion, but of architectural details too.

through the city.

If you turn south at the Sundara intersection, just up the street is the entrance to **Mahabaudha Temple**. Several shops sell fine Buddhist images in the alley leading to this unusual temple.

The surface of this *shikhara-style* temple is covered with hundreds of terracotta tiles depicting the Buddha. It is a 16th century copy of the Mahabodhi Temple of Bodhgaya, where the Sakyamuni attained enlightenment. The 1934 earthquake severely damaged the temple. Unable to restore it completely, the small temple in the corner was built with leftover material.

Exit from Mahabaudha, and continue south to the T-junction, then go left (east) to the gate of **Uku Bahal**. This well-kept monastery combines great art and "historic kitsch." It is worth visiting.

The great art lies in the wooden struts – masterpieces from the 12th and 13th centuries. There are five Mahabuddhas on the struts supporting the first roof, the shrine's main door, and the gilded spires of the top roof.

The *kitsch* is the wonderful menagerie of metal animals that guard the front of the *bahal*. Minding this group of snarling animals and birds is the statue of a pompous-looking Rana.

Uku Bahal will remind you to lighten up and enjoy what you are seeing. Back in the street, head east. Chances are you will see an old brick building being torn down, or maybe one with a timber pushed against a big bulge in a building.

On hearing the noise of striking of metal, you will know that you are in the middle of the metal workers' section. They make devotional statues as well as utensils of any size and design. Some pots are enormous and usually sold by weight; a statue's price is based on craftsmanship and the materials used. Prices quoted are somewhat influenced by the storekeeper's assessment of you, but are always subject to some negotiation.

Westward on the main metal workers' road, past a T-junction, is **I Baha Bahal**, one of Patan's oldest monasteries (1427), now housing a school. Turn right to Durbar Square, then left to a small alley and **Bishwakarma Temple**, the favourite of local craftsmen. It

The torana of Patan's Golden Gate at Durbar Marg.

has a rich gilded facade and an unusual window with a solar disk and interlocking triangles. Turn left and a few minutes ahead is **Lagankhel**, where you can get a bus to Godavari. Past the bus-stop is one of Ashoka's *stupas*. Go around the *stupa* to the east and south. **Patan Industrial Estate** is on your left. Inside the estate are several handicraft factories selling wood, brass and carpets.

Starting south from the T-junction, an 11th century water tap with three spouts comes up on your right. Behind it is **Min Nath Temple**, built in the 16th century, housing a Buddhist deity. Min Nath accompanies *Raato Machhendra* on his annual procession through the city in a smaller child-pulled chariot..

A curved path opposite Min Nath leads to the spacious compound of the *Raato Machhendranath*. This large three-tiered temple, built in the 1670's, is the main home of Patan's most important deity. *Raato Machhendra* is a manifestation of *Avalokiteshvara*, Bodhisattva of Compassion, also known as Lokeswar, and worshipped by Hindus as Shiva. The *Machhendra* also spends several months a year in **Bungamati**, his original home.

A Month of Excitement

In one of the grandest, most exciting festivals of the Valley, both Hindus and Buddhists appeal to *Raato Machhendranath* as a bringer of rain and

The famous St Xavier's school used to be an old Rana palace.

plenty. For several weeks (usually in May), *Machhendra*, represented by a large piece of wood, is pulled through city streets sheltered in his huge roof-crunching chariot with its tall, swaying bamboo and pine bough tower.

The climax comes when the chariot reaches **Jawalakhel**. The *kumari* of Patan sits to one side (Patan's *kumari* is chosen from the families of Bajracharyas, the Newar Buddhist priest caste who preside here) and thousands watch the King in whose presence is displayed the dark bejewelled *bhoto* (vest) entrusted to *Machhendra* for safekeeping by *Karkot Naga*, the serpent king. Its safety guarantees monsoon rains.

Back at the Durbar Square, a main road leads west to another Ashoka *stupa* and the road to Kathmandu. The video libraries, magazine shops, stores selling ready-made apparel and the electric rice-cookers suggest prosperity. But you will see how distorted this perception is when you walk down a side street. Watch for **Haka Bahal** on your left.

Walking south from the *stupa*, you'll see the gates of the Jesuit-run **St Xavier's**, for generations the school of choice for Nepal's elite. A stone's throw away is **Jawalakhel**, where Nepal's zoo is located. Often, football and volleyball games are played in the large open area here. When you come to the *pipal* tree, follow the downhill fork of the road lined with carpet shops. You will then arrive at the **Tibetan Handicraft Centre** and a monastery, behind which is the Tibetan Refugee Camp.

Bhaktapur lies 19km east of Kathmandu. The trolley runs from Tripureshwor to the south of this city of more than 50,000 inhabitants. You'll get a good view of the brick buildings along the east-west ridge north of the Hanumante River. In winter, the Himalayas loom above the city's temple spires. You can also take the frequent (packed) express mini-buses from **Bagh Bazaar** which stop at **Teka Pokhari** on the western edge of the city. It is also possible to bike out to Bhaktapur. Take the **Kodari Road** out and return on the old road that passes north of **Thimi.** On the way out, you will pass an *ayurvedic* medical factory, rice and vegetable plots, the **National Tuberculosis Centre**, and small factories, surrounded by fields, producing or assembling everything from toothpaste to television sets.

Thimi is about halfway to Bhaktapur. It is an old Newar town famous for *papier-mache* masks and pottery, especially animal-shaped flower pots. Thimi has a fantastic New

Bhaktapur

Sun Dokha (golden gate) in Bhaktapur considered a masterpiece in the valley.

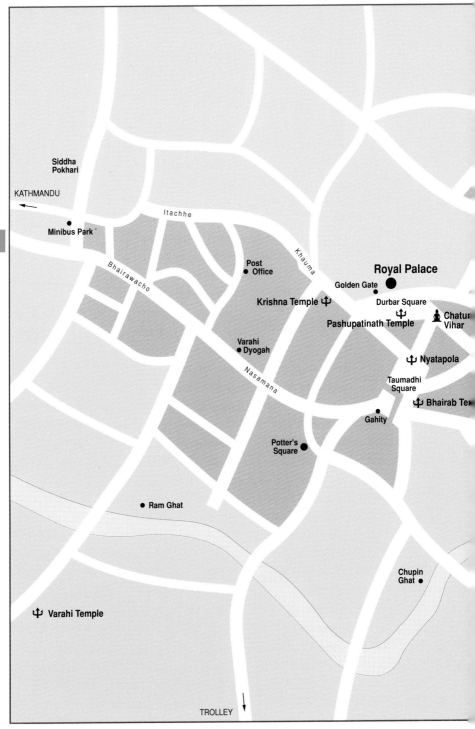

Siddha
Pokhari

KATHMANDU

Itachhe

Minibus Park

Bhairawacho

Khauma

Post
Office

Royal Palace

Golden Gate

Krishna Temple ♆

Durbar Square

♆
Pashupatinath Temple

Chatur
Vihar

Varahi
Dyogah

♆ Nyatapola

Nasamana

Taumadhi
Square

♆ Bhairab Te

Gahity

Potter's
Square

Ram Ghat

Chupin
Ghat ●

♆ Varahi Temple

TROLLEY

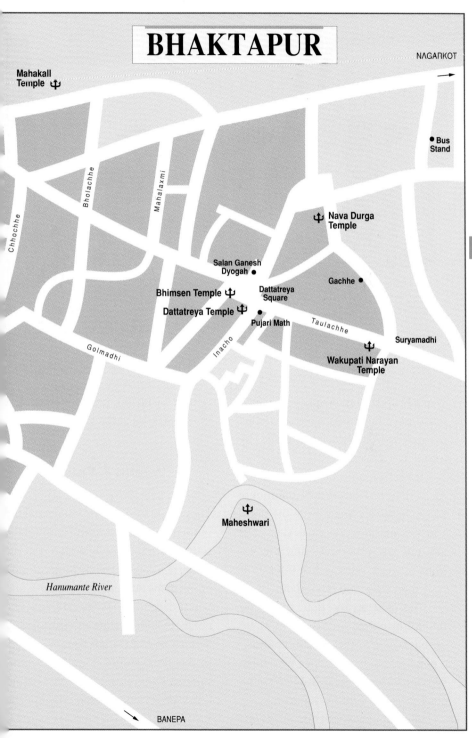

BHAKTAPUR

Mahakall
Temple ♆

● Bus
Stand

Chhochhe

Bholachhe

Mahalaxmi

♆ Nava Durga
Temple

Salan Ganesh
Dyogah ●

Gachhe ●

Bhimsen Temple ♆

Dattatreya
Square

Dattatreya Temple ♆

Pujari Math ●

Taulachhe

Suryamadhi

Golmadhi

Inacho

♆
Wakupati Narayan
Temple

♆
Maheshwari

Hanumante River

→ BANEPA

Bhaktapur's Durbar Square, the heart of the city.

Year's Festival in mid-April when each *tole's* (neighbourhood) god is paraded in a cloud of red powder, surrounded by traditional dancers.

If you are on a bike, take the left road on the fork across the Hanumante River; the trolley line runs to the right. You will come to a playing field on your left, and army barracks and the fire station (check out the fire trucks) on your right. The road forks again.

The road on the right takes you through an old gate into the town. There are buses and, further, **Siddhi Pokhari**, a pond said to be inhabited by a huge *naga* and never drained. Bear left for the quickest way to Durbar Square.

Bhaktapur has been through its ups and downs. Today, it enjoys a reputa-

tion of being the best preserved and most medieval of the Valley's cities.

Wealth & Power

The city grew up around villages on the main trade route between Tibet and the south. It was originally designed in the shape of a conch shell by King Anando Malla in the 9th century. Its wealth and power depended heavily on trade. The palace of this city state was **Dattatrayo Square**, east of Durbar Square.

In the 17th century, King Bupatindro was able to finally integrate the old and new *durbar* (square) area. Though the Valley split into smaller states Bhaktapur remained wealthy and pow erful, and its kings continued their generous patronage. Bhaktapur was the last of the Valley's city states to fall to the Gorkha invaders. With the ascendance of Kathmandu as the country's capital, wealth and status diminished. It stagnated, and became isolated. It grew its own food, made its own cloth and utensils, and produced the best pottery.

Initiatives in business and development were lured by the bright lights of Kathmandu, as were its young people. Until recently, there was little difference between 18th and 20th century Bhaktapur. Surveys showed that Bhaktapur trailed behind Kathmandu in almost every way – education, income and health services.

Help came with the German-funded

Stories captured on the Sun Dokha.

Bhaktapur Development Project, which has done much to improve the city's infrastructure and its economy. Its real success lay in introduction of developments that fully retained Bhaktapur's rich physical and cultural character.

Being a Newar town, you will hear Newari being spoken everywhere. About two-thirds of the city's population are farmers, who walk each day from densely populated *toles* to work their fields outside the city. Much of the social activity takes place in the public square of the *tole*. Houses are small. Animals are kept on the ground floor, the room on top is the kitchen and in-between are living spaces and rooftop terraces heavily used.

The best way to see Bhaktapur is on foot. If you are on a bike, park it in a safe place and walk.

Today's Durbar Square is but a faint reminder of what it once was. The large open area where tourists stroll, amidst cows and kite-fliers, was once a cluster of temples and a wing of barracks. The old palace had at least 12 courtyards, though legend has it as 99! The horrendous earthquake of 1934 destroyed much of the square and only six courtyards remain, most of which are closed to the public.

The Golden Gate

The masterpiece of Bhaktapur's Durbar Square, certainly one of the masterpieces of the entire Valley, is the "Sun Dhoka," the **Golden Gate**, set centrally

Off the main touristic landmarks it is business as usual for the people of Bhaktapur.

in the palaces lining the northern edge of the square. Built in 1753, the Sun Dhoka is often compared to the renaissance Florentine Baptistery doors of Ghilberti. The patron was King Jaya Ranjit Malla, but the artist remains anonymous.

The doors announce the entrance to **Taleju Temple** and the king's personal deity. Its panels of gilded copper show a series of ten divinities. The elaborate decorations are fine examples of repoussé. The door is topped by a gilded roof which is itself topped by lions and

Wooden gates at temples and old palaces are always heavily carved.

elephants and decorated finials.

Enter the gate and walk until you come to the **Taleju Chowk** with its beautiful carved doorway. Entry is forbidden to non-Hindus.

Outside to your left is the **National Art Museum**, with a superb collection of paintings and fine statues. Walking through it, remember these were palaces built in the early 17th century.

At the extreme right of the Sun Dhoka is the **Palace of Fifty-five Windows**, built in 1697 by King Bupatindra Malla.

The building was severely damaged in the 1934 earthquake and was rebuilt. It was probably Bupatindra who built the *shikhara-style* **Temple of Bhagbati** to the right of the palace.

Bupatindra

Bupatindra is remembered as an able monarch, an energetic builder and an active patron of the arts. There is a story that the king himself carved one of the original palace windows from sandalwood. The **Nyatapola Temple** is perhaps his most famous contribution. Another story has it that the king, impatient with the pace of its construction, carried bricks himself, thus inspiring (or intimidating) the townspeople to carry all the construction materials to the site in five days.

It is his statue that sits atop a granite column facing Sun Dhoka, his turquoise-ringed hands joined in front.

Nyatapola Temple stairs lead to a 5-tiered pagoda shrine.

Street life in Bhaktapur, where pictures of gods, heroes and movie stars are on sale beside each other.

Rather than chance the judgment of historians, Bupatindra had the statue built himself. So pleased was he with the result that he had the sculptor's hands ordered to be cut so he could never outdo it. No fool, the sculptor was able to save his hands by convincing the King that the statue was unfinished.

Such stories detract from Bupatindra's reputation as a good and thoughtful monarch. They may just be stories, which proves that then, as now, it is very easy to reduce heroes to mere humans, even downright villains.

Beside Bupatindra stands a large 18th century bell that was used to summon worshippers to the Taleju Temple. Behind the bell is **Batsala Durga Temple**, a stone *shikhara-style* supposedly built by Bupatindra.

Behind the Batsala Durga Temple is the large **Pashupati Temple**, one of the Valley's oldest, built in the 15th century by King Yaksha Malla on instructions from Lord Pashupati himself. It is supposedly a copy of the famous Pashupati Temple. Most of it was rebuilt following the 1934 earthquake. The roof struts of the original building show Shiva and characters from the *Ramayana*.

All along the south side of the Durbar Square runs a low two-storey building which used to be a *dharamsala* and now has a souvenir and handicraft shop and a few government offices.

Behind Pashupati Temple, an alley lined with souvenir stands and clothing shops leads down to **Nyatapola Tem-**

Impressionist touch at a Bhaktapur temple.

ple and **Taumadhi Tole**. Nyatapola, built by Bupatindra in 1702, is Nepal's tallest *pagoda* temple at 30m (98ft). Five receding stone platforms lead to the temple with its five receding roofs.

The steep stairway is flanked by guardians. Jai Mal and Patta, famous wrestlers each with the strength of 10 men, stand guard at the bottom; above them a pair of elephants 10 times more powerful, each pair of guardians 10 times more powerful than the one below. Hidden inside the temple the goddess Siddhi Lakshmi has infinitely more power than all her guardians.

Facing the temple in an old dharamsala is **Nyatapola Cafe**. East of the square is **Kasi Biswanath**, a large three-tiered temple dedicated to Bhairav.

These two temples make the square the spiritual centre of Bhaktapur. During major festivals such as *Gai Jatra*, most of the ceremonies take place here.

Head south and west from **Taumadhi Tole** and you will come to a square which is the pottery centre of Bhaktapur. The entire area is often covered with pots drying in the sun. Potters hunker beside huge whirling platforms that spin black clay into vessels of all sizes and shapes. Women sun the pots and dry and winnow grain while their children play.

Ganesh, as well as being the patron of writers and thieves, is also the god of potters. There is a temple – **Jeth Ganesh**, dedicated to him here. Continue south from the potter's area to **Ram Ghat**, an

Brahmin men singing and selling their songs.

important bathing and cremation place. Further south is the trolley line.

Incidently, be sure to find out why Bhaktapur's yogurt is famous.

Just south of **Nyatapola Square**, a steep flagstone street bends back southeast. Once a year the deep drains of this street become inverted rail tracks for the wheels of the huge Bhairav chariot when it rumbles down to **Khalna Tole** for the god's date with his female consort Bhadrakali. The 25m-high (82ft) *lingam* pole of the Bisket is also erected here. Nearby are temples and *ghats*.

Go east from either Durbar Square or Taumadhi Tole; follow the brick-paved roads lined with two-to-four-storeyed brick houses. You will always see brick when you think about Bhaktapur.

The ground floor usually has a small, specialised shop recalling the neighbourly personal commerce now largely non-existent in the West.

The street goes around a corner to open into **Tachupal Tole**. You will discover that all the roads lead into the square, the original city centre.

Uphill directly ahead is **Dattatraya Temple**, guarded by the wrestlers Jai Mal and Patta. On your left is **Bhimsen Temple**, built in 1605, with an open shelter below and the temple above. A deep water tank stands behind it. You will hear the sound of woodcarvers at work so be sure to go in.

Dattatraya Temple was built by Yaksha Malla in 1427 on an even older foundation. Facing the temple atop a

Multi-coloured wooden carving at Changu Narayan Temple.

pillar is a beautiful image of Garuda. The temple is similar in form and function to Kathmandu's Kasthamandap, in the sense that it serves as a social and religious centre for the community.

Interwoven Faiths

Dattatraya best exemplifies the intertwining and mutual tolerance of the different faiths in the Valley. Inside are images of Brahma, Shiva, and Dattatraya. The Dattatraya cult originated in south India, where Shaivites worship him as Shiva's teacher while Vishnu's followers believe him to be an incarnation of Vishnu. Bhaktapur's Buddhists appeal to Dattatraya as the Buddha's cousin, Devadatta. This illustrates how adherants of different faiths not only tolerate each other but partake of each other's worship. The former importance of **Dattatraya Square** is also indicated by the 10 *maths* (Hindu priest's house) in the area. The jewel of these is the **Pujari Math**, located to the south-east of the **Dattatraya Temple** and dating back to the 15th century. Today, it is the **Woodcarving Museum** of the Bhaktapur Development Project. The **Peacock Window** on the eastern exterior is the most famous woodcarving, though the three floors of woodcarving around the interior court are more impressive. Go up to the roof to see life on the rooftop terraces.

Walk past the square to **Wakupati Narayan** on your right. Go uphill to the

Erotic carvings on roof struts.

home of the local goddess *Nava Durga*, the site of tantric rites involving animal sacrifice. A troupe of dancers from this temple represent the goddess at all local festivals. Join the farmers when they head out to their fields. Remember that you are not walking through some "living museum" but a living community, struggling to achieve a balance between the demands of livelihood and of tradition. The **Kodari Highway** leads east over the Valley to the town of **Banepa**, which, aside from the **Chandeshwari** shrine on the northeast of the town, is uninteresting. **Dhulikhel**, the next town out, is much more interesting and has great mountain views. Locate the **Narayan** and **Bagavati Temples**. **Panauti** is an old centre south of Banepa.

Pokhara Valley

In all my travels in the Himalayas, I saw no scenery so enchanting as that which enraptured me at Pokhara.

Ekai Kawaguchi, **Three Years In Tibet.**

Kawaguchi, disguised as a Chinese *lama* (spiritual teacher), was probably the first outsider to visit Pokhara. Like almost every visitor after him, he loved the place.

"Pokhara looked like a town of villas at home, the site being chosen for the beauty of its natural scenery. ...Another thing notable about that place was that it was the cheapest spot in Nepal."

Hindu pilgrims bathing at the confluence of Kali Gandaki and Trisuli River, south of Pokhara.

The natural beauty, (for the most part), remains as do the cheap prices. Pokhara located by **Phewa Tal** is a roughshorn resort town. It is the place to truly relax, go for leisurely walks (it is mostly flat!), and boat and bicycle rides. Find a nice spot to read, sit on the terrace of a lakeside restaurant eating Thamel-style fare, and, of course, enjoy some of the best mountain views in Nepal. The valley town is 200km (124m) west of Kathmandu, in the centre of Nepal. It

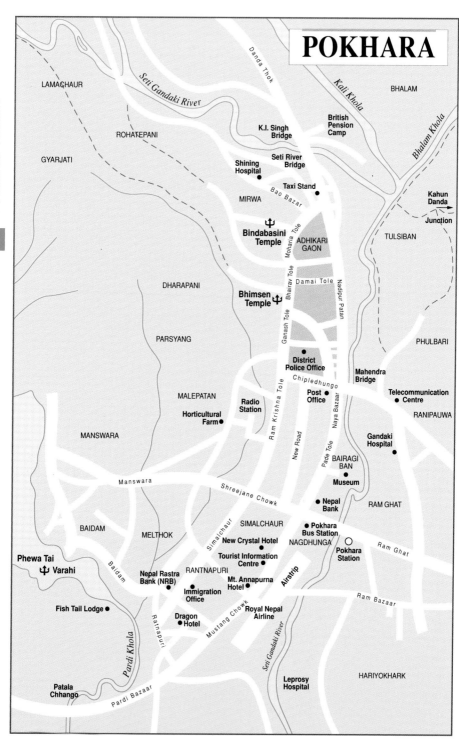

POKHARA

LAMACHAUR

Seti Gandaki River

Danda Thok

Kali Khola

BHALAM

Bhalam Khola

ROHATEPANI

K.I. Singh
Bridge

British
Pension
Camp

GYARJATI

Seti River
Bridge

Shining
Hospital

Taxi Stand

Bao Bazaar

MIRWA

Kahun
Danda

Junction

Bindabasini
Temple

Moharia Tole

ADHIKARI
GAON

TULSIBAN

DHARAPANI

Bhimsen
Temple

Bhairav Tole

Damai Tole

Nadipur Patan

PARSYANG

Ganash Tole

PHULBARI

District
Police Office

Mahendra
Bridge

Chipledhungo

Telecommunication
Centre

MALEPATAN

Radio
Station

Post
Office

Naya Bazaar

RANIPAUWA

Horticultural
Farm

Ram Krishna Tole

Gandaki
Hospital

MANSWARA

New Road

Pade Tole

BAIRAGI
BAN

Manswara

Museum

Shreejane Chowk

Nepal
Bank

RAM GHAT

BAIDAM

MELTHOK

Simalchaur

SIMALCHAUR

New Crystal Hotel

Pokhara
Bus Station

NAGDHUNGA

Pokhara
Station

Ram Ghat

Phewa Tai

Varahi

Baidam

Nepal Rastra
Bank (NRB)

RANTNAPURI

Tourist Information
Centre

Mt. Annapurna
Hotel

Airstrip

Immigration
Office

Fish Tail Lodge

Rathnapuri

Dragon
Hotel

Mustang Chowk

Royal Nepal
Airline

Ram Bazaar

Seti Gandaki River

Pardi Khola

Patala
Chhango

Pardi Bazaar

Leprosy
Hospital

HARIYOKHARK

Phewa Lake.

is the most visited destination after Kathmandu and the hub for treks in the central mountains, the most popular routes. There are frequent day and night bus services from Kathmandu. Take the more expensive buses billed as Swiss and Deluxe tourist buses or the "two-by-two" minibuses – they are more comfortable and drop you off right at the lakeside. When the road has not been knocked around too much by rains, it is about a 6-hour ride, with a *daal-bhaat* stop for lunch at **Mugling**. It is a bumpy but interesting ride, passing river gorges, picturesque villages, and pretty terraced fields. You may consider flying one way and bussing it the other. The 20-minute flight (US$61) comes close to being a "mountain flight."

Pokhara is the largest valley in Nepal, but its handicap has always been the shortage of water for irrigation. At an elevation of 900m (2,955ft), it lies lower than Kathmandu, but the central Himalayas are as close as 30km (19m) north, which accounts for the close-up views. Clouds dumping their rain as they crash into these peaks give Pokhara an annual rainfall of 400cm (157 inches). Pokhara is famous for its rain, so be prepared.

Lakeside

Tourists are drawn to **Baidam**, the lakeside area of **Phewa**. Each year, the line of hotels, restaurants, bookshops,

Clouds plume off Machhapuchhre (Fishtail) 6,993m in Pokhara.

bakeries, clothing and souvenir stalls and travel agents gets longer. There are numerous decent lodges in the US$6-12 range here, offering an attached bathroom with hot water, aside from the top-end establishment. Hotels have also sprung up below the dam at the southern end of the lake. It is easy to rent a boat, with or without a rower, for a leisurely cruise on the lake. Large rowing boats or dinghy sailboats can be rented at US$1-2 per hour, US$4-8 for the day. Enjoy unobstructed views of the as-yet unclimbed and unpermittable — **Machhapuchhre** (Fishtail) at 6,997m (23,000ft) and the **Annapurna** and **Manaslu** *himals*. Visit the small island with a **Temple of Varahi**, and look back across at the large compound and

villa of the Royal Family. Take a short walk south of Phewa Tal to reach the waterfall of **Patle Chhango**, also called **Devi's** (or **Devin's**) **Fall**. This is where the water from Phewa sinks below a channel – with sound and fury in a monsoon and a mere whimper in spring. The story is that a western woman drowned here (while skinny-dipping?), though why it is called Devi (*devi* means goddess in Nepali) no one knows!

The best way to explore Pokhara is on bicycle. You can rent ordinary push-bikes or mountain bikes on the lakeside strip at rates comparable with those in Kathmandu. A favourite evening past time in Pokhara is to sample the array of budget-style "international" cuisine, second only to Thamel. New restau-

A Magar woman in a Gorkha Bazaar.

rants keep popping up, but some tested (and tasted) establishments are **Baba's**, **Don't Cross Me By**, **Hungry Eye**, **Kantipur**, **Phewa**, and **Lhasa**. The fare available includes steak, rosti, pasta, vegetable concoctions, *momo* and *thukpa*, and a long list of desserts.

The Bazaar

The town's main bazaar is a few kilometres north of the lake, past the airstrip and the highway to Kathmandu. Pokhara has grown by leaps and bounds.

Himalchuli framed against delicate white plum blossoms.

Local Courtesies

Namaste is the traditional Nepali greeting. When you board a Royal Nepal Airlines aircraft bound for Nepal, your flight crew will greet you with a *Namaste*. At work, home, or any official or social gathering, wherever you go, you will hear the ubiquitous echo of *Namaste, Namaste*. The word, which is both a greeting and a bidding of farewell, literally means "I salute all the divinity in you." Imbued with the grace and spirit of Nepal's humanist traditions, it is rooted in the belief that everybody has bad and good in his or her nature; the good is divinity, to be saluted.

Within Nepali family life many gestures have become obligatory customs over the centuries. For instance, the daughter-in-law in all households must bend and touch the feet of her husband and in-laws with her forehead each morning. The same gesture is shown to an elder first cousin who is visiting.

Courtesy is observed in speech, too. For members of the royalty, special words are used to address their actions, clothes, food, so forth. For priests and holy men, a whole new set of words are reserved. For those older, equal or lower than yourself, there are different sets of greetings (even for those you despise).

For Nepalis, what to wear and when are of extreme importance. If a parent dies, white clothes must be worn for a year. Married women must wear red, including red vermillion above the forehead where the hair is parted. While attending the wedding of a close relative, women must wear plenty of jewellery to show guests that the bride or groom has rich cousins. Certain customs are observed in eating. A dinner with 18 items is laid for weddings, 12 items for lesser events and 3 or 4 items constitute a regular meal for a family of average means. That is how the importance attached to the occasion is indicated. At a traditional feast or routine meal, the eldest male member sits closest to the east, the others are seated in accordance with seniority. Everyone sits on the floor, usually on straw mats or woolen carpets. The common practice is to sit cross-legged. Generally, women eat only after the men have finished. Before eating, a morsel of every food item is offered to one's deceased ancestors. Only the right hand is used, no cutlery. Everyone remains seated until the entire course is served. It is courteous to remain seated until the eldest person has eaten and leaves his place. After the meal, everyone cleans their mouths and hands with water. As religion is an integral aspect of daily Nepali life, certain codes are strictly adhered to in religious settings. Leather should not be worn in a Hindu temple and shoes are prohibited. One must always go around a Buddhist temple or *stupa* in a clockwise direction.

Every April, on the day of the new moon, Nepalis commemorate Mother's Day. Married daughters come home with sweets, fruits and clothes for their mothers. Those whose mothers have died, go on pilgrimage. A similar celebration is observed on Father's Day, too. In this way, Nepalis extend courtesy to both their living and the dead.

A wedding party in Chayarsa Village.

Looking up the valley of the Kali Gandaki into Mustang.

The first vehicle arrived on a plane in 1958, and the road to Kathmandu didn't open until the early 1970's. People moving down to Pokhara from the hills have more than doubled its population in the past 10 years.

Bike to **Bindyabasini Temple** in the northern part of town to get an idea of Pokhara before the invasion of the ubiquitous concrete box. Also, visit the **Bhimsen Temple** a short way south. A number of treks start here.

A little further north is a good point to view the **Seti River**'s narrow gorge. The **British Pension Camp** for the Gurkha soldiers is nearby. Here too is a museum on the Annapurna area run by the **Annapurna Conservation Area Project** (ACAP). Still further on is the

Tibetan Refugee Camp.

The Tibetan settlements of **Tashi Palkhel** and **Tashiling**, both within easy cycling distance, produce voluminous quantities of carpets for export. Tashi Palkhel, better known as **Hyangja**, is the larger, with 1,000 residents, its own *gompa* and school. Tashiling is half the size, just 2km from the damside, with its own *gompa* and primary school. Tibetans who have settled here have come a long way in the past two decades. Some have opened souvenir shops near the lakeside, others continue to be mobile and work as peddlars.

About 15km east of Pokhara are two small lakes, **Begnas** and **Rupa**, cradled in a ring of hills. Buses run to the lakes from New Road, taking about 45

The leisurely pace at Bindhyavasini Temple in Pokhara.

minutes; or you could cycle out and get there quickly and more enjoyably. Have a boat take you across **Begnas Tal**, then walk back. Or you can walk along the ridge between the two lakes to reach a spot from which you can see both lakes.

Mountain Viewing

The sky over Pokhara generally gets cloudy by mid-morning. You should make it a point to be up at dawn for the best views of the mountains.

Sarangkot (1590m; 5220ft), high up on the ridge north of Phewa Tal, is the most popular destination for a short hike (3 hours). There you can find the ruins of the fort of the Kaski kings who fell to the Gorkhalis in 1781. There are also lodges if you want to stay overnight to enjoy the sunset and dawn. Otherwise it is a day's full excursion.

It takes about three hours to reach **Kahun Dada** (1,520m, 5,000ft). Less spectacular than Sarangkot, the trail is quieter and there is a lookout tower at the top. Cross the **Mahendra Bridge**, and take the paved road north. The road becomes a trail as it goes up and east.

Naudada is reached by walking up from **Suikhet** or **Phedi**, points from which old jeeps operate as taxis. Or start from the **Bindyabasini Temple**. Naudada is as far as you can go without a trekking permit. Still further on is **Chandrakot** (a full day's walk away).

Gorkha

Midway between Kathmandu and Pokhara is **Gorkha**, home of Prithvi Narayan Shah, the unifier of Nepal. The improved 20-odd km road from **Khaireni** on the **Prithvi Highway** makes Gorkha only a half-day ride from Pokhara or Kathmandu. Curiously unvisited, efforts are on the way to put the cradle of modern Nepal on the tourist map.

Prithvi Narayan's Palace still stands above the ridge a steep 20-minute climb from the bazaar. Take a walk around this architectural *tour-de-force* and take in the views of **Manaslu**, **Baudha**, and **Himalchuli**. On Saturdays, Nepali families come to worship at the nearby shrine, bringing a chicken or goat for sacrifice.

Even though Gorkha was the base from which Prithvi Narayan Shah conducted his extraordinary campaigns, it was really a petty hill-state that enjoyed only a flash of glory in Nepal's history. According to historians, Prithvi Narayan's ancestors came to Gorkha in the mid-16th century, fleeing Muslim invaders in their original home in Rajasthan. His father launched an unsuccessful raid on Kathmandu Valley. It is hard to believe that this modest village supported such an active army for almost three decades – only to be supplanted as capital by Kathmandu.

The imposing and impressive **Tallo Durbar** (lower palace) served as the administrative headquarters but is being turned into a museum of Gorkha history. The upper *Durbar*, 300m higher up, housed the king and his court. Prithvi Narayan was born here and upstairs in the east wing you can find his throne and a flame that has remained lit ever since he unified Nepal. The fortress remains a religious place, with the revered *Kalika Mandir* inside, closed to all but priests and the King. Sacrifices are offered on the alcove in front of the entrance, a site of processions and plenty of bloodletting during the *Chaitra Dasain* Festival in late March. Nearby is the holy **Cave of Gorakhnath**, a protector deity of the Shah Kings. In the bazaar, the old brick building with government offices has some noteworthy woodcarving. Of the basic hotels in Gorkha, the

The palace of Prithvi Narayan Shah.

It is usually women tending the fields in Palkhu, Gorkha or anywhere else in Nepal.

Bisauni Hotel, not far from the bus-stop, is the most comfortable, equipped with hot showers. **Dumre** is where you start for the trek to the high **Manang Valley**. Like most places on this road, Dumre seems to have grown out of the leftover road material. Above Dumre on the ridgetop to the south is **Bandipur**. The building of the motor road killed this once prosperous Newar Bazaar as most of the merchants migrated to Pokhara.

Pokhara to Butwal and the Terai

Naudada is where you begin your trek to **Dhorpatan** or **Beni (Baglung)** and up the **Kali Gandaki**.

During the Rana era, **Tansen** was one of the most important towns of Nepal. It was where troublesome Ranas were banished during the frequent inter-familial jockeying for power. An important event in King Tribhuvan's re-taking of power in 1951 was when the Rana commander posted here declared his support for Tribhuvan.

The large Rana palace/government office still stands. The views from the ridgetop are stunning. There is a decent but expensive hotel (**Hotel Srinagar**) and a few basic ones near the bus-stop. Tansen is pleasant to walk through, famous for its Newar brass crafts. Look for the bird and peacock-shaped brass lamps.

Nepal is so integrally associated with the Himalayas that too often the southern Terai belt is completely overlooked, which is unfortunate. While not as spectacular as the snow peaks, the Terai is the vital link or the divide between the mountains and the plains. Thus, it exhibits natural and cultural elements with something of both the mountains and the plains, of the northern Buddhistic tribes and the southern classical Indic sources.

Emerging silhouettes of trees at dawn near Biratnagar.

Terai Sightseeing

If the middle hills and mountains are the heart of Nepal, this narrow plain is the body that works to keep the heart pumping, as the Terai contains 57 per cent of the country's total arable land and is its bread-basket, producing more than 70 per cent of Nepal's total produce. It also contains most of Nepal's young industries as well as the bulk of the country's forest cover.

Not surprisingly, the 18th century traveller Colonel Kirkpatrick called the Terai "an almost inexhaustible source of riches."

Until the 1950s, this strip of land was

mostly made up of inpenetrable jungle infested with malaria. Its only inhabitants were the Tharus, who had somehow acquired an immunity from the disease. With the eradication of malaria, coupled with the steady emigration of hill people in search of new land and the fertility of alluvial plains, the Terai has, in just a few decades become crucially important to the country.

Traditionally, generals and high servants were rewarded with large tracts of land for their service, thus creating a class of *zamindars* (absentee landlords who ruled like feudal barons). A land reform act, (in effect since 1964), has brought changes, but for all that, the pool of landless labourers has increased.

About half of Nepal's 19 million population now live in the Terai, and this growth of population continues to this day. In today's Terai is found a unique amalgam of hill and plains people. The Buddha was born in **Lumbini**, the Hindus' holy **Janakpur** is in the Terai, and the Tharus, (the indigenous people of the area) live here.

A visit to the Terai reveals yet another facet of Nepal. Spring, autumn and winter are pleasant times to visit. Temperatures during May and June can reach as high as 40°C (104°F) even though the monsoon cools the summer months. Winter is the best time to travel there, although nights are wet and cold.

The **East-West Highway**, which links the two ends of Nepal, is nearing completion and long-distance buses run from Kathmandu to the string of towns

Quiet tropical greenery and ponds in the Terai.

The local school bus in Janakpur.

across the Terai. Enquire at the bus-park on the other side of **Tundikhel** and at **Bhimsen Tower** near the Central Post Office. Buses ply daily between all the main Terai towns. The RNAC, too, operates flights to the major towns.

Starting in the east:

Biratnagar is Nepal's second largest city (pop: 180,000) and the main industrial centre of the Terai. Its importance is partly due to its being on a direct line to Calcutta, which is the main seaport for landlocked Nepal. The jute farmed here used to be Nepal's main export but its demand has sharply declined. Like many Terai towns, Biratnagar is just a short rickshaw ride from India. Its proximity to **Naxalbari**, the communist hotbed in India in the 1960s, has influenced it. The Kathmandu-to-Kakarbitta buses stop at **Itahari**, 23km north of the town, other buses go into town. Places to stay: **Hotel Anand**, south of the town, **Hotel Namaskaar**, and **Hotel Geetanjali**. Remember to ask for mosquito netting.

Dharan is a pleasant town about 40km north of Biratnagar, just at the foothills. Until 1989, it was the recruiting centre for Gurkhas, which generated substantial business. The British returned the Gurkha Camp to the Nepalese government and maintains its smaller facility in Pokhara. The camp, now under the Ministry of Health, is a tree-lined campus. The newly opened **Dharan Club** makes use of its golf, tennis, squash and swimming facilities.

Janaki Temple skyline.

You can stay at; **Hotel Evergreen, Hotel Step In**, **Yug Hotel**; also enquire at the Dharan Club.

Janakpur is by far the most interesting and enjoyable town in the Terai. It has historic and religious significance for Hindus as the home of Sita, the wife of Ram, hero of the *Ramayana*. The two are held up as models of the virtuous husband and chaste wife by Hindus who chant "Sita Ram, Sita Ram." Indian tourists visit this important pilgrimage place by the busload, western tourists are rarely seen.

The huge **Janaki Mandir**, with its wedding-cake facade, domes and gilded spires, is one of a kind in Nepal. It was built by the queen of Tikagarh, India. The temple bustles with worship activities in the mornings and evenings. The government offices are located upstairs.

The area around the temple is a typical old bazaar; merchants sit cross-legged, women pass by with their faces hidden behind a sari and bullock carts move languidly. Janakpur is known for its pilgrimage centres, hostels for *sadhus* and its numerous ponds built, as the story goes, for the gods and goddesses attending the wedding of Ram and Sita. Most of the fish sold in Kathmandu comes from these ponds, which also serve as places for ritual bathing.

There are large twice-weekly markets and numerous festivals. The highlight of the latter is the *Bivaha-Panchami*, (the re-enactment of Rama's and Sita's wedding), *Rama Navami* (Rama's birth-

Male performers of the Ramayana at the Janaki Temple.

day) celebrated in March/April and the annual mass *Parikrama* (circumambulation). Janakpur's steam-engine railway, the only rail line in Nepal, goes 52km to **Jayanagar**.

Biruhnj is Nepal's busiest port of entry – and hardly the best introduction to the country. The border is 4km south of the town centre. A few kilometres further is **Raxaul**, the first Indian town from where trains commuted to India. Rickshaws or *tongas* (horse-drawn buggies) are available for the border crossings.

Not difficult to spot the Rhinos at Chitwan.

The town of about 70,000 is a chaotic Terai town with traffic to match, especially the buses and freight trucks. There are frequent bus services to Kathmandu, Pokhara and other points. **Hotel Kailas** and **Hotel Diyalo** are reasonable for comfort and price.

Chitwan, a valley of the inner Terai, is a major destination for most tourists. They come to see the famed Asian One-horn Rhino, Royal Bengal Tiger and other wildlife in the **Royal Chitwan National Park**, reputed to be one of Asia's best. Established in 1962, the 930 sq km (360 sq miles) park is a habitat for leopard, gaur, barking deer, wild boar, sloth bear, python, cobra, otter, langur and rhesus monkey, two types of crocodile – the Needle-Snouted Gharial and the Blunt-Snouted Marsh Mugger, and the Gangetic Dolphin. It is a paradise for birdlife, with as many as 300 species identified. There are a number of extremely comfortable and rustic lodges within or near the park. All offer a number of two to three-day package tours inclusive of transportation, accommodation, meal, and sightseeing activities. You go looking for animals while seated on an elephant back – the only way possible in the 20 to 30ft tall "elephant" grass. Fortunately, the practice of using a live bait to lure tigers while tourists wait in the blind has now been stopped. Many combine a trip to Chitwan with one to Pokhara, or a rafting trip down in the south.

There are a number of inexpensive

Ride through the Thieves Market, Chor Bazaar, Nepalgunj.

lodges just outside the park that are more basic. They, too, will arrange elephant rides and guides into the park.

If you are on a local bus, get off at **Tandi Bazaar** and hop on a bullock cart down to the park's border where the lodges are. A blue *Sajha* bus may cost a little more but it is more comfortable and faster.

Narayanghat was nothing until the early 1980s when the Chinese-built road connecting **Narayanghat**, **Mugling** and **Gorkha** opened and made it the gateway to the Terai and the busiest crossroads in the country. Today, it is a real boom town with one of the largest movie theatres in Nepal.

Earlier, buses and trucks were rowed across the Narayani on two wide boats lashed together. It was fun but the bridge is more efficient. For lodging, there is the **Hotel River View**, **New Bisauni Guest House** and, at the upper end of the market, **Hotel Narayani Safari** at **Bharatpur**, airconditioned with tennis courts and a swimming pool.

Nearby is **Devghat**, a tranquil spot where the **Trisuli** and **Kali Gandaki Rivers** merge to form the **Narayani**, a major tributary of the Ganga. Here wooded hills and lush plains meet. Junctures such as these are considered especially holy. Hundreds of pilgrims walk together for weeks to camp and bathe by the river.

There is a small community with members (who no longer belong – or choose not to) in society. It was founded

Pilgrims camping out at Devghat in Narayanghat, after a 2-week walk.

more than 30 years ago by a sage, Dilli Ram Baba. The site was a jungle where he chose to settle down in after a lifetime of wandering. His first nights were spent under a makeshift shelter of sticks and leaves, with a fire burning to ward off wild beasts. Then he built a temple. People started to arrive and they were welcomed without any questions asked. Now there are homes, fields and even electricity. A sense of peace and calm pervades.

The Central Terai

Butwal and **Bhairahawa** were once the main bazaars for all of central Nepal. Butwal, the centre of the Lumbini administrative zone, was once the start of a trade route to Tibet as well as the pilgrim's trail to **Muktinath**. Gurkha soldiers headed to the recruiting office of Gorakhpur in India and returned home by train, their pockets jammed with money, to cross the border at Bhairahawa. Of course, they wanted to celebrate their return and buy gifts for everyone at home. Bhairahawa and Butwal prospered by helping them to do both. Everyone has heard of hotels adding a few extra empty bottles to an inebriated Gurkha's bill!

Lumbini, 21km west of Bhairahawa, is the birthplace of Gautama Buddha. The local buses are slow and unreliable, so you are better off reserving a local three-wheeler *tempo* if you

Moslem textile traders in Nepalgunj.

have some companions.

The **Sacred Garden** where Buddha was born has deteriorated and was actually lost for 600 years until its rediscovery by German archaeologist RA Fuhrer. The exact spot is the unpretentious white shrine of **Maya Devi**; nearby

is a sacred pond and the ruins of early monasteries.

West of the temple is an **Ashokan Pillar**, recording Ashoka's visit in 249 BC. A recent replica depicts the Buddhist nativity scene, according to which the infant bounced out of the womb, took

Scheme, in which Japanese architect Kenzo Tange is involved, is moving very slowly. You can stay at the *dharamsala* or the **Lumbini Gardens Guest House**.

Nepalgunj, with 50,000 people, has Nepal's second busiest airport, which visitors to this hot western town will find hard to believe. The town is the trade and transport hub of the far west. It also has Nepal's largest Muslim population (about 70 per cent of the town). Prior to the war with the British in 1814-16, this part of the Terai belonged to the Nawab of Oudh, then a principality. It was returned to Nepal for services rendered during the Indian Mutiny of 1857. Moslems here maintain family and business ties with India, just 6 km south.

Nepalgunj has the reputation of being the hottest town in Nepal. In the dry season, a *loo* (hot wind) sweeps through with temperatures of up to 50°C (112°F).

The town very much resembles an Indian town. Hindu worship and trade is carried out near the **Bageshwari Mandir**, behind which Shiva stands like an amateur thespian under a gazebo in the middle of a pond. **Chor Bazaar**, (Thieves' Market), is a series of narrow alleys that dramatise the name.

Most visitors to Nepalgunj pass through the nearby **Royal Bardiya Wildlife Reserve**, probably to the riverside tented camp operated by the Tiger Mountain group. It is a great place for wildlife and bird watching and fishing but the all-inclusive packages, arranged in Kathmandu, are not cheap.

seven steps, and proclaimed his destiny.

The area around Lumbini is predominantly Moslem. Ironically, the Buddhists inhabit the mountainous end of the country. Once a thriving community, Lumbini is as peaceful a place as you can find now. On the grounds are a Tibetan and a Theravada monastery. The famous **Lumbini Development**

Go for it, go for a trek. Go for half a day, go for a couple of months, but go.

In the West, backpacking is usually done in the wilderness, a trek in Nepal is a journey into Nepalese life and culture. The trails you walk were travelled by Nepalis long before the first tourists came.

Trekking
by Wendy Brewer Lama

191

Choosing a Trek

The resilience of the Nepali porters is especially tested on the higher ranges.

Whether you have three days or three months, you will find a trek that is just right for you. Besides time, other factors to consider are the season, your interests, elevation and ruggedness, creature comforts or remoteness, and most important of all, whether you will be staying in local lodges, or camping in a group (see below). If you are trekking on your own, your choices are narrowed to those routes where lodges and food are available; if you are going in a group, you can go anywhere, except for restricted zones.

A summary of the primary trekking seasons and routes:
Best   Trekking Months: January,

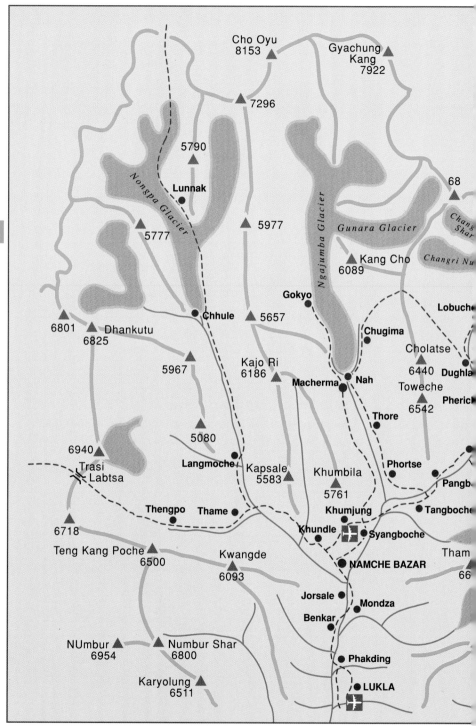

Cho Oyu
8153

Gyachung
Kang
7922

7296

5790

Nongpa Glacier

Lunnak

5977

68

Ngajumba Glacier

Gunara Glacier

Chang
Shar

5777

Kang Cho
6089

Changri Nu

Gokyo

Lobuch

Chhule

5657

Chugima

Cholatse

6801

Dhankutu
6825

Kajo Ri
6186

6440

Dughla

5967

Macherma

Nah

Toweche

Pherich

6542

Thore

5080

Phortse

6940

Trasi
Labtsa

Langmoche

Kapsale
5583

Khumbila

Pangb

5761

Thengpo

Thame

Khumjung

Tangboche

6718

Khundle

Syangboche

Teng Kang Poche
6500

Kwangde
6093

NAMCHE BAZAR

Tham

66

Jorsale

Mondza

Benkar

NUmbur
6954

Numbur Shar
6800

Phakding

Karyolung
6511

LUKLA

Trekking Routes to Mahalangur Himal

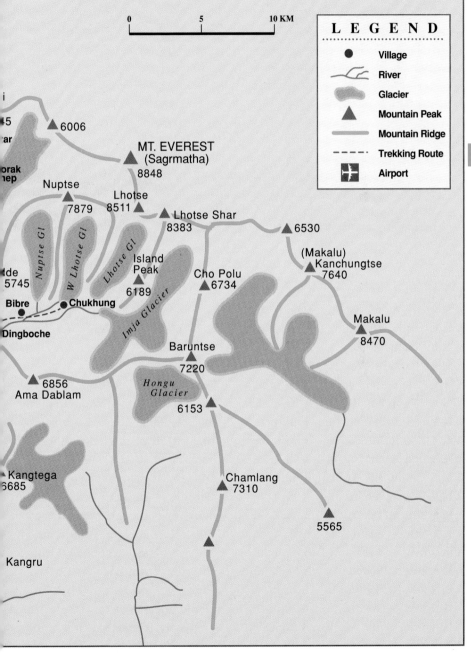

0   **5**   **10 KM**

L E G E N D

- ●   Village
- ～   River
-   Glacier
- ▲   Mountain Peak
- ──   Mountain Ridge
- ---   Trekking Route
-   Airport

▲ 6006

▲ **MT. EVEREST**
(Sagrmatha)
8848

Nuptse
7879

Lhotse
8511 ▲

▲ **Lhotse Shar**
8383

▲ 6530

(Makalu)
Kanchungtse
▲ 7640

Nuptse Gl

W Lhotse Gl

Lhotse Gl

**Island
Peak**
▲
6189

Cho Polu
▲ 6734

Makalu
▲
8470

de
5745

Bibre ● **Chukhung**

Dingboche

Imja Glacier

Baruntse
▲
7220

▲ 6856
Ama Dablam

*Hongu
Glacier*

▲
6153

▲ **Kangtega**
6685

Chamlang
▲ 7310

▲
5565

Kangru

i

45

ar

orak
nep

Vegetation adjusts remarkably with altitude as well as the
different mountain faces.

February, March, April, September, October, November and December (for clear weather).

Most Popular Treks: Annapurna circuit, Annapurna sanctuary, Everest area (Solu Khumbu), Langtang/Helambu, Ghorepani-Ghandruk and Jomsom.

For Mountain Scenery: Everest area, Annapurna circuit, Annapurna sanctuary, Langtang, Kanchenjunga and Makalu Base Camp.

For Cultural Diversity: Annapurna circuit, Solu Khumbu, East Nepal (Chainpur area) and Pokhara-Dolpo-Jumla.

For Spring Rhododendrons and Plant Life: Solu Khumbu, Ghorepani-Ghandruk, Gosainkund-Helambu, Langtang, Arun valley and Kanchenjunga.

For Remoteness: Dolpo, Jumla-Rara Lake, Makalu Base Camp and Salpa Pass.

Seasons

October/November – Clear sky and generally good weather. Warm in the day, cool at night. Above 3,000m (about 10,000ft), nights may be freezing. Major trails are crowded. Get to the day's destination early to ensure a place.

December/January – The coldest months, with nights below 0°C above 3,000m (about 10,000ft). Beautiful days and clear views. Occasionally, at higher altitudes, you can be snowed in for a few days.

February/March – A transitional period – February is cold, March is warm at lower altitudes. Chances of rainstorms,

Rhododendrons, trees at times, mere shrubs at higher altitudes.

high winds, thunder, lightning and hail. Haze and dust are pushed up from India, dimming mountain views from lowlands, but the rhododendron begins to blossom.

April/May – Walking below 1000 m (3,300ft) means dripping sweat (drink plenty of water). Fieldwork makes nearby trails muddy; mountain views are hidden behind the haze. Occasional rain clears the sky for a day or two. Rhododendron blossoms turn entire hillsides red. It is the ideal time for naturalists. Up high, it is still cold.

June/July/August/September – mid-June the monsoon starts and brings relief from the heat. Clouds hide the mountains, but there are occasional magnificent views. Trekking is difficult, with slushy trails often turning into streams or being swept by landslides; leeches are out in full force. Rain-swollen streams may be impassable for hours or days. Rainshadow regions such as the Muktinath-Jomosom, Khumbu and upper Langtang, are trekkable.

Trek Times (maximum altitude reached given in metres):–

Up to one week:

• Treks north of Pokhara. Quick walkers can get to Ghandruk and back.

• Fly to Jomosom (2,800m), spend a few days there and visit Muktinath (3,800m), fly back from Jomosom, though flights are not reliable.

• Fly to Lukla, walk up to Namche (3,446m) and environs, and walk back to Lukla to fly out again.

Nothing like proof.

• Fly to Tumlingtar, walk via Chainpur to Basantapur or Hile, return via bus from Dharan or plane from Biratnagar (2,800m).

8-14 days:

• North from Kathmandu to the Helambu area (3,000 – 3,600m)

• North from Kathmandu to Gosainkund (4,600m)

• North from Kathmandu to Langtang (4,000m). Perhaps return via Gosainkund/Helambu.

• Fly to Lukla, walk to Everest base camp (5,357m), Imja Khola or Gokyo and fly out from Lukla. Side trip to Kala Pattar (5,623m).

• Fly to Jomosom, walk down the Kali Gandaki to Pokhara (3,000m).

• North from Dumre to Manang, cross the Thorung La (5,380m), fly back from Jomsom.

• North from Pokhara to Landruk, Ghandruk, Ghorepani and back via Birethante (2850m).

• North from Pokhara, to Annapurna Sanctuary and back (3,939m).

• Fly to Jumla, walk to Rara Lake (3,000m), return to Jumla, fly back (3,688m). Be warned that flight from the Jumla is chancy.

Up to Two Weeks:

• Annapurna Circuit-Manang, over the Thorang La Pass (5,415m), down Thak Khola to Pokhara (18-21 days). Add a trip to Annapurna Sanctuary for a total of 30 days. Many side trips possible.

• Walk from Jiri to Lukla (about 7 days), and continue on. Walk out to the east via Hile in about 8 days, via Ilam in

Never mind that one's a porter, a lady needs her jewellery.

about 10 days.
• Walk from Pokhara area to Dhorpatan, return via Tansen, spending a few days in Dhorpatan, walking out via Tansen – total time 14-17 days.
• Walk from Jumla to Pokhara via Dolpo, 23-26 days (3,840m).

Remember that flights in Nepal, particularly to high-altitude destinations, can be cancelled at short notice. Also, they may be filled weeks ahead of time. It usually makes more sense to fly in and to walk out.

Do not schedule leaving the country the day after your return flight from your trek. The same applies to buses, which can be cancelled, oversold, delayed, or break down, and are particularly unreliable in the monsoon or the peak holiday travel times of *Dasain* and *Tihar*.

Organising A Trek

Trekking With An Agency – When trekking with an agency, everything is organised for you; what to eat, where to sleep, how far to walk in a day, how much to carry yourself, toilets, medical emergencies, so forth. The food is prepared to suit western tastes, the walking is designed not to be too strenuous and if you get tired or need any help, a guide will appear at your side.

Obviously, with a group there is less flexibility. Unless the group decides so, you will have to stick to your schedule and itinerary. And while the food is wholesome, it may not be exactly what you want. People on group treks also tend to have less opportunities to interact with local people. A trekking party is a self-contained unit, and most of your contact is with group members or with the trekking staff.

What you gain though is more sanitary food, freedom from planning, a knowledgeable guide and a greater assurance of a successful trip.

On Your Own – Surveys show that about 60 per cent of the trekkers to the Annapurna area arrange their own trek.

There are several options when not trekking with a group.

Trekking Alone – Lone persons on the trail will often be asked by Nepalis, "Where is your friend?" Nepalis are seldom out alone on the trail for social and safety reasons. Nepalis know that quick assistance may be needed in the event of an accident on the trail.

Even if you want to walk alone, it is better that someone knows your route and where you plan to be at night.

Women should not go on a trek alone as most Nepali women would not. Certain stereotypes of Western women have spread from popular media – a lone woman trekker may invite awkward situations. What is both safe and enjoyable is to hire a female guide/porter to accompany you. Or else, strike

Portering in the Arun River Valley.

up some kind of "buddy" system with a fellow trekker. This does not necessarily mean you have to be with somebody every moment of the trek.

Travelling With a Small Group – It can be fun to be able to talk with others during your trek. In the high season, it may be difficult to find accommodation for the whole group, so try to reach your destination early, or take turns to go ahead to reserve beds.

Trekking With a Porter/Guide –

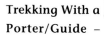

Naturally it is advantageous to travel with someone who knows where you are going. No matter how little English he or she speaks, your porter or guide can tell you things you would otherwise never know. He or she may be your closest contact with the culture you are encountering.

Having a porter/guide would leave you with more freedom for bird watching, taking side trips, and chatting with people. If you plan to stray from the main trekking trail, a guide/porter would be indispensable as trekking maps are often unreliable. Your companion can help you find food and lodging, which are scarce, off the popular trekking routes.

Find out what is a fair wage, and reach a clear agreement before accepting his/her services. Ideally, hire someone who has been referred to you. Or else, get a guide from a trekking agency in Kathmandu or Pokhara and let him hire a porter.

Trekking Macho – They hoist thirty kg on their sweaty backs. They did the "circuit" in 16 days and they are setting off to finish the Sanctuary in eight days so they will have time to "do" Helambu before they leave in two weeks.

The creed of the trekking macho is: carry more, walk faster, walk more places than anyone else and tell everyone you meet all about it!

Whatever you do, you will still be humbled by the Himalayas. So, instead, relax, take your time – that is why you came so far – savour the experience and get a porter if your pack is getting bothersome. Do not worry about how much ground you cover, of more importance is the state in which you covered it!

Annapurna Area

The Annapurna area is the most popular trekking region in Nepal, for good reason. It is highly rated both in terms of mountain scenery and cultural interest, drawing some 35,000 visitors a year.

Nothing like a hot meal before resuming the trek.

Besides, it is easy to get to with daily flights between Kathmandu and Pokhara. Driving by bus or taxi (eight to nine hours) is the cheaper alternative and is a good way to see the countryside. The area also boasts of some of the best tea houses and trekking food in Nepal.

Annapurna Circuit – The Annapurna Circuit follows the **Marsyangdi Khola** and the **Kali Gandaki River** in a loop around the Annapurna massif. The entire circuit is about 330km (150 miles) and crosses **Thorang La** (5,415m, 17,820ft), a snow-bound but not particularly difficult pass. The trek usually takes 18-21 days, or even more if you take rest days or side trips.

Dumre to Muktinath – Most people walk the circuit in a counter-clockwise direction; crossing Thorang La is more gradual from the east side and there are accommodation facilities at the base of the pass.

Dumre can be reached by bus in about five to six hours from Kathmandu or three hours from Pokhara. You can start walking from Dumre, but will have to follow a dusty road for about 10 hours; preferably, catching a ride or a truck to **Bhote Odar** or **Besisahar**.

Besisahar (823m, 2,700ft) is the district centre of **Lamjung District** and was one of the strongest *chhaubisi raja* (24 kingdoms) of old Nepal, a constant thorn in the side of the Kings of Gorkha who ultimately united Nepal in 1769. Looking southwest from a nearby hill, you can see the remains of **Lamjung**

Breathtaking scenery on the trek from Ghandruk into The Sanctuary.

Palace. You will have to show your trekking permit at the Police Checkpost located here (one of several *en route*). There is also a hospital.

You will begin your walk through farmlands of the lower middle hills, predominantly inhabited by caste Hindus.

In autumn, grain ripens a rich golden colour in the terraces. As you gain altitude, you can watch people harvesting and then threshing their crops in their fields and courtyards.

The main trail stays on the west side of the river. Continue on to **Khudi Khola**, where one trail leads to Pokhara, about three days' walk away. Past Khudi, cross the **Marsyangdi** to **Bhulbhule** and climb to the top of **Bahundanda** (Brah-

mans' Hill) in four hours. It sits at 1,311m (4,300ft) in a saddle between two Gurung hillside communities. Now descend and cross the **Marsyangdi**.

The valley begins to feel narrow and cramped. Here the trail has been carved by crowbar into the rock face. In a narrow jumble of rock and trees is the village of **Jagat** (1,341m; 4,400ft). The name Jagat is derived from a customs house that once regulated the salt trade with Tibet.

The trail passes a series of waterfalls amidst a forest that becomes more temperate with oaks as you travel onwards. It gets tighter, and the river is far below. Climb to a rise and you'll look down onto a flat valley called **Tal** (meaning lake, at 1,707m; 5,600ft).

Long ago a landslide blocked the river here, forming a lake. Only its flat bed remains, with a magnificent waterfall on the right and clusters of lodges in the middle.

You are now in **Manang District**. Past **Tal**, the valley narrows again. There is police checkpost at **Dharapani** (about nine hours from Bahundanda).

At **Bagarchhap** (Butcher's Place, 2,164m; 7,100ft), you feel like you have entered another ecological zone. It is cooler and the air is dry as it is in the rain shadow of the Annapurnas. Houses have flat roofs which are ideal for drying crops.

Lattamarang's (2,454m; 8,050ft) big attraction is the hot springs. It is basic but enjoyable. Remember to keep yourself covered while bathing. Another hot springs is located across the river from Chame.

Past Lattamarang you will walk through beautiful blue pine and spruce forests.

But like many places in Nepal, the trees are rapidly being felled. After an uphill walk, the trail bends to the left and **Annapurna II** towers in front. **Chame** (2,713m; 8,900ft) is a few minutes beyond.

Chame is Manang District's headquarters, with government offices, post office, bank, school and electricty. However, mini-hydro electric projects such as this one, only produce enough energy for lights as much wood still goes into cooking stoves.

Pisang's trekker lodges (3,185m;

Watch Khalikot while trekking.

Manangis

The inhabitants of the small valley of Manang are known as the Manangis. Living at over 3,000 m above sea level, their home is a mountain desert. Potatoes, barley and buckwheat are all that grow. The dry, high valleys provide little fodder for sheep or yaks. Unable to support themselves under these severe conditions, the Manangis turned to trade a long time ago.

Tibetan ways run strong in the Manang Valley. Women wear long wrap-around dresses called *chubas* and necklaces of turquoise and coral. Men may have a chunk of turquoise dangling from an ear, giving a pirate touch to their fierce reputation. The edges of towns are marked by *chortens* (Buddhist monuments). There are walls mounted with spinning prayer wheels to spin and the sacred scripture *Om mani padme hum* (Hail to the Jewel in the Lotus) carved repeatedly in stone slabs.

About 190 years ago, the King of Nepal granted the people of **Nyesyang** (the proper name for the Manang Valley above Pisang) special trading privileges. King Mahendra expanded those rights after seeing at first hand the people's poverty while on a hunting trip. Many Manangis have become rich, building palatial homes in Kathmandu.

Some Manangis have adopted the Gurung name to become more Nepalised. Their language is distinct, different from Tibetan and somewhat similar to Gurung.

A modern Manangi.

10,450ft) are set on the river bank near the main trail, about 10 hours walking from **Dharapani**. But the old town, with its stacks of houses and white prayer flags fluttering in the breeze, is across the river and uphill. If you have some extra energy, leave the main trail, which stays low on the left bank, and take the high route through Pisang to **Hongde**. It takes a few more hours, but you will be rewarded with brilliant views of the valley and the Annapurnas. You can drop down and rejoin the main trail at Hongde, or continue on to **Braga**.

Braga, a phantasmagoria of buildings and prayer flags framed by rock cliffs, and dominated by its 500-year-old *gompa*, is, perhaps the most picturesque village on the trek. Ask the caretaker to let you in the *gompa*.

The village of **Manang** (3,351m; 11,650ft) is not as impressive as the amazing view across the river: **Annapurnas II, IV** and **III, Gangapurna**, the glacier and its lake below, and the formidable north face of **Tilicho Peak**. Most of Manang's lodges are between the *chorten* and the main village.

This is the last chance to buy supplies before the pass. Food items will be expensive.

One runs into many peasant workers trekking through the valley areas.

On the snowy trail to Makalu.

Before you go on to the pass, spend at least two nights in Manang to acclimatise.

Take day trips to higher altitudes and return to Manang at night. Should you have any health or altitude problems, visit the Himalayan Rescue Association health post in Manang.

The usual strategy in crossing **Thorang La** is to walk from **Manang** to **Phedi** (4,404m; 14,450ft) in one day (about five hours).

Leave early as there is only one lodge, which is packed in the trekking season. If you want to take more time to acclimatise, stay in **Ledar** (4,176m; 13,700ft), but the lodges there are not very clean.

Most people start for the pass before dawn to avoid a bad wind which rises after mid-morning. It takes about three hours to reach the top.

There are several false summits but the actual pass is marked by a large cairn. Do not attempt to cross the pass if conditions are bad. If in doubt, turn back. Make sure your porters are properly equipped and stay together.

The pass will be difficult or impossible to pass from mid-December to early March. It is also difficult in the monsoon. Make sure you have food and plenty of water with you.

At first, the descent is gradual, but turns steep and can be slippery if the ice is slick. You will need about three hours to reach **Muktinath** (3,802m; 12,475ft) from the top.

The serenity is at times surreal.

Muktinath and South

Just above the small village of Muktinath is a grove of poplar trees with a beautiful spring gushing from the hillside.

This is the sacred pilgrimage site of Muktinath, where both Hindus and Buddhists worship.

Muktinath has been a pilgrimage site since 300 BC, when it was mentioned in the *Mahabharata*. It has a natural spring and a flame of natural gas that seems to burn on water, a gift from the Hindu god Brahma, the Creator.

Behind it the spring's waters are piped out through 108 water spouts. To bathe in these waters is to be given salvation after death.

The flame is located inside a small Buddhist *gompa* below. Crouch down and look under an alter to *Avalokiteshvara*, the Bodhisattva of Compassion. At one time, there were three flames, now only two exist.

Padmasambhava, the great 8th century teacher, who established Tibetan Buddhism in Tibet, is said to have meditated here.

On the full-moon in August-September there is a horse-racing festival called *Pompo Yartung* is held in Muktinath.

About an hour down the trail in **Jharkot** (3,612m; 11,850ft) are the remains of an old castle. The rulers were once the strongest in the Valley, but

Sagarmatha, the great one!

Home on the range – the Annapurnas in the background.

their kingdom later split into three. Look down in the valley to see the ruins of another *dzong* (castle fortress).

As you head down from Jharkot, the town of **Kagbeni** (2,804m; 9,200ft) and its apple orchards appear below you. Kagbeni once controlled a great deal of the trade to Mustang. Walk through narrow streets to the west end of town for a look up the wide valley to the ancient Tibetan kingdom of **Lho** (Mustang). This area is closed to foreigners.

Continuing down the Kali Gandaki and after about an hour you will pass the mouth of a small river emptying into the Kali Gandaki.

One hour up that river is the small village of **Lupra**, one of the last in the region to practice the shamanistic religion of *Bonpo*, (the pre-Buddhist religion of Tibet).

While walking on the river-bed keep an eye out for *shaligrams*, (round black rocks with an ammonite fossil inside). These are valuable to Hindus, who consider them embodiments of the god Vishnu.

If you are walking to **Jomosom** in the afternoon, be prepared for high winds. From here to **Larjung** the winds roar every afternoon as cold air from Tibet rushes under the warmer air coming up from India.

Jomosom (2,713m; 8,900ft) is the main headquarters of **Mustang District**. There is a bank, post office, government and project offices, a hospital, an army camp and an airport with scheduled flights to Pokhara, subject to the usual weather and other delays. The distance from Muktinath to Jomosom is about six hours.

Jomosom also has electricity. It is possible to get a hot shower at many hotels and the food is usually excellent; cheese-bean burritos, spaghetti, apple pie, chocolate cake, bread and great *dalbhaat*. The apple and apricot brandy produced by the **Marpha Distillery** is very potent.

Travelling down from Jomosom to Marpha (2,667m; 8,750ft), the Nilgiris are hidden in shadow on your left, but **Dhaulagiri** and **Tukche Peak** are dramatically apparent. **Marpha** is a pretty white-washed town with impressive drainage canals.

Trekkers camp-site.

The Khampas

Above Jomosom is *Thinigaon* (which also a *Bonpo* community). Past **Thinigaon**, hidden in the shadow of the **Annapurnas** and **Nilgiris**, is the Nepali army's mountain warfare school at **Kesang**.

Following the Chinese takeover of Tibet, bands of Tibetans formed a guerilla resistance movement. Many of them came from the eastern province of *Kham* and thus were known as Khampas. Mustang became their chief refuge. At one time there were as many as 4,000 Khampas operating from bases in Dolpo, Mustang and Manang.

Supported by India, Taiwan and the US, the Khampas inflicted heavy casualties on the Chinese. Throughout the 1960s the Khampas kept up resistance, but world attention (and foreign policy) turned to other matters.

The Chinese put increasing pressure on the Nepalis to expel the Khampas, who were turning the upper Kali Gandaki into their own ministate. Nepal was forced to send a strong force to demand the Khampas' surrender.

Under their leader Colonel Wangdi, the Khampas were headquartered in Kesang. The Nepali troops camped in Jomosom and sent an ultimatum. Colonel Wangdi agreed to surrender the next day. When the army arrived they found a deserted camp. In the night Colonel Wangdi had lead his force over a high pass down to Lupra and fled west.

The Khampas raced westward for India across very rugged terrain. Almost within sight of the safety of India they were caught. Colonel Wangdi was shot and killed from a helicopter and the Khampa resistance was disbanded.

Just below it is the Government Agricultural Farm and its apple and apricot orchards. Many local shops sell packets of dried fruit.

Below Marpha is **Tukche** (2,591m; 8,500ft). Large two-storey houses built around courtyards with elaborately carved wooden balconies are reminders of the town's past importance.

The 500-year old Gompa of Braga in Manang dominates the grey-stoned town.

Tukche was another base of the lucrative salt trade with **Tibet**.

From Marpha and Tukche, side trips to **Dhampus Pass** (5,184m; 17,000ft) and **Hidden Valley** are possible. You will need to carry your own fuel, food and shelter. It is also a good idea to take a local guide.

Below the settlement of **Kobang** – with buildings bridging the trail – is **Larjung**. A *gompa* seems to sit on an island in a river of stone. The wind here can be horrendous. Larjung is the take-off point for excursions to the **Dhaulagiri**

The Thakalis

Thak Khola is the name given to the section of the Kali Gandaki from Ghasa to Tukche. The people native to this area are called *Thakali*. Throughout Nepal their name is synonymous with business entrepreneurship and hoteling.

In the mid-19th century, they were granted a monopoly over the Tibetan salt trade. From there they expanded, sending family members all over Nepal to set up businesses.

To finance their endeavours, they developed the system called *dhigur*. Each of a group of 25 people contributes money to a pool annually, and each year a different member of the *dhigur* receives the whole sum with no obligation to repay it.

Thakalis are equally famous for their abilities as hoteliers. Nepalis know that a *Thakali* hotel assures one of good service, cleanliness, and *daal-bhaat-tarkaari* renowned as the best in Nepal. The amazing international cuisine available on this trek is also the touch of the *Thakalis*. Their hard labour and the increase in tourism have helped develop this area above the normal standards of rural Nepal.

icefall, at the base of the peak.

Kalopani (2,530m; 8,300ft) blends quickly into **Lete**. The southern flanks of Dhaulagiri rise above and the **Nilgiris** and **Annapurnas** stand across the valley. The wind is almost gone and the air feels more alpine.

Ghasa (2,040m; 6,713ft) marks the end of Thak Khola. Here, domestic life takes place on the roofs – children play, grain and vegetables are spread to dry, women sew, men repair tools, everybody gossips and catches the warm winter sun. It is about eight hours' walk from Jomosom.

Kabre (1,707m; 5,600ft) is the northernmost town inhabited by Nepal's middle hill castes. Rice is cultivated; it is noticeably warmer and wetter, and you will see water buffalo again on the trail.

Just before Kabre the river flushes through a gorge right beside the trail. With the roar of the river filling your ears, pause and look up. You are in what is often considered the deepest and narrowest valley in the world. Distance from the valley bottom to the tops of the peaks measures more than five km. Only 40km (25miles) separates the 8,000m (26,000ft) peaks of **Annapurna I** and **Dhaulagiri**.

Below Kabre a few hills mark the base of **Rupse Falls**. Continue descending to **Dana** (1,402m; 4,600ft). The changes in environment are extraordinary, from snow and evergreens to banana trees and rice fields.

Notice the changes in the people too. Nepali *topis* (hats) and Aryan features are again the norm.

Dana's architecture is particularly interesting – solid two and three-storeyed buildings with carved wooden window frames.

The best of them, built generations ago by the Subbha, the king's chief local representative, are reminders of when Dana was the pre-eminent town of the area.

There are good views of the Annapurnas located east across the river. A low ridge hides **Miristi Khola**, famous in mountaineering lore as the route Maurice Herzog and his partner Louis Lachenal were carried down on after becoming the first to climb Annapurna,

An arid part of central Nepal.

and the first ever to scale an 8000m peak (although it nearly cost them their lives).

Tatopani (1,219m; 4,000ft) is the ultimate in Thakali hostelry and as close as you will get to a resort village in Nepal.

The food is as good and varied as you will find in Pokhara or Thamel. Tatopani, which means "hot water," takes its name from the hot springs which first started drawing tourists. With its balmy evenings, citrus trees, patio restaurants lit by strings of bare bulbs, great food and hot bathing springs, it can be a hard place to leave. It is four hours from Ghasa.

From Tatopani, one trail crosses the river and climbs a long hill through Sinwa to Ghorepani (2,850m; 9,350ft), in about five hours. This is the route to the Annapurna Sanctuary and the usual route back to Pokhara (three – five days from Tatopani). Another trail continues down the Kali Gandaki to Beni, Baglung, Kusma and either out to Pokhara (four days) or on to Tansen (six+ days).

From Poon Hill above Ghorepani, you can get great views of the mountains from Machhapuchhre to Dhaulagiri. The name Poon is the clan name of the Magars, famous as Gurkha soldiers. Many of the hotels are run by retired servicemen. It is not unusual to be greeted on the trail by a sharp "Good morning, Sir!" from a smiling ex-soldier.

Glades, gullies and greenery – a trekker's welcome respite.

Gauri Shankar with Dolakha in the foreground.

From Ghorepani, there are even more choices. To Pokhara: head back via a long staircase trail down to **Ulleri** (2,073m; 6,800ft) and **Birethante** (1,097m; 5,250ft) in about six hours. The old trail climbs to **Chandrakot** and **Naudada**, but this route has become largely disused due to the unpleasantness of walking along the new road. Instead, head down river from Birethante, staying on the left side, and catch a Chinese construction truck or a bus from near Nayaphul (new bridge) to Pokhara in two – three hours.

To **Ghandruk**: head east from Ghorepani and climb a nearby ridge, with views to match Poon Hill's. Descend through beautiful rhododendron forests to **Tadapani** (which means "far away water") and continue on the trail through more heavy forest to Ghandruk.

Ghandruk can be reached in one long day from Ghorepani or two easy ones.

Another trail from Tadapani goes directly to **Khimrong Khola**, saving a day *en route* to the Sanctuary bypassing Ghandruk.

Tadapani has lovely views of Machhapuchhre and Annapurna South.

From Ghandruk, you can return to Pokhara via a short-cut to **Birethante** in two days if you drive from **Nayaphul**, or in three days via Landruk and Dhampus to Phedi where you can catch a jeep. Or, head back into the mountains to the spectacular Annapurna Sanctuary.

walk up to Landruk or Ghandruk. Many trekkers do not even enter the Anna-purna Sanctuary but make an eight to ten-day leisurely loop through Landruk, Ghandruk and Ghorepani.

Ghandruk (2,012m; 6,600ft) is one of the largest Gurung villages in Nepal, with more than 700 households.

Almost every family has one of its member in the Gurkha army, and much of the village's prosperity comes from the money they send home. With its superb views of **Machhapuchhre**, **Annapurna South** and **Hiunchuli**, pleasant lodges and opportunities to see village life, it is a great place to spend a rest day or two.

The Annapurna Sanctuary

The **Annapurna Sanctuary** is the single most popular trek in Nepal. Trekkers can walk into an alpine basin, be surrounded by the Himalayas in every direction and be back to Pokhara within about 10-12 days.

Its popularity means that in peak season there is sometimes not enough space (nor food) for trekkers above **Chhomrong**. Try to arrive at your day's destination early. The lodges north of Chhomrong normally shut down after the relatively short season.

Ask around before you leave to find out if they are open.

The trek begins in Pokhara with a

ACAP

The rapid growth of trekking in the mid-1970s required some regulation of tourism and the conservation of the Annapurna area. Proposals were sounded for a national park. But there was strong opposition from local residents who were afraid they would lose their land use rights and perhaps even their homes.

Under a directive of the king, with funding from the World Wildlife Fund, a team consulted with all the major communities in the area before proposing the formation of ACAP, Annapurna Conservation Area Project.

Dividing the area into different use zones, ACAP aims to conserve both the environment and cultures of the area. It works with local communities on development and conservation projects and with tourists to minimise their impact on the area. ACAP also holds seminars for lodge-owners to raise hygiene awareness and to encourage standardised minimum pricing.

Planned and administered by Nepalis, it is an ambitious and innovative project. Plan a trip to the **ACAP Museum** in Pokhara and if in Ghandruk, drop into the headquarters.

The Manangi are keen horsemen, often seen near the Annapurnas.

The Captain's

Down the hill from Chhomrong's sparkling white lodges advertising pizza and apple pie is **The Captain's**. His lodge is a little rough at the edges, but what it lacks in amenities it makes up for in character.

The Captain had a lot of time to get things right. Retired Captain Thaman Bahadur Gurung (6th Queen Elizabeth's Own Gurkha Rifles) opened the first lodge in Chhomrong in 1973 and today it is still going strong. A small man with deep-set eyes, he has a military bearing as he walks in his large courtyard and speaks no-nonsense English.

Take a look at the tiny light bulbs dangling from the ceiling. This is one of the "*bijuli Japani*" (electric Japanese) projects built by Mr Katsuyuki Hayashi, who has used the money he earned driving a taxi in Japan. He has built mini-hydro-electric projects in the Sanctuary.

Stop at **The Captain**'s and try the food, ask the Captain about trekking's impacts – few people have a better perspective or better stories to tell.

It is also the headquarters for ACAP, the Annapurna Conservation Area Project. Visit their exhibit and ask about their activities. Your Rs200 entrance fee will help fund them.

From Ghandruk climb north to a notch on the hill where teashops straddle the narrow pass. Zig-zag down to **Khimrong Khola**; the trail from Tadapani joins at this point. There is a hotel here. Climb up for two to three hours and then turn a corner and enter **Chhomrong** (1,890m; 6,725ft), a thriving resort village. A few years ago trekkers slept on the floor in bamboo and thatch huts.

Now there are masonry hotels with glassed-in viewing decks, solar-heated hot showers, and menus that rival the *Thakali* hotels on the Kali Gandaki. From here Machhapuchhre really looks like a fishtail.

For a bit of that old time trekking flavour, head down the hill to **The Captain's**. Chhomrong is also the site of the Sanctuary's kerosene depot.

From Chhomrong onward, all lodges and trekking groups must cook on kerosene. It is illegal to cut a tree or cook with firewood.

Chhomrong is the last real village on the trail to the Sanctuary. Before trekking made lodges profitable, the Gurungs only climbed higher during summer to graze their sheep, cattle and buffalos.

Pleasant **Khuldighar** (2,499m;

Annapurna South.

8,200ft) is the site of the ACAP tree nursery, vegetable garden and model trekkers' guesthouse. They also have a radio for emergency contact with Ghandruk from where operators can radio Kathmandu.

Descend through heavy forests and bamboo. There are a few lodges in aptly named **Bamboo** (2,347m; 7,700 ft) and further on in **Dobhan** (2,606m; 8,550ft).

Climb up through a dense forest alive with flittering birds and the roar of the river to a small clearing with several lodges called Himalayas (2,873m; 9,425ft).

Beyond the **Himalayas**, the forest opens up as you reach **Hinko** (3,139m; 10,300ft), built in the overhang of a huge boulder. There may be some lodges open at **Deurali** (3,231m; 10,600ft).

Bagar (3300m; 10,825ft) is built on the banks of the **Modi Khola**. Look at the beautiful birch forest glittering across the river and note how sparse trees have become on your side.

Continue to climb through the narrowing gorge till you reach the gates to the Sanctuary. Look back down at the slabs of mountain to see a reminder of the tremendous forces that form these mountains.

As you are gaining elevation, be sure to check yourself and your companions for any symptoms of altitude sickness.If you have a headache or have difficulty catching your breath after stopping for rest, go no higher and spend the night at the nearest lodge.

Dandelion – like plants near Machhapuchhre Base Camp.

When you come to a small stream entering from the west, you are in the Sanctuary. A little ahead is **Machhapuchhre Base Camp** (3,703m; 12,150ft).

Powerful Spirits

Machhapuchhre Base Camp was used by mountaineers only once, in 1957 by a British expedition. Led by Colonel Jimmy Roberts, the expedition was unable to reach the summit and Colonel Roberts turned back with a broken leg. He later remarked, "Powerful spirits inhabit the top of the **Modi Khola Gorge**". The Nepali government later closed the peak, and Machhapuchhre has re-

mained as a sacred mountain, never to be climbed. Roberts went on to found the trekking business in Nepal, starting Mountain Travel in 1965.

Annapurna Base Camp (4,130m, 13,550ft) lies up and to the west. Several lodges are located here. It is cold and damp when the fog rolls up the valley in the evening.

From the centre of this amazing natural amphitheatre, a panorama of mountain views can be enjoyed. Watch the flutes of Machhapuchhre turn pink at sunset. Think how fortunate you are to be here.

On the return, descend to Chhomrong and try a different route back to Pokhara. If you came up via Ghandruk, return via Landruk.

The Everest Region

The Annapurna area may have the numbers but the Everest region has the name. Nowhere else can you immerse yourself so totally among the highest mountains on earth and travel among the legendary Sherpa people.

Flying into **Lukla** (2,827m; 9,275ft) brings the **Khumbu**, (the Sherpa name for Everest region), within 40 minutes of Kathmandu. The alternative is to walk in through **Solu**, the Sherpas' middle hill enclave. Rolling hills are dabbled in forest and pastureland; in spring rhododendron and magnolia blossoms crown the tree-tops. In eight to nine days from **Jiri** (1,905m; 6,250ft), you will cross four

3,000m (10,000ft) passes, and will be in good shape for higher reaches. Another less travelled route begins (or ends) at **Tumlingtar** in east Nepal and crosses 3,414m (11,200ft) **Salpa Pass**, reaching Lukla area in the same eight to nine days. Lodges or homes are available for the night's stay.

Even if you have only 12 or 14 days to trek, you can reach Everest Base Camp (or Kala Pattar) and return, with two to three rest days on the way up, by flying into and out of Lukla. Landing at Lukla (2,827m; 9,275ft) is like bouncing down onto an aircraft carrier in the middle of the Himalayas. The landing strip ends with a mountain on one end and a huge drop-off on the other. If the weather has interrupted the normal flight schedule you will get a taste of rude panic upon landing as the crowd scrambles for tickets for your plane's return. Do not get yourself in the same bind: plan an extra two to three days at the end of your trek in case your Lukla flight is cancelled, and reconfirm your ticket before leaving Lukla on trek.

Plan on two moderate hiking days from Lukla to **Namche Bazaar** (3,446m; 11,300ft), counting your flight day. There are lodges all along the way and a checkpost at **Jorsale** where you will buy a Rs250 park entry permit. One of the many great things about the Khumbu is that it is enjoyable both as a tea-house trek or in a group.

Do not be in a hurry. Be sure to spend two nights in Namche for acclimatisation, or in the vicinity at

Trekkers silhouetted at dawn on Poon Hill.

Khumjung or Kunde. Take a day hike up to Thami (about four hours one-way). In May or June, the **Thami Monastery** stages *Mani Rimbu*, a Tibetan Buddhist dance ritual, as Tengboche Monastery does in November. Another day-trip might take you to Kunde, like Khumjung, a traditional, uncommercialised village located just over the hill. Visit the hospital built by Sir Edmund Hillary's Himalayan Trust and stop in the Khumjung *gompa* to see the *yeti* scalp. Much of what you will need for trekking is available for rent or sale in

Trek help, earrings, nose-rings,
necklaces et al.

momos – (meat or vegetable-filled steamed or fried dumplings) and a cup of Tibetan butter-salt tea. The first cup may be a little rough going down, but it grows on you. While in Namche, be sure to visit the **Sagarmatha National Park Museum**, just above the police checkpost. *Sagarmatha* is the Nepali name for Mount Everest.

Every Saturday is a market day when people come from all over Khumbu, and hundreds of lowland porters ply the

Namche, the "capital" of Khumbu. Down jackets and sleeping bags, hats, mittens, chocolate bars, peanut butter, even ice axes and delicacies such as Spanish canned tongue left over from previous expeditions can be found. But be sure to pick up a Schneider Series Map of Khumbu Himal in Kathmandu; it is incomparably the best around with accurate contour elevations and trail markings.

There are many good lodges in Namche, with tasty food and some with hot showers. Remember that lodges are still using firewood (even though group trekkers must use kerosene for cooking), so try to find a lodge that heats its shower water with hydro-electric power.

Try some Tibetan specialities like

The Sherpas

The Sherpas migrated from east Tibet about 450 years ago; their name means "people from the east" in Tibetan.

Their traditionaly occupation was as traders between Tibet and Nepal/India, and farmers and their name has become synonymous with high altitude portering. Many foreigners mistakenly call any porter a Sherpa, whereas Sherpas have always been lead climbers as well as those who lug heavy loads up to the high camps. Tenzing Norgay Sherpa teamed up with Edmund Hillary in 1953 to become the first men to climb Everest. Among the many excellent Sherpa climbers, Ang Rita Sherpa of Khumbu has scaled Everest six times, more than any person on earth.

Trade between Tibet and Nepal was abruptly stopped when the Chinese closed the border in the early 1960s, and the Sherpas' source of wealth dried up. The boom in mountain tourism has given them fresh opportunities. Many now run trekking agencies or other businesses in Kathmandu.

Sherpas are as serious about their religion as they are about business, and every community has a *gompa*. Followers of the Nyingma sect, the oldest of Tibetan Buddhism, claim the monastery at Tengboche as their spiritual centre. Unfortunately, it burned down in 1989. It is now being rebuilt, with generous contributions from Sherpa and international communities and help from the Himalayan Trust.

The effect is a 'deafening' silence when a trek achieves the altitude such as the area of Rioimo Shar Glacier, Solu Khumbu.

trail from Lukla, to sell their goods in a festive open air exchange.

Gokyo Valley

The Gokyo Valley is off the main Everest Base Camp route, a quiet haven with equal if not better mountain views. The trail begins from Khumjung or Sanasa and reaches a *stupa* on the ridge crest in two to three hours.

On the descent through misty forest, watch for *tahr* (long-haired mountain goats). Near the Dudh Kosi River, a trail connects to **Phortse**, visible across the gorge. Stay to the left and climb to **Dole** (4,084m; 13,400ft) for your first night's stop.

The next overnight stop should be no further than **Machherma** (4,465m; 14,650ft), or even at **Lhabarma** or **Luza** *en route*. It only takes half a day to get there, but remember that you should not sleep higher than 500m (1,500ft) above the previous night's camp once you get above 3,500m (11,500ft). If you feel the altitude, take an extra day and explore the side valleys at any of these settlements. The scenery is spectacular.

Beyond **Pangka**, the trail drops and again climbs after crossing an icy stream. You will soon come to the first of Gokyo's three glacial lakes, about an hour or more before Gokyo itself.

There are several lodges at **Gokyo** and the largest lake (4,791m; 15,720ft), is separated by a high moraine from the

A traditional chain bridge can be a wobbly experience.

giant Ngozumpa Glacier.

From Gokyo, leave early in the morning and climb two hours to the top of **Gokyo Ri** (5,483m; 17,990ft). Views extend north to **Cho Oyu** (8,201m; 26,906ft), east to Everest and south over the lakes at **Ama Dablam** and **Thamserku**. Spend some time before walking down; this may be as high as you will ever get.

Cho La (or Chugima La), at 5,420m (17,783ft), is a short-cut pass between Gokyo and Dughla on the Everest Base Camp side, but should only be attempted in clear weather.

You have to camp overnight at the base of the pass and be self-sufficient as there are no lodges. If no one has marked the trail since the last snowfall, it is advisable to take a local guide. The alternative is to backtrack half a day and spend a night at **Na**, then follow the north side of the **Dudh Kosi Valley** to Phortse (3,700m; 12,140ft) for the high trail to **Pangboche**.

Everest Base Camp

From Namche climb toward the museum but veer off to the left and follow the main trail high above the river. You will stay pretty level for about two hours and then descend to cross the **Dudh Kosi** to **Phunki**. This is a good lunch spot before climbing up about 400m (1,300 ft) through a beautiful forest to **Tengboche** (3,867m; 12,725ft). Watch

The dramatic side of Lingsren.

A trekker's needs are very basic.

for the colourful bird called the *danphe* (Impeyan Pheasant).

The monastery is under reconstruction but you can visit the Sherpa Cultural Centre and see some of the rescued artifacts as well as an excellent display about the Sherpas and the Khumbu. There are fine views of the **Nuptse-Lhotse Wall** and the tip of Everest from the **Tengboche Meadow**. Shortly beyond Tengboche is a nunnery on the right, below a seemingly primeaval forest. The 1½ hour walk to **Pangboche** (3,901m; 12,800ft) is delightful, crossing the **Imja Khola** and climbing gently amidst *mani-carved* boulders. The 350-year-old **Pangboche Monastery** is the oldest in Khumbu. There are superb views of **Ama Dablam** (6,586m; 22,493ft), a much

photographed mountain which takes its name from the small treasure box worn around the necks of Sherpa women.

A good side trip to aid in acclimatisation is an overnight or two at **Dingboche** (4,240m; 13,953ft). Continue for about 1½ hours from Pangboche to a fork in the trail: the fork to the left goes on to **Pheriche** (4,252m; 13,950ft), the right fork to Dingboche. Both are about three hours away. From Dingboche, you can walk another three hours up the Imja Khola to **Chhukung** (4,734m; 15,535ft). It is a good place for exploring, with magnificent views of the back side of **Ama Dablam**. Another three to four hours will take you to **Island Peak Base Camp**. Or, climb the high ridge (5,443m; 17,912ft) to the

Lonely trees and prayer flags in Gupha Pokhari.

north for views of **Lhotse**.

Rather than backtrack to the trail fork, take a high trail above **Pheriche** to **Duglha** and on to **Loboche**. You can visit Pheriche, with its sod-roof hotels and a **Trekkers' Aid Post** on the way down, unless you need medical attention of course. The post is staffed by western doctors during trekking season, and has a decompression bag for emergency treatment of altitude sickness. The final one to two hour climb to **Lobuche** (4,930m; 16,175ft) is made easier by the stupendous scenery. It is better to spend a night at one of the lodges than to continue on to **Gorak Shep** (5,184m; 17,060ft) where the tiny tea-houses are often full.

It is possible to leave Lobuche, climb to the top of **Kala Pattar** (5,623m; 18,450ft) in about four hours for views of Everest and return to Lobuche the same day. You can also do a longer day trip to Everest Base Camp from Lobuche; from Gorak Shep it is about two to three hours across the **Khumbu Glacier**, but if your days are limited, Kala Pattar is the preferred choice.

The way back to Namche is a breeze: from Lobuche to Pangboche in one day, and to Namche another. A hot shower will never feel so good.

Langtang-Helambu

The **Langtang Valley** lies due north of Kathmandu, and is one of the best places

and the south side on the way back. You will see a vast difference in vegetation: the south facing hillsides are dry while the opposite slopes are lush and shady.

After your second night at **Lama Hotel,** you can climb through thick forests of birch, pine and rhododendron to **Ghora Tabela** (2,880m, 9,450ft) from where the army watches over the national park. The valley has opened up and high ridges parallel the long meadows. Few trekkers stay at Ghora Tabela, whose name means "horses' stable," though it is a nice peaceful setting. Soon you will see **Langtang Lirung's** white triangle top (7,245m; 26,770ft) peeking over the dark ridge to the north. A couple of hours further is **Langtang Village** (3,307m; 10,850ft) with pleasant lodging.

It is not long before the yaks begin to appear, so you know it is time to slow down. It is only two to three more hours to **Kyangjin** but it is better to spend a night in Langtang to acclimatise. Hike up the valley slopes for some good views of the **Langtang Himal.**

Kyangjin (3,749m; 12,300ft) is as far as most trekkers go; beyond you must have tents and food. But it is a great place from which to take day trips, further up the valley or up one of the nearby "hills" such as **Yala Peak,** at 4,700m (15,400ft). A small *gompa* and yak cheese factory, which also makes delicious creamy yoghurt, is just down from the national park lodge.

On the return, try the southern trail through **Syabru** (2,118m; 6,950ft), a

to get high into yak country in a short time. A five-hour bus ride gets you to Trisuli, a hot valley-bottom town where you will want to catch the quickest bus to Dhunche (1,966m; 6,450ft). Take a minute to visit the **Langtang National Park** interpretive centre before Dhunche (Rs250 entrance fee) to learn about the wildlife and flora of the area.

As in all national parks, there are regulations against cutting firewood in Langtang, so try to reduce your consumption by taking adequate clothing and ordering meals when others do.

There are two trails into the Langtang Valley, joining the second day. You might go up via **Syabrubensi** and **Khangjung** (3,177m; 7,300ft) on the north side of the river and via Syabru

Dawn reveals each peak, minute by minute, a daily Himalayan drama.

linear village of wooden houses stretched along the hilltop. You can reach it in one day from **Lama Hotel**. From there you can reach **Dhunche** via **Bharku** in a day and head back to Kathmandu, completing the trek in nine days without rest, but would be better in a relaxing 10-12 days. If you have another six to seven days, consider a trek to the **Gosainkund Lakes** and through **Helambu**, coming out either on the **Kathmandu Kodari Road** or at **Sundarijal** in the eastern Kathmandu Valley. With tea-houses at Gosainkund, it is now possible to do the whole route staying in lodges.

From Syabru, or straight from Dhunche if you skip Langtang, you can reach the first night's stop at **Sing Gompa** (3,254m; 10,675ft) in about five hours. You will pass through rhododendron forests ablaze in spring and climb steadily. Reward awaits you with a cheese factory and lodgekeepers who have learned to make cheese turnovers and other delicious concoctions.

Beyond *Sing Gompa*, the mountain views start to open up. On a clear day you can see west to the Annapurnas, Himalchuli, Ganesh and east to the Langtang Himal. Keep climbing and soon you will come to the lakes, the largest of which is **Gosainkund** (4,298m; 14,100ft), the site of a yearly Shiva festival where hundreds of Hindu devotees bathe in the sacred waters.

To continue on to Helambu, stay to the left of the lakes and cross the 4,602m

(15,100ft) **Laurebina Pass**. It can be difficult to follow the route in fresh snow. You will come to a group of *goths* or herders' shelters at *Tharepati* (3,475m; 11,400ft) where you can find food and shelter.

There are two choices here; you can follow the ridge south to **Kutumsang, Gul Bhanjyang** and **Pati Bhanjyang** and then climb up and over **Burland Bhanjyang** at 2,438m (8,000ft) to **Sundarijal** (four days), or descend to the east, cross the **Melamchi Khola** and return through **Tarkeghyang** (2,560m; 8,400 ft) and Helambu proper (five days). The eastern route better conveys the Sherpa lifestyle; you will stay in lodge-homes with heavy wood beam floors and shelves lined with shiny copper and brass pots, the pride of a good Sherpani housekeeper.

From Tarkeghyang there are two trails. The high route passes through Shermathang; climb to the ridge-top for views of the nearby **Jugal Himal**. The other drops to the river via Talamarang and can be hot in late spring. The trails meet in **Melamchi Phul Bazaar** and soon become a dirt road, following the **Indrawati Khola** through **Bahunepati** and on to **Panchkaal**. You can get a ride for most of it. Buses ply regularly from Panchkaal to Kathmandu.

Life goes on in the fields.

wildlife, soaring mountains and raging rivers.

Rai and *Limbu* descendants of the *Kirantis*, a people thought to have settled in the Kathmandu Valley more than 2,500 years ago, populate the undulating hills, alongside Tibetans, Sherpas, Newars and *Brahmins/Chhetris*. Trekking in east Nepal offers you the chance to see original lifestyles uncommercialised by tourism, and to taste a bit of wilderness.

Makalu Base Camp

The Arun Valley-Makalu Base Camp Trek is a classic: 21-25 days of hiking through an amazing cross-section of the

East Nepal

East of Everest are some of Nepal's lushest landscapes, complete with prolific

The beautiful children of Simikot.

Himalayas, beginning at less than 1,000m elevation and peaking at over 5,000m. From the **Tumlingtar airstrip**, the path follows the mighty **Arun River**, whose origins are located high on the Tibetan plateau, to **Num** below which a giant dam is proposed. There the route turns west and climbs gradually to the **Tashigaon**.

At around 2,500m (8,200ft) it is the last settlement, still farmed by Sherpas. This trek can only be done by groups self-sufficient with all provisions including fuel. Tea-house trekkers can go as

Green Trekking

The Nepalis have a phrase "*Hariyo Ban, Nepalko Dhan,*" which means "A green forest is Nepal's wealth." Conservation is nothing new to the Himalayan peoples; it has been a necessity of survival for centuries.

But new factors are at play today – plastics, a fast-growing population, a cash economy and an influx of trekkers whose demands for food, shelter, fuel and canned, bottled and plastic-wrapped goods put added stress on the environment.

If the 62,000 trekkers who visit Nepal each year were spread evenly across the hills from east to west over twelve months, their needs would be less apparent; but with 90 per cent of trekkers using the three main trekking areas, the Annapurnas, Everest and Langtang, for only four to five months a year, their impact is beyond the regions' ability to absorb them.

"Green Trekking" is beginning to take hold among some of the more conscientious trekking agents and among a few lodge-operators, primarily in the Annapurna Conservation Area Project (ACAP).

Many trekkers would like to do more to prevent litter, pollution, cutting of trees and damage to the environment, but are not sure how to go about it.

Here are some tips on how to tread lightly.

Pick up a copy of ACAP's Minimum Impact Code when you get your trekking permit at the Department of Immigration, or ask your agent to provide one. Even if you are not going into the Annapurna area, it gives some excellent suggestions.

Support the use of kerosene for cooking by going with a trekking agent who regularly uses it. Encourage the agent to use kerosene for porters' cooking also but expect to pay a bit more for its cost and transport.

Choose a lodge that cooks with kerosene or a fuel-efficient stove; few outside of the Annapurna Sanctuary do.

In that case, try to coordinate menu selections and eating times with other trekkers to reduce the use of firewood.

Be sure to dress warmly and see that your porters have some form of wrap so that none of you are dependent upon firewood for night-time warmth.

Encourage your staff or lodgekeeper to properly dispose of wastes – burn burnables (not including metals or plastics), bury biodegradables (food wastes) and site latrines or toilet tents a safe distance (100ft) from any water source.

Minimise the non-biodegradables you bring into the hills and plan to carry them out, especially batteries. Be sure your staff properly cover toilet holes.

Do not leave toilet paper in the bush or along trails; burn it (carefully!) or carry a plastic bag and dispose of it properly. Be conscious of not picking a toilet spot near a sacred site.

Bathe away from drinking sources; carry a bucket of water away from the river and remember to bring bio-degradable soap.

Avoid buying hot shower water from lodges that do not have a back boiler or hydro-electric water heating system.

Dress modestly while bathing. Women can wrap in a *loongi* (cotton tube skirt) like the locals do, and should wear a swimsuit only if well isolated (never bathe nude). Men should wear underwear or swim trunks while bathing.

Modesty extends to the trail. Notice how the Nepalis cover themselves: women in calf-length or longer skirts and men with shirts on at all times.

Loose pants have become acceptable for women but shorts are definitely not. Men's shorts should be bermuda-length. Do not encourage begging, for *paisa* (money), *mithai* (candy), or *won dot pen* (pens) – the common *mantras* heard along trekking corridors! Begging erodes self-pride and feeds a hand-out mentality.

Instead, give donations to a school or monastery, or to people who cannot work because of handicap or religious devotion.

Respect people's privacy while photographing. Put yourself on the other side for a moment.

In the dining room of an old hotel in Chame.

far as Tashigaon, but should expect only the basics in food and lodging in this less touristed area.

Above Tashigaon the terrain becomes more challenging. In two days you cross two high passes, **Khongma La** and **Shipton La** (4,500m; 14,764ft), with another, **Barun La**, to go before reaching base camp, some five to six days from Tashigaon. The views from high are other worldly: 360°C panoramas of Everest and the Khumbu Himal, Makalu, Kanchenjunga and north into Tibet.

You are now walking through forests of birch, rhododendron and oak, camping in alpine meadows of the **Barun Valley**.

Base camp is pitched further up this glacial valley; on day hikes visit **Camp** I or the **Barun Glacier**. Peaks of 6,500m (21,000ft) surround you. All seems blissful, but beware of a turn in weather which can block the passes on the only way out.

Return to **Tashigaon** and back via **Num** and **Khandbari** to **Tumlingtar**, where you can catch a plane to Kathmandu or walk out to **Hile**, or even walk over **Salpa Pass** to Khumbu. Eventually a dam service road will reach Num and you will be able to drive in and out.

Chainpur Area

A less demanding trek favoured for its interesting bird life and lively market

The shrubbery struggles for survival but manages to add colour to barren stoney mountain-sides.

days begins with **Chainpur** (approximately 1,600m, 5,250ft), a prosperous town known for its generations-old brass industry. Fly to Tumlingtar and walk for five to six hours to this charming ridge-top town reminiscent of a Mediterranean villa: wrought iron railings and orange trees loaded with fruit line the flagstone pathways. The Friday *haat* (bazaar) is a colourful scene worth waiting for, with *Rai* women in their flower gathered skirts and coin necklaces.

A five to seven-day loop is possible for the tea-house trekker who can live without western food and is not too fussy about the board.

From Chainpur, continue east along the historical trade route between Kathmandu and Darjeeling and Sikkim to **Nunkdhaki** at about 2,000m (6,560ft). The next day climb steadily to **Gupha Pokhari** (3,000m; 9,843ft), a frontier trade town with few tourist amenities but a simple lodge and several tea and *tongba* (fermented millet drink) shops. It is named after a sacred cave (*gupha*) and lake (*pokhari*). In the clear morning, **Kanchenjunga** (8,586m; 28,169ft) and **Makalu** (8,463m; 27,766ft), third and fifth highest mountains in the world, rise to the east and west.

Turn west from **Gupha Pokhari** and reach the roadhead at **Basantpur** in two days via **Chauki**. Buses or taxis will take you to **Biratnagar** for a flight to Kathmandu, or to Dharan where you can pick up an overnight bus.

Loads are heavy, and winds can be a fight on a trek in open country.

Kanchenjunga

Basantpur-Gupha Pokhari is also the main approach route for the Kanchenjunga trek. In 1988, two routes were opened to trekkers: northeasterly along the **Tamur Kosi** to **Pangpema**, the north side base camp, and to **Yalung Glacier** and the south camp.

It is also possible to combine the two by crossing one of two high passes, **Lapsang La** (5,932m; 19,460ft) or **Sinion La** (4,800m; 15,750ft). You will need a minimum of 22-25 days to do so, if you can get a flight into and out of Taplejung airstrip. The more reliable alternative is via Gupha Pokhari or the road to Ilam.

Take along all food and fuel, and keep the environment clean, the trails and campsites are already suffering from litter and the forests are being cut for firewood. Do your part in abiding by conservation codes.

The Wild West

West Nepal is indeed untamed frontier and trekking can be both fascinating and frustrating. Half the problem is getting there. Royal Nepal Airlines flies to **Jumla** and **Dunai**, but neither is foolproof; it is wise to count on losing several days to flight delays. To compound the transport issue, all food and provisions should be brought from Kathmandu as the entire area does not have enough food. People are less inclined to invite you into their homes, some believing that a stranger's presence "pollutes" the hearth. There are no hospitals, no hot showers and certainly no pizza and apple pie.

But if you are prepared and flexible, the west is a marvel of its own. Although the Himalayas are more distant, there are dramatic lakes, Tibet-like landscapes and incredible finds in this region rich in history and of unique religious beliefs.

Jumla-Rara Lake

Rara National Park is the centrepiece of this short but interesting trek. Fly to **Jumla** (2,347m; 7,677ft) from **Nepalgunj** and hire your porters there. There is no road access so you are at the mercy of locals whose demands reflect the captive market. Do not start off later than November or earlier than mid-March as the winters can be harsh; expect snow at any time. There are two trails to **Rara Lake**, making a pleasant loop trek of about eight to nine days with a rest at the lake. One path heads westerly to **Sinja**, an ancient capital, then north, crossing several moderate ridgelines (up to 3,800m, or 12,500ft) before reaching the lake, at 2,980m (9,777ft). There is a simple government guest-house for visitors on the northern shore but no food. Lovely pine and fir forests frame the deep (literally, the bot-

Trekking Tips

It is amazing how many "essentials" stay unused at the bottom of our pack. When you are finished packing, go through your baggage again and throw out one third. If it is your first trek, go back and take out another third. Your loaded backpack should not weigh more than 15 – 20kg (33 – 44 lbs).

Trekking Gear: What to Take

Footwear: Nothing ruins a trek than sore feet. Bring at least one pair (preferably two) comfortable, well-broken-in shoes. You are asking for trouble if you expect to break in a new pair on a trek.

For most walking, a pair of running or walking shoes with some traction is fine. The shock-absorbing soles of running shoes will serve you well, especially going downhill. In wet conditions, fabric shoes dry quicker. If your shoes have replaceable inner soles, bring an extra pair. Change and wash them during your trek.

If your trek is longer than two weeks, your shoes will take a real beating. Light but sturdy boots of ankle-height with vibram soles are perfect, in addition to a heavier pair for rocky and icy trails, depending on where you are going.

Definitely wear high top boots if you have ankle trouble, and make sure the heels are shock-absorbing if you have knee trouble. Try different lacing and knots if you are troubled by rubbing and blisters.

Thick socks of synthetic fabrics tend to cause blisters. Wool and cotton are best. If you wear two pairs, wear thin synthetic socks under thick woollen ones.

You will have clean socks if you wash them and satefy-pin them to dry on your pack as you walk.

At camp or at the lodge, it is nice to have

something to slip on and off easily. Many use *chapals* (rubber thongs).

Clothing

Remember you are in a conservative society. Loose pants for men, long skirts or pants for women, loose shirts or T-shirts are good basic-wear.

How much to carry? A general rule of thumb is "a couple": that is, two T-shirts, two shirts, two sweaters (or a sweater and a wool shirt), two pants and shorts. The rule doesn't apply to socks and underwear.

A Nepali *lungi*, the 2m piece of cloth Nepalis often wear comes in handy. You can wear it, use it as a sheet, change clothes in it and women often use it while bathing.

Layering is the best way to keep warm. You will probably go through huge temperature changes in a day (remember you are at about the same latitude as Florida and Kuwait). Add or strip off layers to suit changing temperatures.

The temperature drops 1.95°C for every 300m altitude gained (3.5°F for every 1,000ft). In December, January and early February, it gets cold at even lower altitudes and severely cold at higher altitudes. Your long underwear will come in handy. The new pile clothes are good, but many believe wool is better. Sweaters bought in Kathmandu fare well.

A down vest is handy but a down parka is essential for the higher altitudes in winter. Also bring a windbreaker large enough to go over a thick sweater.

A wide brimmed hat will keep out the sun at low and high altitudes, and a woollen hat is needed for colder weather. Remember 40 per cent of body heat is lost through your head. Also, mittens are better than gloves.

The sun's intensity increases as the air gets thinner. Up in the mountains, bring sunglasses for protection from ultraviolet rays. And if you wear prescription glasses or contact lens, bring spares and a safe case to store them in.

At lower altitudes, lighter clothes, particularly cotton shorts and cotton skirts, are best – Bermuda shorts, not running shorts and knee-length skirts. These can be bought at Thamel.

Sleeping Bags: A good sleeping bag is essential, but just because you're going to the Everest area, don't buy a bag with 60 ounces of down. If you stay in lodges, a good medium bag is enough.

Sleeping Bag Liner: A cotton sleeping bag liner will keep you warm and keep your bag cleaner. In lower altitudes, it might be all you need.

Packs: If someone is carrying your gear, use a lockable duffel bag and carry a daypack big enough to hold camera, plasters/moleskin, binoculars, diary, water-bottle, raingear, and layers you strip off. It is always wise to carry (depending on the weather) a down parka or sweater with you.

If you are carrying your own pack, make sure it has pads and webbing to keep it off your back or else, when it is warm, your sweat will wet your gear. A pack with at least one lockable compartment will help.

An external frame pack may be best for trail walking but internal frames packs are nearly as good and they are easier when travelling. Have good pads as most of the weight should be distributed on your hips.

Mattress: Almost all lodges on the main trails provide foam mattresses but you may want to use your own. On remote routes, carry a foam pad or an air mattress.

Plastic Sheets: Buy different sizes in Kathmandu. They are handy to cover the hotel mattresses (from lurking bugs!), your porter and his (your) load from rain, for packing wet things, or as a groundcloth.

Umbrella: Essential for rain or sunshine! Buy the sturdy bamboo stem ones available in Kathmandu's Asan area. Even a loose pancho traps heat and sweat. Umbrellas make good walking staffs, and they will keep the village dogs at bay.

Flashlight: Bring a spare bulb and batteries.

Handkerchiefs: Use them as sweatbands, towels and whatnot.

Mug: A large mug is handy to drink or wash from. Large enamel ones can be found in Kathmandu. Sierra-style cups burns your lips and do not hold enough.

Pocket knife: Useful as a bottle-opener, can-opener and cutting blade. Bring a table-spoon.

Toilet Kit: Bring toothbrush, dental floss, shampoo,soap (though most of these are available on the trail). A small washcloth-size towel can double up as a washcloth and towel. Wet tissues are also good, but do not throw their roll on the trail.

Toilet Paper: Bring a roll or two; bring matches to burn the paper after use on the trail.

Stuff Bags and Plastic Bags: Nylon, cloth or plastic bags will help you keep organised.

Diary/Notebook: A small spiral notebook to jot your inspired lines or just simple observations, your expenses, etc.

Water bottle: A water bottle with a minimum of one litre capacity is essential. Translucent plastic with a water-tight screw top and wide mouth is best.

Medical Kit: Besides your usual prescriptions, plasters, moleskin, an elastic "Ace" bandage, aspirin, decongestant, cough and cold tablets, stomach medicine, diamox for altitude sickness (see below); also bring a lip balm and a good sun screen.

Trekking Expenses

Most of the gear you need can be rented in Kathmandu. You can equip yourself with the basics – pack, sleeping bag, down jacket – for about US$3 per day.

On the main trekking routes, allow yourself from US$5 – $10 per person per day, more if you want cokes, bottled mineral water, beers and/or hard liquor.

On a less patronised trail, your dietary options (temptations) will be reduced, and so will your expenses, but pay a fair price if you eat at private homes.

If you hire a porter, allow roughly US$3 – $5 for him/her, and a tip at the end of the trek. An organised trek will cost you anything from US$30 to U$50 or more per day, depending on where and from whom you buy the package. Usually, each group member pools in US$25 and upwards to be distributed among the trek crew, depending on the arduor and length of the trek, and of course, the service.

Old clothes can be divided by the *sardar* (tour leader).

Note: There is a national park fee of Rs.250 and Rs200 for the Annapurna Conservation Area Project (ACAP).

Staying Healthy On The Trail

You should get regular exercise (running, swimming, walking, etc.), and plan on several all-day hikes up and down steep hills before you begin your trek. Get into a rigorous exercise program a few months before your trek.

Make sure you have all your innoculations; polio, cholera, typhoid, paratyphoid, and tetanus.

If you have not had measles, mumps or rubella, innoculations against them are recommended. Rabies occurs in Nepal and you may want to consider the (expensive) vaccine.

If you are bitten by a rabid dog, you have about a week to get treatment started, 10-14 days if you have the vaccine. Likewise, for tuberculosis you may want to consider a BCG innoculation.

If you have any chronic ailment, consult your doctor before signing up for a trek. People with heart and respiratory problems should be particularly careful. Also, if you have serious knee or back problems, you should seek advice on what medicines to bring with you.

Before leaving for your trek, get a serum globulin (gamma globulin) shot for protection against hepatitis. It will not provide total protection, but it is effective.

Its effectiveness decreases over time, so an additional shot is recommended if you are in Asia for more than four months.

This shot is also available in Kathmandu at the CIWEC Clinic, Nepal International Clinic, and Kalimati Clinic.

On the Trail

Stomach problems are a trekkers' most common ailment. Your chances of suffering from some stomach bug can be reduced to almost nothing if you take a few precautions.

Water

Never drink any water that has not been boiled for at least 10 minutes or treated with iodine, even for brushing your teeth. Unless you actually see the water boiling, do not consider it boiled water.

The most effective way to treat water is with iodine. Lugol's iodine is available at pharmacies in Kathmandu. Put five or six drops in one litre of water, and wait 20 minutes before drinking. If the water is very cold or seems really murky, use 8 to 10 drops and wait about 40 minutes.

Water purification iodine tablets are also available. The colder the water, the longer you should wait before drinking.

If pregnant, consult your doctor before using iodine. Water filters alone are not effective; boiling is also necessary. The new small pump filters are available but expensive and clog. Halazone® or other chlorine agents are not effective against amoebic cysts, but iodine is.

Bottled mineral water, soft drinks and beer are safe to drink. The plastic mineral water bottles can be reused as water bottles if need be.

Since most Nepali liquor is diluted with water, there is some risk in drinking it.

Food

Freshly cooked food is generally safe to eat. Fruit and raw vegetables should be washed with clean drinking water and peeled. Soak for 20 minutes with about 5 drops of Lugol's per litre.

Eating cold and uncovered food in teashops is risky. The chances of contamination from flies is great. Ask yourself where those flies were before they landed on the food and you will lose your appetite anyway.

Milk in Nepal is generally boiled but since water might have been added to it, it may need to be boiled again.

Fresh yoghurt is safe, but if it has not been covered, skim the film off the top before eating. Drinking *mahi* (buttermilk) is chancy.

It is the rare trekker who does not lose weight on a trek, no matter how much they eat. So do not hold back if you feel hungry: you will need plenty of fresh carbohydrates and protein to get you up those hills. See how the experts (your porters) fill up.

Chew your rice carefully in case of small stones in it.

Stomach Problems

The most common stomach problems are diarrhoea and dysentery (stool with mucus and blood). Diarrhoea is more common of the two.

Above all, keep your body rehydrated. Drink plenty of liquids. "Jeevan Jal," available at any chemist, will replace the salts you lose and give you sugar for energy. Gator Aid® is a rehydration powder that does the same thing but tastes better. Use as directed with treated water. Drink weak tea and clear soup. Avoid dairy products, alcohol, spicy or sweet food – think bland.

Unless you are in great pain and incapacitated, do not start gulping medicine right away. If the diarrhoea persists, try two to three Lomotil® tablets (or codeine which is even better).

But remember that taking drugs to plug yourself up may actually prolong or mask your illness.

If in serious discomfort (fever, nausea, vomiting, extreme diarrhoea), you might start a course of antibiotics as per your doctor's recommendation.

Diarrhoea is caused by bacteria or parasites producing toxines in your intestines. The most infamous is a nasty protozoan known as *giardia*. Its most common symptom is hideous rotten-egg burps (and flatulence) and a swollen stomach feeling. Your stool may contain mucus and smell even worse.

Treatment: Tinidazole® or Tiniba® (not available in the US) is available in Kathmandu and is very effective. Two grammes taken in a single dose should be enough, but another dose may be needed after 24 hours. But make sure you are suffering from *Giarda* before taking this drug.

Equipment and supplies checked out at Annapurna Base Camp.

...Trekking Tips

Different treatment is required for other forms of diarrhoea and dysentery.

Treatment: Consult your doctor. You should probably have two different types of antibiotics. Co-Trimoxazole® and Norfloxacin® are recommended, as is Naladixic Acid®. Tetracycline® is also common but this may cause increased sensitivity to sunburn.

Altitude Sickness

Three thousands metres (about 10,000ft) is often considered to be the altitude when problems start, but you can get altitude sickness at as low as 2,450m (8,000ft).

More than two-thirds of trekkers going to high altitude are somehow affected by it, but only 2 per cent are seriously affected. The higher and faster you go, the greater your chances of being affected.

People flying to a high altitude airport and proceeding higher are especially susceptible and should pay close attention to their condition. Even those in top physical condition can be affected by altitude; neither does prior high altitude experience count. Each time is a first time.

Symptoms of altitude sickness include:—
• Insomnia
• Loss of appetite
• Headache
• Shortness of breath, irregular breathing
• Dizziness,lightheadedness
• Swelling of hands and/or face
• Irritation, emotional behavior
• Decline in urine
• Heartbeat of more than 110/m minute even while resting

It is common to experience mild attacks of one or more of these symptoms. A slight headache after a sizeable ascent is common and it may be gone by the next morning. If it is not, you should spend a day sleeping at the same altitude for proper acclimatisation.

Pay attention to yourself and the other members in your party. If symptoms continue or

become more severe, DESCEND IMMEDIATELY. Severe symptoms include:
    Severe headache
    Severe nausea and/or vomiting
    Extreme lassitude, (including loss of appetite)
    Extreme fatigue, (loss of coordination when walking)
    Shortness of Breath, (even at rest)
    Abnormal behavior or speech
    Bubbly breath, (coughs with coloured sputum)
You must descend as much as possible. Do not wait for helicopter rescue, do not wait till the next morning, do not rely on any medicine. You must go down until your symptoms are gone. This means descending a few thousand feet. It is best for the sick person to be carried down.

Never let someone in this condition go alone. Improvements after descent are often dramatic.

Gain altitude gradually with rest days at higher altitudes. Above 3,000m (10,000ft), limit yourself to a 300m – 500m (1000 – 1500ft) rise in altitude per day. When you gain an additional 900m (3000ft) in altitude, spend an extra night there. Use this rest day for a day trip up higher but return to sleep at the lower elevation.

Drink plenty of liquids. You should be passing more than half a litre of urine a day; one litre is even better. Eat plenty of carbohydrates. A good appetite indicates that you are acclimatising. Take your time. Besides rest days, allow yourself plenty of time while walking. While making your schedule, allow for a pace that is comfortable for you.

Helicopter Evacuation

Before you can be evacuated, payment must be guaranteed. If you have medical insurance, make sure it covers an evacuation. An hour of helicopter time costs over US$750 dollars and upwards; estimate 2½ hours for either Annapurna or Everest. Do not expect your embassy or trekking company to vouch for you.

Send a message with the injured person's

name, passport number, nationality, insurance company and policy number, the nature of the injury (say "most immediate" if death seems likely in 24 hours), exact location, and the name of the person sending the message. Ask that Himalayan Rescue (222906, 418755) be contacted.

If you do not have insurance, give the name and telephone of someone who will act as guarantor. Do not expect a helicopter in an hour; sometimes it can take a day or longer.

Trekking with Children

Trekking families are becoming slightly more common on Nepal's trails. It is better if they have some overnight hiking experience before they try it in Nepal. Pre-school children should probably not be taken.

Consult your physician before you go. Make sure you have all the necessary immunisations (allow several months). Be aware that there is periodic occurrence of meningitis epidemics in Kathmandu Valley.

You can catch colds, sore throats, and coughs easily in Nepal; have the medicine and basic know-how to treat your child if he/she comes down with something.

Children seem more susceptible to altitude than adults. If your child starts to have symptoms of altitude sickness, start descending. You may have trouble determining whether the problem is altitude – related or something else.

The recommended altitude limit for children is 4,000m (13,000ft). Small infants are advised not to go above 3,050m (10,000ft).

Gastro-intestinal sickness is the biggest cause of death among Nepali children. Sanitation standards are low, and oral-fecal contamination is the biggest hazard for child trekkers. If you heed the proper precautions, you should not (and most families do not) have problems. Give only cooked and heated food. Dry and rinse plates with boiled or iodised water.

If your child has diarrhoea or is vomiting, it is crucial to keep him/her rehydrated. Use "Jeevan Jal," which you can buy in Kathmandu to take with you. As in the case of adults,

Tengboche Village.

children need to take in the same volume of fluids they are losing. Do not give children drugs (opiates, for example) to stop the diarrhoea.

Handicapped Trekkers

Handicapped trekkers should be prepared for a lot of attention from curious Nepalis and fellow trekkers.

It may be just that Nepalis have not seen many Westerners who are disabled.

It is best to have some trekking/hiking experience at home before you try it in Nepal. Consider the trekking routes, keeping in mind your handicap.

tom has never been found) blue lake and bird life abounds in the reeds.

On the return, leave from the southern rim and descend to **Pina**. On this three to four day hike back to **Jumla**, you will cross two passes of 3,400 – 3600m (11,000 – 12,000ft).

Flat-roofed houses reflect the dry climate and rough home-made clothing indicate a much less prosperous lifestyle than in the central or eastern part of Nepal. The landscape is also different; valleys are broader, oak and spruce forests form patchworks with high pastures and an occasional carved human image guards a bridge crossing or a temple entrance, reminders of the animist faith practiced here.

Dolpo Area

Like Kanchenjunga, the Dolpo area was opened two years ago to trekkers within a defined route and who abide by self-sufficiency regulations. Long hidden from the outside world, inner Dolpo paints a picture much like Tibet with stark landscape and pre-Buddhist *Bon* sites.

A Dolpo trek is not for the first-timer; it crosses numerous high passes and negotiates sketchy trails through remote mountainous regions. There is no easy turning back if you decide this is not your holiday dream nor a Himalayan Trust Hospital – should your body balk at your demands. Be sure to go with a reliable and experienced trekking agency. The short-cut flight to **Dunai** will save you more than a week of walking but remember the uncertainity factor. Otherwise, you can hike for 10-12 days from Pokhara or Tansen, each with 3,000m (10,000ft) passes.

On the high banks of the Thulo Bheri River around **Dunai**, district headquarters and checkpost stop, you will see *kots* (hilltop fortress ruins) from where early kings ruled before Nepal was united under the Shah family.

To reach **Phoksundo Lake** (3,630m; 11,900ft), inside **Shey-Phoksundo National Park**, you will take a short steep trail from Dunai up the **Suli Gad River** to **Ringmo**. Here, life revolves around the yak, supplier of milk products, wool, skin, dung and transport. The inhabitants of this seemingly god-forsaken land are originally from Tibet and still practice *Bon* religion, which was largely integrated into Tibetan Buddhism when the latter spread up from India in the 8th century.

Climb up to one of the hilltops above the lake for a view of **Kanjiroba Himal**, highest of the western ranges.

Return to the **Thulo Bheri River** and, if time permits, follow it west and then cross the **Kagmara Lekh** (3,840m; 12,590ft) on a five to six-day hike to **Jumla**.

Deep in central-west Nepal, this region sees few foreign tourists or development projects. From Jumla, continue on to Rara Lake or fly back to Kathmandu. Plan on taking a minimum of 23 to 26 days.

To take up the challenge or step back in awe?

R iver-running, relatively late in getting started, has quickly grown popular and is a fixture in adventure holiday itineraries. Nepalese rivers are ideal for rafting as they flow in a natural gradient, dropping from the northern mountains, with its snowmelt, to the southern lowlands, contouring the base of hill after hill but always heading down. There are some thrilling areas of whitewater to get you wet, but plenty of calm stretches too.

Entrusting it to an elephant's memory or just being led by the nose.

At present, seven rivers are rafted of which the **Trisuli River**, west of Kathmandu, is by far the most popular. Most rafting operators offer a 3-day trip, putting in at the north of **Mugling** (half-way between Kathmandu and Pokhara), and pulling out at **Narayanghat** down in the Terai. Most of the rapids are above Mugling – you will be given ample notice of them by your crew, and you will remember their names: *Ladies' Delight, Surprise* and *Upset*. A motor road follows the river almost the whole way – but it doesn't seriously detract from the scenery. You can stop by little villages that happen to be re-

Whitewaters provide an exhilarating time.

mote just because the river comes between them and the highway.

If you opt for the Trisuli, you're better off taking the 3-day trip, as the drive to and from the put-in and pull-out points takes three hours or so. If wilderness is what you missed while rafting, then continue to **Chitwan National Park** from Narayanghat. Most operators who sell trips to the Park in fact stop at Narayanghat, from where it is another hour's drive.

After Trisuli in popularity comes the **Sun Kosi**. A few operators offer an 8 to 11-day trip on the Sun Kosi, depending on the season and the river's swiftness, starting at **Dolalghat**, 2½ hours east of Kathmandu, and pulling out in the eastern Terai. The trip is obviously

for real river lovers. The river courses through contrasting landscapes that include some remote country, and it offers both rapids and flat water.

Rafting on the other rivers are offered only by the better established operators, mainly because of the difficulty of access and providing support. They include the **Seti**, east of Pokhara, and farther afield, **Karnali** in far western Nepal, **Bheri**, also in the west, **Arun** in the east, and lower **Kali Gandaki**, south of Pokhara. Most of these trips are more expensive and need to be arranged in advance, whereas a Trisuli trip can be booked at short notice, especially if you are a group of four and the raft is a smaller capacity "paddle-raft." Some companies offer day or two-day trips for

Mountaineering not only demands fitness, but proper outfitting and equipment.

Rapid sensation captured on oil.

those wanting just a taste of Nepali rivers.

Most operators use the smaller "paddle" rafts, holding four persons, on which passengers help with a paddle and the guide in the rear steers. This can be exciting because you take part – and you're more likely to get wet. Others use bigger rafts, holding seven persons, which are rowed and steered by one oarsman. Operators generally carry supplies and cooks; and provide tents, sleeping bags, mattresses, a waterproof bag for clothes and an "ammo" box to store camera and valuables. All you need to bring are a change of clothes, towel, sneakers and slippers, rainwear, hat, sunglasses and other personal items.

Generally, you are on the river for about six hours. The day passes with a stop for lunch and a little loitering. Camps, usually sandy beaches, are reached by 4 pm, leaving you free to relax or to explore the environs.

Among the numerous rafting operators, some are good and charge US$30 per day and up, which includes transportation, well-prepared meals, and equipment. Of course, for rivers in remote areas, the cost is higher. Other operators go down to US$15 per day, with obviously lower standards, probably many hidden "extras," and worst of all, may entail more risk. Ask around before booking a trip and avoid those not registered by the Nepal Association of Rafting Agents, which sets standards and prices.

Trekking above Ghorepani with Annapurna South (7,219m) in the background.

The best time for whitewater is in October when rivers are high and fast from the monsoon; they may be too rough in July to September. Generally, any time from October to April is good, with slight variation in water level, temperature (though it never gets chilly as most rafting is done at lower altitudes), swiftness of flow, and in opportunities for birdwatching, generally best in spring.

A list of recommended rafting operators is given in the Directory.

Bicycle Touring

It is now possible to rent 15-speed (or more) mountain bikes in Kathmandu and even in Pokhara. These bikes are fine for touring on Nepal's limited and rough road system. Many trekking agencies now offer tour packages for bikers. It is also possible to bike independently. Make sure both you and your bike are ready.

• *Bell:* Make sure you have a working bell on your bike.

• *Traffic Rules*: Right of way is determined by size, so bikes lose out to trucks, cars, buffaloes and cows. You can usually lord it over pedestrians, but do not count on getting any respect from goats.

• *Trucks:* seem to drive on "assume": they "assume" they can take as much of the road as they want, they assume you are going to give the road to them, and they "assume" a margin of 5cm is

Mountain biking, speedier but not necessarily requiring less stamina.

enough. After a few episodes of seeing that "do not kiss" sign on the rear of most trucks, you will be inclined to tell them what they can kiss.

• *A lock:* A cable that goes through the wheels is best. Lock anytime you stop.

• *Repairs:* Most towns have bike shops capable of repairing punctures, but that is it. Do not expect to find anything else.

• If your bike is a *rental*, make sure it is in excellent shape before you go. Nothing will be available outside of Kathmandu. You should know how to maintain and repair the bike yourself.

Some popular routes from Kathmandu are to **Nagarkot** and **Sankhu** (65km, 2 days), **Dhulikhel**, **Namobuddha** and **Panauti** (75km, 2 days), **Kodari** or the Tibet border (230km, 4 days), and Pokhara (400km, 5 days).

Contact an agency operating mountain bike tours (see Directory).

Real Mountain Biking

People have in the past taken All Terrain Bikes (ATBs) on the Everest trek to **Kala Pattar** and around the **Annapurna Circuit**, including over **Thorung La Pass**, but now permission is not given for such cycle-trekking in the national parks.

You are better off taking on **Helambu** and the **Pokhara-Gorkha** trail. The Annapurna region is said to be quite daunting, requiring you to carry your bike much of the time.

But if you should go on a cycle trek, here are a few pointers:

Your bike should be in top shape, as should you. You should be totally self-reliant and assume spare parts and maintenance/repair help will not be available.

Be prepared to carry your bike over some long sections. Let a porter carry the rest of your stuff. Just arrange where you will meet him during the day.

Remember that you will be sharing the trails with villagers old and young, some carrying large loads or babies; also animals that become skittish on seeing this strange "thing" approaching them.

Use the utmost caution on blind curves, and stay on the well-worn trails. No sooner have Nepalis got used to trekkers, when tourists tear up or down the narrow mountain trail on ugly

Just plain fishing on the Kali Gandaki.

Taking it all in on a mountain flight.

For something less energetic, contemplate the Fishtail
from Lake Pokhara.

(though sturdy) contraptions that many have never seen.

Mountain Flights

Of all the compelling reasons to visit Nepal, the mountains may rank on top for most visitors. In clear weather, which is frequent enough all year round except in summer, some of the central Himalaya can be seen from Kathmandu itself.

Or else, you can drive out to a ridgetop of one of the hills standing sentinel around the Valley, where magnificent views can be had. But for close and truly dramatic views of a wide stretch of the Himalayas, the Mountain Flight is unbeatable.

The Mountain Flight is Royal Nepal Airlines' hour-long ride, mostly by Boeing 727, sometimes by the pressurized 44-seater Hawker-Siddeley AVRO 748, operated once or more times a day in season (all year except summer) when the weather is clear.

The aircraft flies at about 8,000m for about 100 miles east of Kathmandu, turning around about 15 miles from the Eastern Himalayas. You will see most of the eight 8,000m peaks – there are 14 of them in the world that fall within Nepal, including Sagarmatha or Everest, Cho Oyu, Lhotse, and Makalu.

RNAC offers a refund (US$94) if you take off and the weather turns bad. You are best-off booking with a travel agent.

One of the great things about Nepal is the food. Your choice may be limited while trekking, but you have more variety in Kathmandu as in most cities around the world.

Daal-Bhaat

The national cuisine is *daal-bhaat-tarkaari* (lentil curry with curry). The centrepiece of this meal is the rice of which numerous varieties are used. This includes a red rice in the far west that was formerly reserved for royalty. The rice is crowned with the *daal*, a lentil soup, in which several types of lentils are used, *kaalo daal* being a favourite of many people. Besides the rice, a portion of *tarkaari*, curried vegetables, accompanies the dish.

Corn sundried and stored eventually keep many a Nepali well-fed.

With your right hand, mix a little of the *tarkaari* with a small amount of rice/ *daal*, then, using your thumb, push the mixture in your mouth.

There may be a meat curry – chicken or goat but never beef, which Hindus

Pictures of past & present kings grace the walls of a humble restaurant.

do not eat.

Yoghurt is another common side dish. It is served over the rice and mixed in, or eaten separately. Small amounts of *achaar* (pickles) are eaten on the side for a sour and hot taste.

In some places *chapaatis*, a small flat roasted bread is available.

Nepali yoghurts are delicious, especially when made from buffalo milk. Scrape the top crust off if it has been in the open.

Nepali sweets resemble Indian sweets. Favourites are *jelebis* – which look like orange pretzels – *ladus*, and *kala jamun*. *Pedas* are small cakes of milk that have been boiled down. *Sale roti*, a ring-shaped sweet bread, is available during Dasain Festival and *khapsay*,

a Tibetan biscuit is available during the Tibetan New Year. Tibetan cooking includes *thukpa*, a heavy noodle soup, *momo*, a meat dumpling and *teen momo*, a steamed bread. Most of these are served in restaurants in Kathmandu and on the popular trails.

Alternative Fare

Kathmandu has an amazing variety of restaurants, mainly centered in Durbar Marg and Thamel. It is possible to get Indian, Tibetan, Chinese, Japanese, Italian, French, Mexican, Austrian, Korean and Thai food here should one wish to take a break.

There is a wide variety of bread and

Street treats.

every kind of cake and pie you can think of, all of which are excellent.

Outside Kathmandu, the possibilities thin out. Pokhara is almost as good for variety, and you can sample some of the tastiest food on the Jomosom trail. The main trekking trails offer some variety, but basically it is *daal-bhaat-tarkaari* (see Trekking p.191).

Something Stronger

There are several types of liquor you can try. *Raksi* is distilled usually from millet and corn. *Newari raksi* will light up with a match! The country stuff is weaker. Try it warmed with a little butter and roasted rice thrown in. A beer called *chaang* is fermented from rice, wheat and corn. In Kathmandu and some places in eastern Nepal, *tongba* is popular.

Hot water is repeatedly poured over fermented millet and sipped through a bamboo straw until the drink becomes weak. An afternoon can be pleasantly whiled away with a few *tongbas*.

Restaurants

There are restaurants for a wide range of tastes and budgets. Locally brewed beers are good and include Star, Iceberg, Leo, San Miguel and Tuborg among others. Local spirits – rum and vodka in particular – are good with mixers.

Measuring out one "paati" of rice, the traditional measurement.

wining Nepali style. Expensive.

Nepalese Kitchen, Thamel. Nepali music, nice setting; decent food and decent prices.

Others

The Chimney Room, Hotel Yak & Yeti. Charming setting; sit around the fireplace and have a variety of continental fare, including borsch. Fairly expensive.

Himthai, Thamel. Nepal's first Thai restaurant, nice garden setting, good food, reasonable prices.

Mike's Breakfast, off Hotel Yak & Yeti entrance. Big servings, tasty, wholesome food at moderate prices, with refills of real coffee; for breakfast and lunch only.

K.C.'s, Thamel. An institution, still serving steak, lasagne, pies, etc., at moderate prices.

Nanglo's, Durbar Marg. Another institution, great rooftop terrace, good western style food at reasonable prices.

Copper's, Thamel. Quality Western food at reasonable prices.

Utse, Thamel. One of the earliest restaurants in Kathmandu; try the steamed or fried *momos*, and other Tibetan dishes. Inexpensive.

Rumdoodle, Thamel. Lively bar and restaurant, with mountaineering motifs for decor.

Narayan's, near Chetrapati. Western fare, including Mexican, and good desserts. Colourful patrons, lots of ambience and best of all reasonable prices.

Breakfast of rice flour doughnuts.

Nirula's, Durbar Marg. Better than the pizza are the numerous-flavored ice-creams.

Pumpernickel, Thamel. Good bread, good breakfast place.

Shangrila's Bakery, Lazimpat. Excellent French pastries and bread.

Pokhara

There are dozens of restaurants along the lake. Personal favourites include **Don't Pass Me By**, **The Kantipur**, **The Phewa**, **The Hungry Eye**, and **Baba Lodge**.

F ortunately for shoppers, Kathmandu keeps growing – in shops; if you take the time to explore, you will get what you want and have fun in the process. Main shopping areas are Thamel, Durbar Marg, Kupondole, Indrachowk, Patan, Boudha and Bhaktapur.

Gift Possessibilities

Nepali women are seldom without their bangles, which also make wonderful souvenirs.

Paper products – calendars, stationery, cards and gift-wrap make good and easy-to-carry gifts. Brass sculptures and woodcarvings are equally visible though bulky to carry. You will see them on a stroll through the main shopping areas – Asan, Thamel, Patan and other small streets.

To get a rough idea of prices for wood and brass handicrafts, visit stores in the **Patan Industrial Estate**. Also see the **Bhaktapur Crafts Center** in Dattatraya Square. The **Chainpur Brass Store** on Durbar Marg sells excellent brass.

Nepali textiles have recently come into their own. Interesting modern apparel is available in boutiques such as **W h e e l s**, **Yasmin** and **Mandala**,

Marketplaces are often brightened by colourful ethnic fabrics and made-up clothing.

most of them are located in the Durbar Marg. Nepali silk is available at **Everest Handloom Silk**, across from Central Immigration near Thamel.

A mini-industry has sprung up making Tibeto-Nepali woollen sweaters, mittens, caps, jackets, trousers, Kathmandu or Nepal T-shirts with your favorite slogan or embroidery, and a fascinating array of hand-stitched and hand-woven bags of all sizes and colors. Most of these are found in Thamel.

Nepal's woollen carpets have improved tremendously; what is more, their

in a tighter weave, and is more expensive. Old carpets from Tibet are often antique pieces and priced accordingly. By all means please bargain.

The Boudha area is a good place to find Tibetan items, anything from images, silver bowls, mandalas and other ritual objects to jewellery and stones. Other Tibetan items are *thangka* paintings, *choktse* tables, prayer-wheels, old costumes and brocades. Jewelry of turquoise and coral with silver – earrings, pendants, rings, bracelets are attractive and good buys. Thamel and Boudha are the best places to look for these. Most of the gem stores are on New Road, selling jewellery with semi-precious stones such as garnet, amethyst, black star, moonstone, lapis lazuli, topaz, alexandrite, etc, most of which are from the subcontinent.

$$$ Souvenirs

For more expensive and quality Tibetan artefacts, visit the **Tibet Ritual Art Gallery** on Durbar Marg, and the Tibetan stores in Thamel.

Other worthwhile items are copper, brass and bronze statues of deities, *papiermache* dance masks, cloth puppets, terracotta animals used as flowerpots, embroidered wall-hangings, silver filigree work, pieces of woodcarving, and a Newari chess-set called *bagh chal* (tigers and goats) made of brass pieces. Hunt for all the above at Patan, Bhaktapur, Thamel and Durbar Marg.

dollar price remains what it was 10 years ago. They are found in Thamel, Indra Chowk, Patan and near the Tibetan Refugee Camp at Jawalakhel. Dyes may be chemical or natural, the wool a mix of highland Tibetan and New Zealand wool. The designs are Tibetan, Tibeto-Nepali, or geometric. A higher knottage (knots per inch) results

The Indra Chowk area has many shops selling *pashmina* (shawls, scarves and jackets, made from the wool of a particular goat from northern Nepal) they come in colours or in natural grey and beige. The softer the better.

Indra Chowk is also the place for *potes* (glass bead necklaces worn by married women).

The generally Moslem *pote* will custom-string them for you in a few hours. They are pretty, exotic though sufficiently modern looking, and inexpensive.

A word of caution, when buying, be aware that any religious image that is an antique or resembles an antique must have a clearance certificate from

Nepalese silver jewellery is intricate and beautiful.

Bring plenty of $$$ to buy unique masks as souvenirs.

the Department of Archaeology before it can leave the country.

Most Nepali art originated as devotional art, objects of religious worship. Appreciate them for what they are. Treat them with respect when you take them home.

On the other hand, many items you buy may be acceptable representations of the real thing. Do not expect the genuine thing for very little money.

A real *khukuri* (curved Nepali knife) generally has a notch at the bottom to drain blood. Two smaller knives for skinning and sharpening come with it. Avoid putting your hand over the blade side of the scabbard when you withdraw it.

However, a real prayer-wheel, (the object actually used for prayer), has

Tika powder of all colours are sold by the teaspoonful in the market.

printed mantras rolled inside the cylinder.

Such a "real" consecrated prayer-wheel will not generally be available for sale, however. So, be content with one that seems well-made; after all, you may not use it.

The vast majority of "old" *thangkas* are aged over a sooty flame. There are good new *thangkas* in the better shops – and they cost more. Real old ones, in any case, are not exportable.

You may see some stores selling fur coats. A whispered enquiry may even bring you a coat of Snow Leopard, an endangered species. Before you buy such an item, be aware of your own country's import regulations, and ask yourself if you really want to support such a business.

Most definitely, visit the **Mahaguthi, Hastakala** and **Dhukuti Handicraft Stores** in Kupondole, opposite the **Hotel Himalaya**. They carry excellent utility items made of traditional methods and material, things like sweaters and dresses, cushion covers, scarves, shawls, table cloth and napkins, quilts, mats, bags, all kinds of kitchenware, and many other knick-knacks. Mahaguthi is also located on Durbar Marg and in Patan's Durbar Square.

There are several art galleries in the city and at hotels exhibiting and selling the works of contemporary Nepali artists, such as **Siddharta on Kantipath, Contemporary Art Gallery** on Jamal, and **Nepal Art Council**, near Babar Mahal, and **Sirjana** in Blue Star Hotel.

Look for advertisements in the Nepalese newspaper, *The Rising Nepal.*

Shipping

You can pack your parcel and send it

Clay models, terracottas, brass artefacts of 'travel' size make interesting conversation pieces after a trip.

through the Foreign Post Office; do not seal it before it is inspected. Or, you can entrust your parcel to one of the many shipping agents in Thamel and Durbar Marg to pack and send by air or by surface. Use a recommended shipper. The best advice is for you to carry your shopping back with you.

G E T   P H Y S I C A L

These itineraries are helpful for first-time visitors. Most travel agencies offer them, but you can follow them independently by hiring a taxi. They are suggestions for stays of 3, 5, 7, 10 or more days in Nepal. Use your discretion to mix the components; also, vary them between cultural sights and excursions to the countryside. For details, refer to the relevant sections on Kathmandu, Patan, Bhaktapur and the Valley.

Suggested Itineraries

One of the many splendidly carved doors in Patan.

3 DAYS

Day 1: *Morning*: Visit the old part of Kathmandu City **Durbar Square**, **Hanuman Dhoka**, **House of the Living Goddess**, **Kasthamandap** (House of Wood), and **Swayambhunath** or "Monkey Temple."

Afternoon: Visit Patan, the "City of Golden Roofs," founded in 250 A.D. Highlights include the **Durbar Square**, **Krishna Mandir**, **Mahabaudha**, the golden **Temple of Hiranya Verna Mahabir**, and carpet weaving at the Tibetan Refugee Camp in nearby Jawalakhel.

Day 2: *Early morning:* Mountain Flight, an hour-long flight to view the mountains at

Temples of hundreds of years are not just monuments but remain fully functioning to this day.

close range. For this, you should book in advance, though it is possible to get seats at short notice. RNAC operates this flight regularly from October to March (except in bad weather) and, sometimes, unscheduled flights. If the flight is on time, take the time to stop by the **Pashupatinath Temple**, the most sacred of Hindu temples, on your way back from the airport.

Day 3: *Morning*: Visit **Bhaktapur**, also known as Bhadgaon, the "City of Devotees," and its **Durbar Square**, the **Palace of Fifty-five Windows**, the **Golden Gate**, etc. On your return, stop by the colossal *stupa* of **Buddhist Boudha**, to see the area's monasteries and shops.

Keep an evening free for one of the cultural shows – the **New Himalchuli Culture Group** or the **Everest Cultural Society** (see Directory). And, definitely,

stroll around the city on your own, to the shopping and commercial New Road area and Thamel, hub of tourist activity.

5 DAYS

Day 4: *Morning*: Drive to **Nagarkot**, or **Kakani**, or Dhulikhel, and have an early lunch out. See the sunrise and a little of rural Nepal.

Afternoon: Drive 12km east of Kathmandu to the **Temple of Changu Narayan**, with a 5th century statue of Garuda, Vishnu's mount, and other images from the Licchavi and Malla periods.

Day 5: *Morning*: Drive to the ancient settlement of **Sankhu**, 19km beyond **Boudha**, to visit the **Temple of Bajra Jogini**.

Afternoon: Drive to **Panauti**, 35km

There's always something ...... any which way you wish.

from Kathmandu, a charming traditional village with the massive three-tiered **Indreshwar Mahadev Temple**, which some say date back to 1294.

7 DAYS

Add to the 5-day itinerary an overnight trip to **Nagarkot**, **Kakani**, or **Dhulikhel**, with the opportunity to catch both sunrise and sunset.

Alternatively, fly to **Pokhara** (35 minutes) for a night, and drive back (200km, 6-7 hours) the following evening. You could stay for two nights, fit in some hill-walking, then fly back.

10 DAYS

Options: Definitely include 2 nights/3 days in Pokhara, making sure to do some walking. Or, take an overnight trip to **Nagarkot**, **Kakani** or **Dhulikhel**, and have time to visit **Chitwan National Park** for 2 nights/3 days, including five hours each way.

15 DAYS

Take a short trek of 4 to 7 days, either around the Kathmandu Valley rim, to **Helambu** (5 days), or the so-called Royal Trek (4 days) – or around **Sarangkot/ Kahun Danda/Naudana** from Pokhara, with a night at the lakeside.

Or, if a trek is what you really want, allot up to nine days, in which case **Khumbu**, **Ghorepani**, and **Langtang-Helambu** are possible.

Alternatively, you may opt to combine a 3-day rafting trip with two nights in **Chitwan National Park**. In both cases, you'd have time for the cultural sights in the Valley.

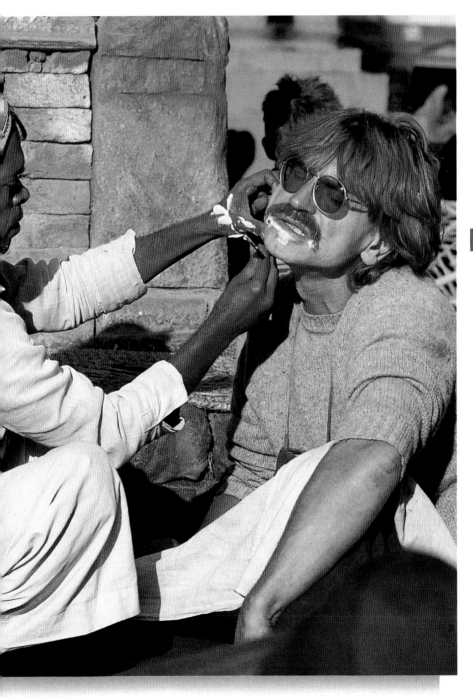

A no-frills quick shave out in the street gets the job done at a bargain price.

Beyond Nepal

You can take the land or air route to New Delhi. Both Indian Airlines and Royal Nepal Airlines fly daily. The best land route is via **Bhairahawa** to **Sunauli** (10 hours), then **Gorakhapur**, from where there are frequent daily Delhi-bound (22 hours) buses and a broad gauge train connection to Delhi and other points.

Delhi has plenty of historical and cultural sights, museums and art galleries, superb shopping, first-class hotels and good restaurants. Sightseeing highlights are the five-tiered **Qutb Minar**, **Jama Masjid**, **Humayun's Tomb**, the **Red Fort** where a sound-and-light show is held every night, and **Hauz Khas Village**. Delhi has very many upper-end hotels; for medium, try **Nirula's**, **Marina** or **York's** (all on **Connaught Place**), or **Ashok Yatri Niwas** on Ashok Road. If you are arriving by air, enquire at the airport hotel counter.

Possibilities From New Delhi:

Agra: Home of the **Taj Mahal**. Indian Airlines and **Vayadoot** fly daily, the latter frequently. Take the tourist bus

The Taj Mahal, Agra, one of India's greatest landmarks.

The Gateway to India in Bombay.

to Agra (204km) or go by train — the Taj Express and the Shatabdi Express. Accommodation: **Mughal Sheraton** and **Clarks Shiraz** (upper end)and **Mumtaz, Shahanshah Inn** and **Mayur Tourist Complex** (medium and lower end). Season: all year round though summer is hot.

Rajasthan: Of maharajas and palaces, chivalry and romance, art and culture. The Rajasthan Tourism Development Corporation (RTDC) offers several package tours from Delhi. A sample: Hawa Mahal tour of Agra/Fatehpur Sikri/Bharatpur/Deeg/Sariska/Jaipur/Delhi (3 days); Golden Triangle tour of Sariska/Jaipur/Bharatpur/Fatehpur Sikri/Agra/Delhi (3 days); Desert Triangle tour of Bikaner/Jaisalmer/Jodhpur/Ajmer/ Pushkar/Delhi (7 days). Contact RTDC in New Delhi, tel:3322332.

Season: all year though warm in summer.

Kashmir Valley & Ladakh: Indian Airlines flies twice daily to **Srinagar** in Kashmir; daily buses run from Delhi to Srinagar via **Jammu** (876km); the Shalimar Express goes to Jammu, from where you continue by bus or taxi. The state tourism corporation and private travel agents offer tours to **Gulmarg** and **Pahalgam**, **Sonamarg/Kangan**, **Wular Lake** etc. Shikara boats on **Dal** and **Nagin Lakes** will transport you and take you sightseeing. Kashmir offers wonderful trekking opportunities and the novelty (for this part of the

Varanasi on the Ganges.

world) of skiing and toboganning (equipment and instruction available at low cost). There are hotels to suit different pockets, but you cannot miss staying in a houseboat (also of different standards) on the lakes. Contact travel agents in Delhi or Srinagar for details and booking.

Season: March to October.

Leh (1,154ft elevation), capital of Ladakh, can be reached by air – five times weekly from **Srinagar** – or two days (434km) by bus from Srinagar via **Kargil**, though the road is open only from June to September. Highlights are **Leh Palace**, the monasteries or *gompas* of **Alchi**, **Spiti**, **Hemis**, **Thiksey**, **Phiyang**, **Spituk** and a landscape simi-

lar to the mountainous desert of Tibet. Agents in Leh can arrange treks in **Ladakh** and **Zanskar**. Accommodation from up to lower-end includes; **Gaidan Continental**, **Shambala**, **Kanglachen**, **Ladakh Sarai**, **Himalayas**, **Yak-Tail**, **and Dragon**.

Season: May to October.

Varanasi: Indian Airlines flies to Varanasi daily from Kathmandu. You can take a bus (8 hours) or train from **Gorakhpur** near Sunauli, the border point across **Bhairahawa** in Nepal. Travel agents offer tours to the river front, **Alamgir Mosque**, **Vishwanath Temple**, **Durga Temple**, **Benares University**, **The Archaeological Museum and Deer Park** in nearby **Sarnath**. Ac-

The Red Fort in New Delhi.

commodation: **Taj Ganges** and **Clarks Varanasi** at the top end, and hotels **Gautam** (Ramkatora), **De Paris** (Mall), and **Ajaya** (Lohurabir) at the lower end.

The Indian Airlines flight ex-Kathmandu continues a hopping service to **Khajuraho**, then **Agra** and **Delhi**. The **Temples of Khajuraho**, dating back 1,000 years to the Chandela period, display the very finest examples of Indian architecture and erotic sculpture.

Also, from Varanasi, you can hire a taxi (or bus it) to **Bodhgaya** (243km), where the Buddha attained enlightenment. From **Patna**, to which Indian Airlines flies twice a week, Bodhgaya is much closer (115km); also, **Vayadoot** flies thrice-weekly from Patna to **Gaya**, 16 km from Bodhgaya.

Darjeeling: Take Indian Airlines to Calcutta and then catch a flight to **Bagdogra**, where you can get on a state tourist coach or hire a taxi to Darjeeling (90 km). Buses run to **Kakarbhita** mornings and evenings (12 hours), where you cross the border, an hour's jeep ride to **Siliguri**, gateway to the northeastern hill stations. At Siliguri, there are buses and taxis (on share-basis) to Darjeeling (80km). A narrow gauge railway line (nicknamed the "toy train") also connects Siliguri with Darjeeling, which is fun but takes twice a car's time (8 hours!). Places to visit are **Tiger Hill**, the **Himalayan Mountaineering Institute**, **Ghoom Monastery**, **Lebong Race Course** and Darjeeling's famous **Tea Gardens**. Stay at **Sinclair's**, **New Elgin**,

Windamere and **Pineridge** at the upper end, and **Flora**, **Apsara** and **Capital** at the lower lend. An India visa is sufficient for Darjeeling.

From Darjeeling, consider a 2-day excursion to the beautiful hill-station of **Kalimpong**, 55km away, once a bustling town from the Tibet trade. Visit its fine flower nurseries, **Durpin Dara, Dr Graham's School, The Arts and Crafts Centre** and enjoy the general ambience of the town. **Himalayan Hotel or Park** for comfort; budget lodges are **Gompu's** and **Crown**, among others. *Season*: all year round; Darjeeling tends to be misty, both towns are a bit chilly in winter. Until recently, foreigners could stay in Kalimpong for only 2 days; there is no such restriction now.

Gangtok: The nearest airport to Gangtok, capital of Sikkim, is **Bagdogra** (124km). Either take a taxi directly to Gangtok or go via **Siliguri**, from which it is 114 km. Highlights are the **Orchid Sanctuary** (with 250 varieties of orchids in bloom in April/May and December/January), **Rumtek Monastery** (seat of the Kargyu Karmapa sect of Tibetan Buddhism), and the **Chogyal's Palac**e. Treks to the **Pemayangtse** region, toward **Kanchenjunga**, can be arranged by operators based in Darjeeling and Gangtok. Hotels: **Tashi Delek, Mayur, Tibet** and **Orchid**.

Season: All year round; monsoon in summer and a bit chilly in winter. Besides an Indian visa, you need a special permit for Sikkim, but it can be processed with

Whirr, flutter and flap as Himalayan winds play with the prayer flags
and take their messages to the gods.

your visa overnight.

Tibet

From north of the Himalayas, Tibet beck-

ons, but travellers have to put up with
certain conditions. You must go with a
group, though two persons apparently
fulfils that condition. You must book a
tour with an approved Kathmandu
agency, which contacts Tibet Travel

Bureau in Lhasa, which in turn distributes the actual handling among several government travel operators, namely China International Travel Service, China Youth Travel, China International Sports Travel, China Workers' Travel and Tibet Travel Company.

In season (March or April to November), there are twice weekly flights from **Kathmandu** to **Lhasa**, operated by RNAC on Wednesday and Southwest China Airline on Saturday.

The round-trip costs US$380.

Kathmandu agencies offer standard 4-day, 8-day, 12-day, or 16-day itineraries, which include a few days in

Monastic ruins in Lhasa, Tibet.

Lhasa, the capital, **Tsethang** in **Yarlung Valley**, where early Tibetan civilisation began, **Samye**, Tibet's first monastery **Shigatse**, seat of the Panchen Lamas, and **Gyangtse**. You can fly one way and go by land the other, fly or go by road both ways. Advance booking is needed for trips to far-off **Kailash** and **Mansorovar** in western Tibet, **Derge**, **Chamdo**, **Golok**, **Bathang** and **Gyelthang** in what was Eastern Tibet, and **Kumbum**, **Kokonor Lake**, and **Labrang** in what was **Amdo** (north-eastern Tibet).

Treks of up to 20 days to the Everest Base Camp on the Tibetan side and **Shishapangma Base Camp** are also operated. Nepali operators wisely take a veteran Sherpa crew; plan a few months in advance. Cost for tours, excluding airfare, ranges from US$120 to US$150 per day; trek costs go up to US$180 per day, depending on the logistics entailed.

Some Kathmandu agencies require you to arrive five days in advance to finalise your visa and travel arrangements. Contact any of these Kathmandu agents; Adventure Travel Nepal, Arniko Travel, Asian Trekking, Tibet Travel, Yangrima Trekking, Nepal Travel Agency and Yeti Travel

Bhutan

With Druk Air operating flights from Kathmandu to **Paro** (coming from Bangkok and Delhi), getting to **Bhutan** is

Ornate eaves end at the Jokhang Temple in Lhasa.

easier, which is fortunate as the Dragon Kingdom remains pristinely beautiful. But Bhutan, perhaps wisely, is averse to letting in tourist hordes. Consequently, there is a fixed quota of 3,500 tourists per year, filled by so-called "high-yield" tour groups.

Paro has the only airstrip in the kingdom although **Thimpu** is the capital. Paro is absolutely charming and unspoilt in spite of its hosting the only airport! Thimpu being the capital, bustles with markets and trading activity, and at this time, modern living is coming into evidence among the cityscape.

All tours are handled by the state-run Bhutan Tourism Corporation, though it parcels out trekking contracts to a few private operators. These private operators are listed in the Tibetan Telephone directory.

This includes a pre-selection of your hotel, cultural shows, meals and tours with Bhutanese guides Most common is the one-week tour covering **Paro**, capital **Thimpu**, and **Punakha**; longer tours take in **Wangdiphodrang**, **Bumthang Valley**, and **Tashigang**. Tour costs range from US$130 to US$170 per day per person. Druk Air flies to Paro weekly from Kathmandu; airfare US$105 oneway, US$210 roundtrip.

Contact a Kathmandu-based travel agent – Shambala Tours, International Trekking, Yeti Travel and Adventure Travel Nepal. Visas, after agents' groundwork, are issued upon arrival in Paro. *Season*: March to November.

TRAVEL TIPS

USEFUL INFORMATION

There are air connections to Kathmandu from Bangkok, Delhi, Calcutta, Varanasi, Patna, Dhaka, Dubai, Singapore, London, Frankfurt, Hong Kong, Lhasa, Paro (Bhutan) and Karachi.

Airlines serving Nepal are Thai Airlines International, Singapore Airlines, Pakistan International Airlines, Civil Aviation Administration of China, Biman Airways, Indian Airlines, Dragon Air of Hong Kong, Druk Air of Bhutan, Royal Nepal Airlines (RNAC), Lufthansa and Aeroflot.

RNAC is the only airline operating within Nepal. Tickets for domestic flights are best bought through a travel agent.

RNAC operates a special Mountain Flight to the Everest region just to look at the mountains. It is offered daily, weather permitting, from October to April. Cost is US$94.

ARRIVAL

When flying in from the east, sit on the right for mountain views, including that of Mount Everest; from the west, sit on the left for the western Himalayas.

As you enter the new terminal, look for the currency exchange counter. If you do not have a visa, you can get one upon arrival at the airport. You need a photo and US$10 cash or the equivalent in Nepali rupees.

In the lounge, after customs clearance, there is a counter to the right of the exit where you can book a taxi or bus that goes downtown and to the major hotels. The bus costs about US$1, the taxi about US$4, for the 10-minute ride into town.

Or, outside the terminal, weed out a taxi driver from everyone barraging you. The non-metered fare is about Rs80 (US$3) for a ride to the centre of town.

BUSES

Either minibuses or blue *Sajha* buses will take you almost anywhere in the Valley for Rs1 to Rs6. Most Valley buses leave from **Ratna Park**, near **Rani Pokhari**. Long distance *Sajha* buses leave from **Bhimsen Tower**. Tickets are sold next to the main post office.

Tourist buses to **Pokhara** (about US$4) also leave from here. Most long distance buses leave from the central bus-park, east of Ratna Park. There are services mornings and evenings to the more important destinations. Front-seats are more comfortable. (Remember to book at least one day ahead).

BUSINESS HOURS

Most tourist-related offices are open from 9am to 5pm. Government offices start at 10am and close at 5pm; shops stay open from 10am to 7pm. Saturday is a holiday, Sunday is like a regular weekday.

In winter, offices close at 4pm. If you must visit a government office, get there at 10.30am , with lots of patience. The *bholi* (tomorrow) syndrome is pervasive in Nepal.

CLIMATE

Nepal has almost every kind of climate, ranging from semitropical to arctic.

Kathmandu is cold from early November to early March. Temperatures can dip below freezing in January, and there is a cold morning fog. Winter days are crisp, but temperatures drop in the evenings.

May to mid-June is the hot season. It can get over 33°C (91°F) in Kathmandu. A hot dry wind stirs up the dust. Pre-monsoon showers arrive in May.

The monsoon arrives at the end of June. Daytime temperatures drop slightly, but nights are hotter. The monsoon does not ruin valley sightseeing; in fact, the rice fields are breathtaking during the monsoon! There are downpours, but plenty of clear weather too. However, it is not the best time to trek, unless you go to the high rainshadow areas. Trails are slushy, views poor and leeches out in large numbers.

CLOTHING

Casual. Your only concerns are comfort and respect for Nepali customs: no ultra-short shorts or revealing tank tops. When visiting a temple, women should have their shoulders and knees covered, men should wear trousers.

Most important is a pair or two of comfortable walking shoes. No dress shoes and high heels are needed.

During spring, summer, and fall, light clothing, with a sweater or jacket, is sufficient. For winter, woollens and winterwear, including a parka, are needed. Take a sweater or jacket even while visiting the generally warm Terai.

An umbrella beats the fanciest raingear and it is cheap (it is also useful as a sun shield).

CURRENCY

The unit of currency is the *rupee*. There are 100 *paisa* to a rupee; 25 *paisa* is a *sukaa*, 50 *paisa* a *mohar*. There are 5, 10, 25, 50 and one-rupee coins. Denomination of rupee notes: 1, 2, 5, 10. 20, 50, 100, 500 and 1,000.

Money can be exchanged in Kathmandu at the **Nepal Bank** on New Road or at **Rastriya Banijya Bank** inside the New Road Supermarket and their branches. Private banks include **Nepal Indo-Suez**, **Nepal-Arab Bank**, and **Grindley's Bank** on Kantipath and Durbar Marg which are more efficient. Banking hours from 10am to 2pm, 12noon on Friday; closed Saturday. The bigger hotels are authorised to exchange money.

The Nepali rupee is tied to the Indian rupee; exchange rates are posted daily at the banks and in "*The Rising Nepal*".

CUSTOMS REGULATION

You can import one bottle of liquor, two bottles or 12 cans of beer, 200 cigarettes; a pair of binoculars, a musical instrument, a transistor radio, a Walkman and 4 tapes, camera and a reasonable amount of film.

You may not bring in guns or ammunition, radio transmitters, or walkie-talkies without a permit from the Foreign Affairs or Home Ministry.

The rules for video cameras and cassettes are not clear-cut. These items may be written into your passport, to be shown while departing the country.

Drugs are strictly prohibited, as is bringing in large amounts of gold.

Make sure you get a clearance from the Department of Archaeology for any artefact that is or looks old. If it is more than 100 years old, it cannot be exported. It is illegal to take out precious stones, gold, silver, weapons, animal hides, fangs, etc.

DEPARTURE

Be at the airport at least two hours before your flight; when there is overbooking, late-comers' names fall victim! Airport tax is Rs450.

The bank counter in the departure lounge will change 10 per cent of your excess rupees back to a hard currency, provided you show bank receipts for what you changed into rupees.

DISABLED TRAVELLERS

For those with physical handicaps, travel in Nepal is difficult but not impossible. Most streets are in poor condition and have high curbs. Few hotels have facilities, such as special stairs, for the disabled.

There are no special toilets for the handicapped.

Disabled travellers are sometimes the subject of open stares and whispered comments. No one means to be rude; nevertheless, this is often the response (also see Trekking).

ELECTRICITY

Voltage fluctuation can be expected; power cuts and blackouts are common. Bring a small flashlight and keep it handy.

HIRE BICYCLES

Mountain bikes or regular Indian or Chinese bicycles can be rented from lodges and locations in Thamel. They cost US$1-3 per day, and they can be rented for longer trips.

CAR HIRE

Day rental cars (with driver) are available through any travel agency. Expect to pay about US$25 for half a day and US$50 for a full-day. You can expect a car that can hold three to four people and an obliging driver who speaks a little English. (Nepal Tourist Service, tel: 225508, hires cars out at reasonable rates).

Taxis can be hired for long trips, but check their condition and its driver. Have a clear agreement before you start out on any journey.

MOTORCYCLES

Motorcycles can be hired at about US$10 per day in **Thamel** and **Khichapokhari**. They are not that safe a form of transportation for those unfamiliar with Nepali traffic.

LOCAL CUSTOMS

Nepalis greet or bid farewell by putting their hands together as if praying and say *Namaste*. Remember to:-

- Remove your shoes before entering shrines, temples and monasteries.
- Walk around temples, stupas and altars in a clockwise direction.
- Ask before using your camera/video in religious sites.
- Dress with propriety, especially while visiting temples.
- Certain public displays of affection between couples are not considered good taste in Nepal.
- Always take and give with the right hand or with both hands. In Nepal, the left hand is used to clean up after toilet.
- Do not pat children on the head, the most sacred part of their body.
- Not to point your feet at anyone. If you are sitting on the floor and must stretch your feet, keep them somehow covered.
- Do not show anger or raise your voice when frustrated. It will only make the situation worse.
- Do not give money, sweets, balloons, etc, to children or adults who beg. If encouraged, they will become beggars.

LOCAL LAWS

If anything is stolen from you, report it to the police. You will be required to provide a detailed statement in writing. If the stolen property is recovered, it may not be returned for a long time. Nepali law does not recognise it as evidence once it leaves police possession.

Also, you will have to pay 10 per cent of the value ascribed to the items as per your statement, a sort of finder's fee for the police.

If your passport is lost/stolen, procure a statement from the police for your embassy which states that your passport was indeed lost/stolen.

MEDICAL ASSISTANCE

Injections against hepatitis, tetanus, and typhoid are recommended. These are available at CIWEC and Nepal International clinics.

The **CIWEC Clinic** (tel: 410983) is a Canadian clinic run by foreign doctors and nurses. It is reputable and also charges much more than Nepali clinics. The **Nepal International Clinic** (tel: 412842), run by an US – trained Nepali physician, caters to a mostly expatriate clientele and is well-regarded.

Be careful of what you eat: no raw vegetables, peel all fruit; no ice cubes, only boiled or bottled water. Cooked food should be eaten warm.

Some minor ailments are part of adjusting to the different water and air, or caused by jetlag. If the trouble persists, get a stool test before you start taking medicine.

Among the hospitals in Kathmandu, two of the better ones are **Patan Hospital** (tel: 522266, 521048) in Lagankhel, Patan, and the **Teaching Hospital** (tel: 410983) in Maharajgunj. Most of the doctors work evenings at private clinics. Consultation fees and the cost of drugs are generally low.

If you need to get to a hospital/doctor quickly, flag down a taxi. There are two ambulance services: the **Red Cross Service** (tel: 228040) and the service (tel: 211959) at **Bhimsensthan**. Ask your hotel staff for help.

For medical evacuations while trekking, contact **Himalayan Rescue Association** (tel: 222906, 418755) (see Trekking).

Some cases of AIDS have been reported in Nepal. Hygiene standards being what they are, insist on seeing syringes and needles opened before your eyes. Or bring your own 5cc and 10cc disposable syringes and needles.

NEWSPAPERS & MAGAZINES

The Rising Nepal is the semi-official English daily newspaper. Other publications in English are *The Independent* a weekly, *The Commoner* daily, the fortnightly *Spotlight*, and a few tourist magazines. Pick up the bi-monthly *Himal*, a reputable regional publication devoted to politics, development and environmental issues . *The International Herald Tribune, USA Today, Newsweek, Time, The Economist, Far Eastern Economic Review* and *Asiaweek* are available. A wide range of Indian newspapers and magazines such as *India Today, Illustrated Weekly, Sunday, The Times of India*, etc., are also available at newstands and bookshops.

Nepal is a great place to buy books; there are plenty of bookstores in Kathmandu and Pokhara. Try **Ratna Pustak Bhandar** in Bagh

Bazaar, **Educational Enterprises** across from Mahakali Temple, **Himalayan Booksellers** near the Clock Tower and in Thamel, **Saraswati Books** in Pulchowk and **Pilgrim's Bookshop** in Thamel and near Yak & Yeti. The rupee equivalent of US and UK prices are charged. For used books, try **Nightingale Books**, next to **KC's Restaurant** in Thamel. You get 50 per cent back on returning the book.

PHOTOGRAPHY

Bring as much film as you think you need and some extra. Bring spare camera batteries. All kinds of film are available in Kathmandu, including Kodachrome. Film is expensive and you should check the expiry date, (for camera batteries as well).

Several studios in Kathmandu do colour printing, black and white, and E-6 slide processing.

Use a polariser to cut reflected glare. Up in the mountains, put your camera in your sleeping bag with you at night.

POSTAL SERVICES

The **Central Post Office** is on the corner of Kantipath and Khichapokhari Road. Hours are 10am to 5pm (4pm in winter), closed Saturday. You must stand in line to buy stamps and again to have your letters stamped. Many hotels provide basic postal services.

The post office has a Poste Restante service. Ask those sending you mail to have your family name written in big letters. It is better not to have anything of value sent.

Next to the Central Post Office is the **Foreign Post Office**, where parcels can be sent or received. Procedures tend to be exasperating.

RADIO & TELEVISION

Radio Nepal broadcasts news in English at 8am and 8pm. A shortwave radio will pick up *BBC* and *VOA* mornings and evenings.

Nepal Television broadcasts in Nepali in the morning and in Nepali and English in the evenings. The English broadcast is at 9.40pm.

TAXIS

Taxis are usually *Toyotas* and *Datsuns* with black license plates. Pay according to the meter. They are available until 10pm. After that and when it rains, cabbies are reluctant to use the meter, in which case negotiate a fixed price. Tips are not expected.

TELECOMMUNICATIONS

The **Telecommunications Office** in Tripureshwor across from the National Stadium handles international calls, telexes, and cables. Book your call and wait a bit. International connections are excellent.

International calls can also be made from most Kathmandu hotels. The bigger towns (sorry, not on the trek routes!) have facilities for placing international calls.

Most hotels in Kathmandu have telefax service as well. Phone, telex, and fax services are being offered by independent "communication" centres.

TIME

Nepal is 5 hours 40 minutes ahead of Greenwich Mean Time, 15 minutes ahead of Indian Standard Time. If it is noon in Kathmandu, it is:

6.20am today in London
1.20am today in New York
10.20pm yesterday in Los Angeles
4.20pm today in Sydney
3.20pm today in Tokyo
2.20pm today in Hong Kong
1.20pm today in Bangkok

The official calendar of Nepal is the **Vikram Sambat Calendar**, which is 56 years ahead of the Gregorian Calendar; hence 1992 will be 2048 in Nepal. It is widely used, including by government offices. The Nepali New Year is in mid-April.

Baisaakh: mid-April to mid-May
Jeth: mid-May to mid-June
Asadh: mid-June to mid-July
Srawan: mid-July to mid-August
Bhadra: mid-August to mid-September
Ashwin: mid-September to mid-October
Kaartik: mid-October to mid-November
Marga: mid-November to mid-December
Poush: mid-December to mid-January
Maagh: mid-January to mid-February
Phaagun: mid-February to mid-March
Chaitra: mid-March to mid-April

The Nepali fiscal and budgetary year starts in mid-July.

TIPPING

In Kathmandu restaurants, it is customary to leave a tip of 5 – 10 per cent. You are expected to tip guides, drivers, and bell-boys, but not taxi drivers.

TOURS

There is no dearth of travel agencies in Kathmandu, located in Durbar Marg and everywhere else. They offer a number of standard half and full-day tours, overnight packages, and they can help you with ticketing, and book you on any of the different visitor activities offered in Kathmandu, such as trekking, rafting, mountain flight and so forth.

There are many options for longer tours. A trip to Pokhara via Gorkha, on to Tansen and Lumbini from there, back to Kathmandu after a few days in Chitwan via Hetauda, for example. Travel agents can tailor a package to your interest.

Consider combining a visit to Pokhara with a rafting trip and a few days of a jungle experience in Chitwan.

Several agents now arrange mountain bike tours to as far away as Lumbini.

For help, comments, complaints, contact the **Tourist Guide Association of Nepal** (TURGAN), **Yak & Yeti Plaza**, tel: 225102, or the **Nepal Association of Travel Agents** (NATA).

VISA & HEALTH

A one month visa can be obtained from any Nepali Embassy or Consulate. Present your passport, two passport-size photos, and a fee of US$10.

A 15-day visa can be obtained at the point of entry for the same fee, and it will be automatically extended for the full month at **Central Immigration Office** (tel: 412337) in Keshar Mahal, near Thamel. Applications are accepted from 10am to 4pm (3pm Friday), except on Saturday and government holidays.

India-Nepal border crossing points are **Kakarbhitta**, **Birgunj** and **Sunauli**. You can also enter at **Kodari** on the Tibet-Nepal border.

You may extend your visa to remain in Nepal for up to three consecutive months. You are required to present bank receipts showing you have exchanged an equivalent of US$10 for each day of further intended stay. The fee for extending your visa is Rs75 per week in the second month, Rs150 per week in the third month.

After 3 months, you will have to stay out of the country for 30 days, before a new visa is considered. In any given year, you may stay in Nepal for a total of 4 months.

Visas can be extended up to 15 days in Pokhara as well.

TREKKING PERMITS

You must have a trekking permit for each trek you plan to go on. This is obtained at **Central Immigration** in Kathmandu. The cost is Rs90 per week in the first month, Rs112.50 per week in the second and third months. Two passport-size photos are required. Your trekking permit substitutes for a visa. The same rules regarding currency exchange proof applies.

You may obtain a 15-day trekking permit for the Annapurna area in Pokhara.

There is no real health screening for entering Nepal.

WEIGHTS & MEASURES

Weights are measured in kg. A common measure is one *pau* for a unit weight of 200g. One *dharni* equals 2.4kg.

In the hills, a volume measure is commonly used for rice, sugar, and lentils. One *manna* equals about a half litre; 8 *mannas* is one *paati*, about 3.75litres.

The term *muthi* denotes a handful. It can refer to one load of firewood.

For precious metals, one *tola* equals 11.5g; for precious stones, one carat equals 0.2g.

For lengths, it is inches, feet or metres. The term *kos* is used for long distances. One *kos* is about 3.2km (2 miles).

GLOSSARY

Ananda	Buddha's chief disciple
Ananta	cosmic serpent upon which *Vishnu* reclines
Annarpurna	Goddess of Abundance and an incarnation of *Mahadevi*
Ashoka	Indian Buddhist emperor who spread Buddhism throughout the empire
arak	whiskey fermented from potatoes or grain
Asadh	third month of the Nepalese year (June-July)
Ashwin	sixth month of the Nepalese year (September-October)
Avalokiteshvara	*bodhisattva* of this era, also the Hindu/Buddhist God of Mercy whose incarnation is *Machhendranath* or *Manjushri*
avatar	incarnation of a deity living on earth
bahal	Buddhist monastery, usually two storeys high and built around a Buddhist monastery,many are used as schools
bahil	a smaller *bahal*
bakba	Tibetan clay mask
Balkumari	one of *Bhairav*'s consorts
Baisakh	1st month of the Nepalese New Year (April-May)
Bajra Jogini	Tantric goddess
bazaar	market area, a market town is also called a *bazaar*
bell	tantric female symbol equivalent to the male thunderbolt or *dorje*
bel tree	customary marriage of young girls to this tree so that they are never widowed
betel	mixture of areca nut and white lime wrapped in betel leaf and chewed, makes a red splash when spat out
Bhagavad Gita	one of the most important Hindu religious scriptures in which *Krishna* spells out the importance of duty to *Arjuna*. It is contained in the *Mahabharata*.
Bhadrakali	tantric goddesss who is also *Bhairav*'s consort
Bhairav	tantric form of the god *Shiva*
Bhimsen	deity noted for strength and courage
bodhisattava	an enlightened person who has forsaken heavenly *nirvana* to help mankind
bon	animist pre-Buddhist religion of Tibet
brahmins	highest Hindu caste
Buddha	first name Gautama, born of princely stock in Lumbini c.6 BC
caste	social hierachy divided into four main castes and numerous sub-castes
Chaitra	12th and last month of the Nepalese New Year
chaitya	small *stupa* which usually contains a *mantra* rather than a Buddhist scripture
chang	Tibetan rice beer
chappati	Indian unleavened bread
chhetri	Hindu warrior caste (Rana and Shah royalty) second in status to the *brahmins*
chorten	small Buddhist shrine usually located in mountain regions

chowk	palace or market courtyard
chuba	long woollen Sherpa coat
crore	10 million
Dalai Lama	reincarnated high priest of Tibetan Buddhism and the Tibetan political leader
Dattatraya	deity considered the incarnation of *Vishnu, Shiva*'s teacher or *Buddha*'s cousin
Devanagari	Sanskrit Nepali script
devi	*Shiva*'s *shakti* in many forms
dhal	lentil soup
dharma	Buddhist teachings
dharamsala	public rest-house for travellers and pilgrims
doko	basket carried by porters
dorje	the "thunderbolt" symbol of Buddhist power
durbar	palace, usually with an accompanying square
Durga	*Shiva*'s *shakti Parvati* in one of her more fearsome forms
Falgun	11th month of the Nepalese year (February-March)
Ganesh	*Shiva* and *Parvati*'s son who is recognised by his elephant head
Ganga	goddess of the River Ganges
Garuda	mythical human-eagle who is *Vishnu*'s vehicle
Gelugpa	yellow-hat sect of Tibetan Buddhist reformed under the *Dalai Lama*
ghanta	tantric bell which is the female equivalent of the *dorje*
ghat	river platform with steps used for bathing and cremation
gompa	Tibetan Buddhist monastery
Gorakhnath	a 11th century yogi who founded a Shaivaite cult and is now regarded as the reincarnation of Shiva
gurkha	Nepalese mercenaries traditionally from the hill region of *Gorkha* known for their courage
Gurungs	western hill people predominantly from *Pokhara* and *Gorkha*
guthi	*Newari* community group offering mutual support to its members and their families
Hanuman	monkey god and Ram's friend
hiti	water conduit or a tank with water spouts
Impeyan	also called the *Danphe Impeyan*, Nepal's national bird
incarnation	a life form governed by *karma* for humans, deities have several incarnations
Indra	king of the *Vedic* gods and God of Rain
Jagannath	*Krishna* worshipped as "Lord of the World"
janai	sacred thread worn by *brahmin* men looped over one shoulder and replaced once a year
jatra	festival
Jesth	2nd month of the Nepalese New Year (May-June)
jhankri	shaman or sorcerer
jogini	mystical goddess
jyapu	*Newar* farmer caste

Kali	Shiva's shakti Parvati in her most terrifying form
karma	Buddhist and Hindu law of cause and effect of one's thoughts and deeds that follow one from one reincarnation to the next
Kartik	7th month of the Nepalese year (October-November)
Khas	Hindu hill people
kinkinimall	temple wind bells
khukuri	the long curved knife used by the Gurkhus
Krishna	the 8th incarnation of Vishnu
kshatriyas	the warrior caste (the Hindu equivalent of the chhetris)
kundalini	female energy principle
kumari	a young girl worshipped as a living, peaceful incarnation of Kali
la	mountain pass
lakh	100, 000
Lakshmi	Goddess of Wealth and Vishnu's consort
laliguras	Nepalese rhododendron, the Nepalese national flower
lama	Tibetan Buddhist monk or priest
lingam	phallic symbol of Shiva's creative might
Lokeswara	Lord of the World and an aspect of Avalokiteswara
Machhendranath	patron god of the Kathmandu Valley and an incarnation of Avalokiteswara or Lokeswara
Magha	10th month of the Nepalese year (January-February)
Mahabharata	one of the major Hindu epics, the other being the Ramayana
Mahayana	school of Buddhism that predominates east Asia, Tibet and Nepal
Maitreya	Buddha that is to come
Malla	royal dynasty of the Kathmandu Valley
mandala	Tibetan Buddhist astrological and geometric diagramme that works as an aid to meditation
mandap	roofless tantric shrine
mandir	Nepali word for temple
Manjushri	god who cut open the Chobar Gorge so that the Kathmandu Lake became the Kathmandu Valley, he is now revered as the God of Learning
mani (stones)	stone carved with the Tibetan Buddhist chant "Om mani padme hum"
Mani Rimbu	Tibetan dance drama
mani wall	wall built with mani stones, walk by it clockwise
mantra	prayer formula or chant
math	Hindu priest's house
mela	country fair
moksha	Hindu version of spiritual release (likened to the Buddhist nirvana)
naga	serpent deity
namaste	Nepalese greeting
Nandi	bull that is Shiva's vehicle
Narayan	Vishnu represented as the creator of life
Narsingha	man-lion incarnation of Vishnu
Newaris	people of the Kathmandu Valley
nirvana	when the self has finally exited from all the cycles of existence
Nyingmapa	one of the three red-hat sects of Tibetan Buddhism
Om Mani Padma Hum	sacred Buddhist mantra which means "hail to the jewel in the lotus"
oriflammes	prayer flags

pagoda	multi-storeyed Nepalese temple
panchayat	government non-party system consisting of elected councils
Parvati	*Shiva's* female consort
Pashupati	*Shiva* as "Lord of the Beasts and symbolised by the *lingam*
path	a small raised platform (on important routes) which shelters travellers
pokhari	large tank
Pausch	9th month of the Nepalese New Year (December-January)
parjna	female counterparts of male Buddhist deities
porters	hill people (usually Sherpas) who carry goods on the trek trail
prasad	food offerings to the gods
prayer flags	a flag carrying a sacred mantra which is said whenever the flag flutters
prayer wheels	cylindrical wheel inscribed with a prayer which is said as it spins
puja	prayers
raksi	homemade rice or wheat liquor
Rama (Ram)	7th incarnation of *Vishnu*, hero of the *Ramayana*
Rawana	demon King of Langka and *Rama's* adversary
rimpoche	abbot of a Tibetan buddhist monastery
sadhu	Hindu holy man
Saraswati	*Brahma's* consort, worshipped in Nepal as the Hindu Goddess of Learning
shakti	*Shiva's* consort, but more literally the dynamic element in a male-female relationship
Shiva	ultimate destroyer of good as well as evil so that new creation can take shape
Sita	*Rama's* wife and the heroine of the *Ramayana*
Srawan	4th month of the Nepalese New Year (July-August)
stupa	hemisherical Buddhist structure
sundhara	fountain with a golden spout
Surjya	Sun God most closely associated with *Vishnu*
sudras	lowest Nepalese caste
Taleju Bhawani	Nepalese goddess imported from south India, an aspect of *Devi*
tantric	form of Buddhism which evolved in Tibet in the 10-5th centuries
Tara	Nepalese princess deified by Buddhists and Hindus
Terai	fertile lowland regions of Nepal
Thakalis	people of the Kali Gandaki Valley
thangka	religious scroll painting
tika	caste mark applied on the forehead as a symbol of the divine
tole	street or quarter in town
topi	traditional Nepalese hat
torana	decorative crest suspended over a door with the figure of a deity enshrined in the centre
Tribhuvan	last king of the Rana era who ended Nepal's isolation
vihara	Buddhist monastery encompassing a *bahal* and a *bahil*
Vishnu	preserver in the Hindu trinity who is also worshipped as *Narayan*
yoni	hole in a stone symbolising the female, occurs with the *lingam*

DIRECTORY

AIRLINES

Air Canada
Durbar Marg – 222838
Air France
Durbar Marg – 223339
Alitalia
Durbar Marg – 223339
Aeroflot
Kamladi – 212397
Air India
Kantipath – 212335
Air Lanka
Kamaladi – 212831
Biman Bangladesh
Durbar Marg — 222544
British Airways
Durbar Marg – 222266
Cathay Pacific
Kantipath – 226765
CAAC
Kamaladi – 411303
Druk Air
Durbar Marg – 225166
Indian Airlines
Durbar Marg – 223053
Japan Air Lines
Durbar Marg – 222838
KLM
Durbar Marg – 224896
Korean Air
Jamal – 212080
Lufthansa
Durbar Marg – 223052
Northwest Airlines
Lekhnath – 226139
PIA
Durbar Marg – 223102
Pan Am
Durbar Marg – 228824

Philippine Airlines
Kantipath – 215814
Royal Nepal Airlines
New Road – 220757
Saudi Airlines
Kantipath – 222787
Singapore Airlines
Durbar Marg – 220759
Swiss Air
Durbar Marg – 222452
Thai International
Durbar Marg – 220759
Trans World Airlines
Kamaladi – 411725

BANKS

Nepal Bank Limited
New Road – 224337
Rastriya Banijya Bank
Supermarket New Road – 222437
Nepal-Arab Bank
Kantipath & Durbar Marg – 227181
Nepal Indo-Suez Bank
Durbar Marg – 228229
Grindley's Bank
Kantipath – 228474/5
Standard Chartered Bank
Durbar Marg – 220129
American Express Jamal Tole - Durbar Marg. Card holders can while traveler's checks and receive mail (after 2 pm).

CINEMA

There are no English language cinemas. For a Hindi or the occasional Nepali film try:

Biswojyoti Cinema across from Rani Pokhari
Jai Nepal Cinema near Narayan Mandir
Kumari Cinema near Kamalpokhari

The **French Cultural Centre** in Bagh Bazaar (224326) shows a French film with English subtitles every night.

COURIER SERVICE

The **DHL** agent is located in Kamladi behind the Clock Tower (220215)
Nepal Air Courier Express (225854) on Putalisadak is the agent for United Parcel Service (UPS)

DEPARTMENT STORES

The **Bluebird** in Tripureshwor is the closest thing to a department store/supermarket; Bluebird has a branch in Lazimpat and there are several smaller such stores in the city.

FOREIGN MISSIONS

Austrian
Hattisar – 410891
Australia
Bhat Bhateni – 411578/417566
Bangladesh
Naxal – 414943/414265
Belgium
Lazimpat – 414760
China

Baluwatar – 411740
Denmark
Kantipath – 227044
Eygpt
Pulchowk – 524812/524844
France
Lazimpat – 412332
Germany
Kantipath – 221763/222902
India
Lainchaur – 410900/414913
Israel
Lazimpat – 411811/413419
Italy
Baluwatar – 412280/412743
Japan
Panipokhari – 414083/410397
Korea (North)
Jhamsikhel – 521855/521084
Korea (South)
Tahachal – 270172/270584
Myanmar (Burma)
Patan Dhoka – 524788
Netherlands
Kumarpati – 522915/524597
Pakistan
Panipokhari – 410565/411421
Sweden
Khichapokhari – 220939
Swiss
Jawalakhel – 523468
Sri Lanka
Kamalpokhari–414192/416432
Thailand
Thapathali – 213910/213912
United Kingdom
Lainchaur – 411590/414588
United States
Panipokhari – 411179/412718
USSR
Baluwatar – 412155/411063

ACCOMMODATION

In Kathmandu you can stay in 5-star luxury hotels, with swimming pool and tennis, or spend about US$.50 for a dormitory bed, or the wide range in between. Pokhara and the Chitwan area also offer a wide range of accommodation. Beyond these, accommodations are more basic. Hotels in the Terai may have mosquito nets and ceiling fans,

in the middle hills a wooden bed with a foam mattress is all you should expect (see Trekking, p.191). Toilets may be western or subcontinental style. Sometimes, airconditioning is available in the larger towns.

In the off season, huge discounts are offered by most hotels in Kathmandu and Pokhara. The tourist season extends from mid-September to end of May. First-class Hotels (double US$90-110):

Hotel de'l Annapurna
Durbar Marg, central location
Tel: 221711
Tlx: 2205
Fax: 977-1-225236

Everest Hotel
Baneswar
Tel: 220567
Tlx: 2260
Fax: 977-1-226088

Hotel Soaltee Oberoi
Tahachal
Tel: 272550
Tlx: 2203
Fax: 977-1-272205

Hotel Yak & Yeti
Durbar Marg, central location
Tel: 228255, 413999
Tlx: 2237
Fax: 977-1-227782

Four-star (double US$55-90):

Hotel Himalaya
Patan, best mountain views, pool, tennis
Tel:523900
Tlx:2566 HOHIL NP

Hotel Kathmandu
Maharajgunj
Tel: 413082
Tlx:2256 NP
Fax: 977-1-416574
Hotel Malla
Lekhnath Marg

Tel:410320
Tlx: 2238 NP
Fax:977-1-418382

Hotel Shangrila
Lazimpat, pool, charming garden
Tel: 410051
Tlx: 2276 NP
Fax: 977-1-414184

Hotel Shanker
Lazimpat, old Rana palace, beautiful lawn
Tel: 410151
Tlx: 2230 NP

Dwarika's Hotel
Battisputali, beautiful setting
Tel: 414770
Tlx: NP 2239 KTT (DWARIKA)
Fax: 977-1-225131

Hotel Sherpa
Durbar Marg, central location
Tel: 228021
Tlx: 2223 NP Nepcom
Fax: 977-1-222026

Hotel Woodlands
Durbar Marg, pool, central location
Tel: 222683
Tlx: 2282 HOTOOD NP

Three-star (double US$50-60):

Hotel Blue Star
Tripureshwar
Tel: 211470
Fax: 977-1-226820

Hotel Narayani
Pulchowk, pool
Tel: 521711
Telex: 2262 NARANI MP
Fax: 977-1-521291

Hotel Crystal
New Road, near Hanuman Dhoka
Tel: 220337
Tlx: 2268 Pagoda NP

Hotel Yellow Pagoda
Kanti Path, good location
Tel: 220337
Tlx: 2268 PAGODA NP

Summit Hotel
Kupondole Heightspool
Tel: 521894
Tlx: 2342
Fax: 977-1-523737

Two-star (double US$20-300):

Hotel Ambassador
Lazimpat
Tel: 410432
Tlx: 2321

Hotel Vajra
Swayambhu
Tel: 272719
Tlx: 2309
Fax: 977-1-271695

Budget Hotels:

Kathmandu Guest House
Thamel, a long time favorite
Tel:214167
Tlx: BASS 2321 NP

Hotel Garuda
Thamel
Tel: 416776
Fax: 977-1-223814

Hotel Gautam
Kantipath
Tel: 215016

Garden Guest House
Jyatha Thamel
Tel:213366

Potala Guest House
Chhetrapati
Tel: 220467
Fax: 977-1-223256

Hotel Tridevi
Thamel
Tel: 412822

VALLEY AREA
Hotel Flora Hill
Nagarkot
Tel: 226893
Double about US$40

Golden Gate Guest House
Durbar Square, Bhaktapur
Tel: 610534

Shiva's Guest House
Durbar Square, Bhaktapur
Tel: 610740

Hatiban Pine Ridge Resort
Hatiban
Tel: 415652
Double US$90 (include meals)

Dhulikhel
Hotel Sun-n-Snow
Tel:225092

Dhulikhel Mountain Resort
Tel: 226779
Tlx: 2415
Double US$44

Dhulikhel Lodge, Dhulikhel bazaar, an old budget favorite.

Pokhara
Top End (double US$30 and up):

Fish Tail Lodge Lakeside
Tel: 20984

Hotel Mt Annapurna
Tel: 20027

Hotel Dragon
Tel: 20391

Hotel New Crystal
Tel: 20035

Kantipur Resort Lakeside
Tel: 227043

Tiger Mountain Lodge Pokhara
(to open in 1992)
Tragopan
Tel: 20910

Budget Hotels
Hotel Fewa, Devistan
Tel: 20151

Hotel The Hungry Eye, lakeside
Tel: 20908

Hotel Kantipur, lakeside
tel: 20886

Alka Guest House, lakeside
Tel: 20887

Hotel Garden, damside
Tel: 20870

Tansen
Hotel Shree Naga,
Tel:-20045

GOVERNMENT & BUSINESS
Ministry of Foreign Affairs
Sital Niwas – 416023
Finance
Hari Bhawan – 215099
General Administration
Harihar Bhawan – 521572
Forest & Soil Conserv.
Babar Mahal – 220067
Agriculture
Singha Durbar – 223440
Home
Singha Durbar – 228024
Panchayat & Local Dvlp.
Shree Mahal – 521873
Health
Ram Shah Path – 215302
Communications
Panchayat Plaza – 212441
Industry
Tripureshwar – 215027
Commerce
Babar Mahal – 223489
Labor
Singha Durbar – 226899
Tourism
Tripureshwar – 211286
Law & Justice
Babar Mahal – 224633
Works & Transport
Babar Mahal – 221319
Housing & Phy Planning

Babar Mahal – 225978
Water Resources
Babar Mahal – 228933
Education & Culture
Kaiser Mahal – 411599
Defense
Singha Durbar – 226282
Prime Minister
Singha Durbar – 228555

INTERNATIONAL ORGANISATIONS
UNDP
Pulchowk – 523220
FAO
Pulchowk – 523239
UNICEF
Pulchowk – 523200
WHO
Pulchowk – 523200
ICIMOD
Jawalakhel – 522839
CARE Nepal
Pulchowk – 522143
Save the Children Fund
USA
Maharagunj – 412120
United Missions of Nepal
Thapathali – 212179
USAID
Rabi Bhawan – 270144
French Cultural Centre
Bagh Bazaar – 224326
British Council
Kantipath – 221305
Goethe Institute
Sundhara – 220528
US Information Service
New Road – 223893
World Bank
Kantipath – 226792

TRAVEL AGENTS
Adventure Travel Nepal
Lazimpat – 415995
Annapurna Travel & Tours
Durbar Marg – 223940
Everest Travel Service
Gangapath – 221216
Gorkha Travels
Durbar Marg – 214895
Himalayan Travels & Tours
Durbar Marg – 226011
Kathmandu Tours & Travel

Gangapath – 222985
Nepal Travel Agency
Ram Shah Path – 413188
Natraj Tours & Travel
Durbar Marg – 212014
Tiger Tops
Durbar Marg – 222706
Trans Himalayan Tours
Durbar Marg – 213854
Universal Travel & Tours
KantipatH – 214192
Yangrima Tours & Travel
Kantipath – 215814
Yeti Travels
Durbar Marg – 221234

TREKKING AGENTS
Above the Clouds Trekking
Thamel – 416923
Annapurna Mountaineering & Trekking
Durbar Marg – 222999
Everest Express Trekking
Durbar Marg – 223233
Gorkha Adventure Trek
Durbar Marg – 221532
Himalayan Adventures
Lazimpat – 414344
Himalayan Journeys
Kantipath – 226139
Lama Excursions
Durbar Marg – 220185
Makalu Trekking
Thamel – 226499
Mountain Travel Nepal
Durbar Marg – 414508
Nepal Treks & Natural History Explorers
Gangapath – 224536
Rover Treks & Expeditions
Naxal – 412667
Sherpa Co-operative Trekking
Durbar Marg – 224068
Trans-Himalayan Trekking
Durbar Marg – 224854
Wilderness Experience
Kantipath – 220534
Yangrima Trekking
Kantipath – 227627

MOUNTAIN BIKE TRIPS OPERATORS
Himalayan Mountain Bikes
Thamel – 413632

Makalu Trekking Jyatha
Thamel – 226499
Discover Nepal Trekking
Durbar Marg – 224142
Marco Polo Travels
Kamalpokhari – 413632

RIVER RAFTING OPERATORS
Great Himalayan Rivers
Kantipath – 216913
Himalayan Encounters
Thamel – 413632
Himalayan River Adventure
Lazimpat – 410219
Himalayan River Exploration
Durbar Marg – 418491
Himalayan White Waters
Thamel – 225371
Journeys Whitewater Rafting
Kantipath – 225969
White Magic Nepal
Thamel – 226855
Wild Waters
Naxal – 410561

SPORTS
Golf – **Nepal Royal Golf Club**
(212836) near the airport
and **Gokarna Safari Park**. Both
are 9-hole courses.
Tennis – For a fee visitors can
play at these hotels: **Everest** (clay)
Yak & Yeti (hardcourt) **Soaltee
Oberoi** (hardcourt) **Annapurna**
(hardcourt) **Himalaya** (clay) and
Oasis (clay); there are courts at
the national stadium too.
Swimming – There are pools at
the following hotels: **Annapurna,
Soaltee, Yak & Yeti, Everest,
Himalaya, Shangrila, Woodlands, Summit** and **Narayani**;
there is a pool at the **National
Stadium** and one at **Balaju Gardens**.
Squash – At **Hotel Oasis, Woodlands** and at **Battisputali**.
Sports Fishing – **Asla** a type of
snow trout and *mahseer* which
weigh up to 30 kg. Late fall and
early spring are best times to fish
in Terai streams. Contact **Tiger
Tops** about fishing in **Royal

Bardiya Reserve in the far west. Obtain a permit from the National Parks Department in Baneswar.

TOURIST INFORMATION

There is an office at Tribhuvan Airport and on Ganga Path near Basantapur; in Pokhara and in Jomosom near the airstrip.

The **Department of Tourism** behind the National Stadium often offers free posters for visitors.

CAR HIRE

Nepal Tourist Service (tel: 225508) in the alley behind Durbar Marg offers reasonable rates. **Avis** is represented by Yeti Travels (tel: 221234) on Durbar Marg and **Hertz** by Gorkha Travels (tel: 214895) on Durbar Marg. Or ask any reputable travel agency.

HOSPITALS

Bir Hospital
Kantipath – 221988
Emergency – 221119
Red Cross Ambulance – 228094
Kanti Children's Hospital
Maharajgunj – 411440
Maternity Hospital
Thapathali – 211243
Nepal Eye Hospital
Tripureshwor – 215466
Patan Hospital
Lagankhel – 522266
Emergency – 522286
Teaching Hospital
Maharajgunj – 412505

PRIVATE CLINICS

CIWEC
near Russian Embassy – 410983
Nepal International Clinic
near Durbar Marg – 412842

DENTAL CLINICS

Phora Durbar (Dr Elliot Higgins) – 221517

Dr K K Pradhan – 221142

LIBRARIES

British Council (221305)
Kantipath
Kaiser Mahal
Indian Sanskrit Library
RNAC Building Kanti Path

CONVENTIONS

All the 5-star hotels have large rooms capable of seating several hundred people. Besides them **Hotel Blue Star** is a popular. A convention centre is under construction in **Baneswar** near the Everest Hotel.

NIGHTSPOTS

Pumpkins at the **Everest Hotel** admission to couples only.

The *Damaru* at the **Hotel Woodlands**, charges Rs350 (for non-guests per couple)

Casinos Hotel: **Soaltee Oberoi**. One of the few in this part of the world. Your ticket-jacket and passport will entitle you to some free-play coupons. You will be able to see rich Indians throw their money away; Nepalis are not allowed in.

Several Indian restaurants feature live *ghazal* singers or instrumental music with the meal. The best are at:
Far Pavilions at Everest Hotel
Ghar e Khabab on **Durbar Marg**
Moti Mahal on **Durbar Marg**

TRADITIONAL MUSIC AND DANCE

The **New Himalchuli Culture Group** (tel: 410151) near Hotel Shanker every night from 7pm for Rs80 per person.

The **Everest Cultural Society** (tel: 220676) near Hotel Annapurna every evening from 7pm.

PHARMACIES

Almost any medicine can be

bought over-the-counter. Good pharmacies near New Road gate or visit *Saajaa* open 24 hours near **Bir Hospital**.

MUSEUMS

Museums are open from 10.30am to 4pm closed Tuesdays.

The **National Museum** near Swayambhu – an interestingly eclectic collection.

The **Tribhuvan Museum**, Hanuman Dhoka – the entry-fee lets you climb **Basantapur Tower**

The **National Art Museum** Bhaktapur, Dubar Square – well worth the trip.

The **National Woodworking Museum**, Bhaktapur, Dattratraya Square – beautiful building and exhibits.

The **National Brass and Bronze Museum**, Bhaktapur, Dattratraya Square – extremely interesting.

WORSHIP

Roman Catholic: **St. Xavier's School**, Jawalakhel, Patan, Annapurna Hotel Durbar Marg.
Protestant: USIS (213996) **Rabi Bhawan**.
Jewish: **Israeli Embassy** (411811) Lazimpat.
Islam: **Main Mosque**, Durbar Marg.

POLICE

Police headquarters (tel:211162)
Hanuman Dokha
in Patan tel:521005
in Bhaktapur tel: 610284
Police Emergency tel: 226999

POST OFFICE

Central Post Office (tel: 211073) is on the corner of Kantipath and Khichapokhari Road. Hours are 10am to 5pm.

PUBLIC HOLIDAYS

There are many holidays in accordance with the Nepali Vikram

Sambat calendar. The corresponding date on the Gregorian Calendar changes each year.

December-January
Poush
King's Birthday
(January-February)
Maagh
Basanta Panchami

February-March
Phaagun
Rastriya Prajatantra Divas
Holi

March-April
Chaitra
Ghorejatra

April-May
Baisakh
Raato Machhendranath
Buddha Jayanti

June-July
Asaad
Tribhuvan Jayanti

July-August
Srawan
Naga Panchami
Janai Purnima

August-September
Bhadra
Krishnaastami
Gaijatra
Indrajatra
Teej (women only)
Father's Day
Dasain

September-October
Asoj (Dasain often falls here)

October-November
Kaartik
Tihar

November-December
Margha
Queen's Birthday
Tihar may fall here

PHOTO CREDITS

Chris Beall : cover, backcover (top left), endpaper (front), endpaper (back), viii (bottom), ix (top), ix (bottom), 24, 34/35, 36, 40, 61 (top), 72, 173, 199, 205, 207, 208/209, 214, 223, 224, 226, 231, 243, 264

Jon Burbank : vii (bottom), x (top), (middle), x (bottom), xi (top), xi (bottom), xiii, 9, 19, 20/21, 27, 32, 42/43, 50, 56, 58, 65, 66, 70, 78, 80, 81, 84/85, 86, 87, 90/91, 91, 92/93, 94, 96/97, 100, 105, 106, 108,109, 110/111, 112, 114/115, 118/119, 119, 120, 123, 129, 130,142, 143, 144, 146, 147, 149, 150/151, 152, 156, 157, 158, 159, 161, 162, 163, 165, 166, 170, 171, 172, 174, 175, 176, 177, 178, 180/181, 182, 183, 184, 186, 187, 188/189, 198, 201, 203, 204, 210, 212, 216/217, 218, 220/221, 222, 225, 227, 230, 232, 234, 235, 236, 241, 251, 254/255, 258, 260, 261, 262, 265, 266, 267, 268, 272, 273

Kiran Chitrakar : 14/15, 17

Susan Harmer : viii (top), 8, 116, 158

Wendy Brewer Lama : 6, 59, 60 (top), 185, 202/203, 211, 219, 228/229

Gilles Massot : 13, 69 (top), 77, 145, 148, 160, 164

John May : 22, 28, 29, 30, 122

Ashvin Mehta: backcover (top right), viii (middle), 25, 36/37, 136, 215, 245, 257, 292

Francesco Milanesio : 132/133

Fiona Nichols : backcover (bottom), vii (top), xiv, 10/11, 26, 38, 125, 194, 246, 256, 274/275

R. Mohd Noh : vi (top), vi (bottom), 4, 71, 88, 116, 121, 250, 272

Steve Powers : 2/3, 39, 46, 47, 48, 51, 54/55, 63, 68, 128, 195, 248, 249

Maura Rinaldi : 49

Morten Strange : 53 (top left), 53 (top right), 53 (middle), 53 (bottom)

Michelle Tan : 69 (bottom)

Trans Globe : 169, 263

The Image Bank/P & G Bowater : 284

The Image Bank/Gerald Champlong : 282

The Image Bank/Martin & Newman : 196/197

The Image Bank/Paul Slaughter : 124, 285, 286

The Image Bank/Steve Satushek : 135

The Image Bank/Harald Sund : 288/289, 290, 291

The Image Bank/Nevada Wier : 44, 190, 206

The Image Bank/Frank Wing : 137

Eric Yeo : xii (top), xii (bottom), 60 (bottom), 61 (bottom), 64, 74/75, 83, 95, 113, 127, 131, 138, 270/271, 276, 278, 279, 280/281

Pradeep Yonzon : 252/253

INDEX

A

Adinath Lokeswar, 123
adolescence, 72
adventure holiday, 247
Agra, *283*, 284
agriculture, 23, 24, 49
air connections, 293
airlines, 293
Akash Bhairav, 107
alluvial plains, 180
altitude sickness, 242, 243
Ama Dablam, 225, 227
Amnesty International, 18
Amshuvarma, 9
Ananda, 298
Ananta, 127, 298
Anapurnas, 218
Ancient One, 72
angtang, 121
animal, 36, 165
Annapurna Base Camp, 220, *241*
Annapurna Circuit, 43, 253
Annapurna Conservation Area Project (ACAP), 55, 174, 217, 218, 233, 239
Annapurna I, 213
Annapurna II, 203
Annapurna massif, 36
Annapurna Sanctuary, 214, 216, 217
Annapurna South, 216, 217, *219*, *251*
Annapurna, 41, 49, *63*, 121, 170, 174, 199, 203, 204, *210*, 211, 213, *218*, 220, 221, 230, 233, 242, 253, 297, 298
annual rainfall, 169
apple orchard, *123*

arak, 298
architecture, 126
area, 5
arhat-hood, 76
Ari Deva, 11
Arniko, 89
arrivals, 293
art theft, 137
Arun, 37, 42, *199*, 231, 232
Aryan, 34, 65
Asadh, 85, 296, 298
Asan Tole, *83*, 87, 104, 105
Asan, 237, 269
asana, 95
Ashok Binayak, 67, 104
Ashok Road, 283
Ashok Yati Niwas, 283
Ashok, 115
Ashoka Cinema Hall, 141
Ashoka, 8, 134, 137, 139, 151, 188, 298
Ashokan Pillar, 188
Ashwin, 86, 296, 298
Asia, 42, 43, 104, 113
Asian Development Bank, 31
atman, 70
Avalokiteshvara, 76, 77, 105, 149, 207, 298
avatar, 69, 111, 298
ayurvedic, 153

B

baaisi rajas, 12
Babar Mahal, 274
Bagar, 219
Bagarchhap 203
Bagavati Temples, 165
Bagdogra, 287
Bageshwari Mandir, 189

Bagh Bazaar, 153
Bagh Bhairav, 126
bagh chal, 126, 271, 295
Baglung, 214
Bagmati, 86, 87123, 135, 136, 137, 139
bahal, 109, 139, 141, 148, 298
bahil, 298
Bahundanda, 202, 203
Bahunepati, 231
Baidam, 169
Baikuntha, 128
Baisaakh, 85, 296, 298
Bajra Jogini, 124, 298
Bajracharyas, 151
bakba, 298
Bala Chaturadasi, 86
Balaju Gardens, 128
Balaju Jatra, 85
Balaju, 85, 127
Balkumari Jatra, 85
Balkumari, 85, 298
Balmiki, 84
bamboo, 219
Bandegaun, 121
Bandipur, 177
Banepa, 165
Bangkok, 290
bangles, *269*
Barahchhetra, 42
Bardia Wildlife Reserve, 48, 52
Barh-Mangrant, 64
barley, 64
Barun Glacier, 234
Barun La, 234
Barun Valley, 234
Barun-Makalu, 49
Basant Panchami, 87, 135
Basantapur Square, 108

Basantapur Tower, 90, 108, 112
Basantapur, 107, 108, 235
Basantpur-Gupha Pokhari, 236
Batsala Durga Temple, 161
Baudha, 176
Bazaar, 186, 296, 298
beers, 261
Begnas Tal, 175
Begnas, 174
bel tree, 65, 298
bell, 65, 298
Beni (Baglung), 177, 214
Besisahar, 201
best trekking, 191
betel, 298
beyond Nepal, 283
Bhagavad Gita, 71, 298
Bhadra, 85, 296
Bhadrakali, 83, 163, 298
Bhagbati, 134
Bhai Dega, 146
Bhai Tika, 80
Bhairahawa, 187, 283, 285
Bhairav, 69, 81, 83, *110*, 126, 135, 162, 298
bhajan, 105
Bhaktapur Crafts Centre, 269
Bhaktapur Development Project, 94, 157, 165
Bhaktapur Tower, 112,
Bhaktapur, 9, 12, *65*, 82, 91, 94, 118, 141, 163-165, 186, 269, 271, 277, 278
Bharku, 230
Bhattarai, 21
Bheri, 248
bheti, 67
bhikkhus, 75
bhikkunis, 75
Bhimsen Temple, 147, 163, 174
Bhimsen Thapa, 41, 107
Bhimsen Tower, 107, 182
Bhimsen, 298
Bhimsensthan, 295
bholi, 293
Bhote Odar, 201
Bhotiya, 26, 59, 60, 64
bhoto, 82, 151
Bhrikuti, 9
Bhulbhule, 202
Bhutan Tourism Corporation, 291
Bhutan, 290-291
Bhutanese, 133

Bhuteswara, 135
bicycle, 251-253, 294
Bidghgaya, 287
Bldya Temple, 144
bija mantra, 77
biking, *252*
Binayak, 115
Bindhyavasini Temple, *175*
bindu, 133
Bindyabasini Temple, 174, 175
Biratnagar, 16, *179*, 182, 235
bird life, 1, 46, 52-53, *128*, 234, 244
bird watching, 120, 189, 200, 251
birding sites, 52
Birds of Nepal, 53
birds of prey, 52
Birendra Bir Bikram Shah, *20*
Birethante, 216
Birgunj, 16, 297
Birpalendra Malla, 136
Biruhnj, 184
Bisauni Hotel, 177
Bishnumathi River, 104
Bishwakaram Temple, 148
Bishwanath, 147
Bisket, 85, 163
Biskhet festival, 82
Bisnumati, 115
Bivaha-Panchami, 183
black stone Buddha, 68
Blue Sheep, 50
Blue Star Hotel, 274
bhotiyas, 59
Bodinath, *68*
Bodhgaya, 74, 148
Bodhi Tree, 74
Bodhisattva Manjushri, 7
bodhisattava, 76, 298
Bombay, *284*
bon, 64, 244, 298
Bonpo, 210, 211
books, 295
Boudha, 269, 271, 278
Boudhnath Stupa, 137
Boudhnath, 85, 87, 97, *130*, 131, 134, 135
Braga, 204
Brahma, 68, 69, 135, 165, 207
brahman, 58, 59, 70, 71, 72, 79, 142
Brahmins, 163, 231, 298
Braksha Bandhan, 85

bratbandh, 72
British East India Company, 13, 31
British Pension Camp, 174
British resident, 13, 104
British, 13, 16, 41, 107, 126, 189
broadleaf forests, 48
buck-wheat, 36, 61, 64
Buddanilkantha, 89
Buddha Amitabha, 133
Buddha images, 126
Buddha's birthday, 85
Buddha's Life, 74
Buddha, 8, 85, 133, 134, 135, 137, 148, 180, 188, 298
Buddhism, 2, 5, 9, 12, 73, 77, 124
Buddhist Boudha, 278
Buddhist centre, 134, 139
Buddhist Chilanchu Vihar, 126
Buddhist deity, 149
Buddhist gods, 132
Buddhist images, 148
Buddhist monasteries, 12
Buddhist monuments, 204
Buddhist nativity, 188
Buddhist sects, 132
Buddhist temple, 173
Buddhist, 59, 60, *61*, 65, 68, 76, 79, 82, 94, 94, 95, 119, 121, 132, 141, 149, 151, 165, 207
Buddhistic, 179
Budhanilkantha, 127
bulla, 264
Bumthang Valley, 291
Bungamati, 121, 123, 149, 82
Bupatindra Malla, 159
Bupatindra, 159, 161
Buri Gandaki, 133
Burland Bhanjyang, 231
buses, 293
business hours, 293
Butwal, 177, 187

C

Calcutta, 182
calendar, 296
Camp I, 234
camp-site, *211*
capital, 5, 24
captain, 218
Capuchin monks, 13
car hire, 294

carpets, 27-29, 174, 277
cash crop, *24*
caste, 58, 61, 65, 72, 73, 91, 202, 298
caste-less, 62
cavalrymen, 62
Cave of Gorakhnath, 176
census, 68
Central Immigration, 270, 297
central Nepal, *40*, 64
Central Post Office, 107, 182, 296, 296
central terai, 187
central-west nepal, 244
chaang, 261, 264
Chabahil Bahal, 137
Chabil, 9
Chainpur Brass Store, 269
Chainpur, 234, 235
Chaitra Dasain, 176
Chaitra, 87, 296, 298
chaityas, 105, 121, 134, 136, 298
chaku, 133, 264
Chame, 203, *234*
Champadevi, 126
Chandeshwari, 165
Chandrakot, 176, 216
chang, 298
Changu Narayan, 9, 23, 69, 89, 118, 146, *164*, 278
Channa, 74
chapaatis, 260, 298
charka, 127
Charumati, 8, 137
Chaturadasi, 128
Chatwin, Bruce, 51
Chaubas, 127
chaubisi raja, 12
Chauki, 235
Chayarsa Village, *173*
chemical fertilisers, 24
Chenrezi, 76
Chhaubisi raja, 201
chhetri, 58, 59, 72, 142, 231, 298
Chhomrong, 217, 218, 220
Chhuking, 227
Chialsa, 27
child labour, *30*, 31
child marriages, 58
China, 43, 76
Chinese, 130, 211
Chisopani, 42

chitrakar, 91
Chittogarh, 12
Chitwan National Park, *46*, 52, 248, 280
Chitwan, 49, 52, 64, 185, 297, 297
chiura, 264
Cho La, 225
Cho Oyu, 41, 225, 257
Chobar, 7, 123, *123*, 126
choktse, 271
Chor, *186*, 189
chortens, 204
chowk, 299
Christian, 68
chubas, 133, 204, 299
Chyasal, 147
civil service, 59
CIWEC Clinic, 239, 295
Clarks Shiraz, 284
climate, 293
climatic range, 1
Clock Tower, 104
clothing, 294
coalition cabinet, 21
colonialism, 3
colour, 296
commingling, 68
Communist Party of Nepal, 21
communists, 26
conch, 127
Connaught Place, 283
conservation, 48, 55, 217, 233, 236
constitution, 16, 21
Contemporary Art Gallery, 274
corn, *24*, 24, 61, *259*
cottage industries, 27, *29*, 126
craftsmen, 91
cremate, 60
crocodiles, 46
crops, 36
crore, 299
cross-cousin marriages, 61
cuisine, 171
cuisine, Chinese, 265
cuisine, Indian, 263
cuisine, Italian, 263, 265
cuisine, Japanese, 265
cuisine, Nepali, 265, 266
cuisine, others, 266-267
Cultural Centre, 227
culture, 57, 64, 117, 142, 191, 277, 280, 283

currency, 5, 294
cusine, local, 264
customs regulation, 294
customs, 173, 294

D

daal, 259, 299
daal-bhaat, 37, 169
daal-bhaat-tarkaari, 259
Dakshin, 124
Dakshinkali, 95, 123, 124
Dalai Lama, 76, *86*, 133, 299
damais, 73
Dana, 213, 213
Danphe Pheasant, 50, 53, 227
Darheeling, 62, 235, 287
dark ages, 10
Dasain, 79, 85, 113, 264
Dasain pujas, 264
Dasin, 199
Dattatraya, 91, 156, 163, 165, 269, 299
daura-surwal, 135
death, 60
deciduous forests, 38
deforestation, 38, 48, 49
Degu Talle, 144, 146
Delhi, 19, **290**
Democracy Day, 87
Deoghat, 42
Deopatan, 8, 9, 137
Department of Archaeology, 272, 294
departure, 294
Deurali, 219
Devadatta, 165
Devanagari, 299
Devapala, 8
Devghat, *187*
Devi Fall, 170
Devi, 170, 299
Devin Fall, 170
dhami, 83
Dhammapada, 75
Dhampus Pass, 212
Dhampus, 216
dharamsala, 161, 189, 299
Dharan, 52, 182, 235
Dharapani, 203, 204
Dharma, 72, 75, 299
dharni, 297
Dhaulagiri, 41, 121, 211, 212, 213, 214
dhido, 63

dhigur, 213
Dhobi Khola, 128, 129
Dhorpatan, 27, 49, 177
Dhukuti Handicraft Stores, 274
Dhulikhel, 165, 165, 253, 278, 280
Dhum Varachi, 89, 128, 129
Dhunche, 229, 230
dhyani, 134
dialects, 57
diet, 58
Dilli Ram Baba, 187
Dingboche, 227
Directory, 251
disabled travellers, 294
divorce, 59, 65
Dohhan, 219
dokos, 63, 299
Dolakha, *216*
Dolalghat, 248
Dole, 225
Dolpa, 133
Dolpo, 211, 244
domestic market, 29
doon, 39
Dor Bahadur Bista, 65
dorje, 134
Dragon Kingdom, 291
drugs, 294
Druk Air, 291
Dudh Kosi River, 224
Dudh Kosi Valley, 225
Dudh Kosi, 225
Dughla, 225, 228
dukkha, 73
Dumre to Muktinath, 201
Dumre, 177
Dunai, 236, 244, 244
Durbar Square, 86, 115, *142*, *156*
Durbar Marg, *77*, 85, 97, 139, 142, 143, 147, 148, 149, 151, 157, 161, 269, 271, 271, 274, 275, 277, 278, 294
durbar, 91, 110, 156, 176, 260, 263, 269, 299
Durga, 69, 77, 79, 80, 109, 299
dzong, 210

E
earth, 223
East Asia, 90
east Nepal, 19, 231
East-West Highway, 180

Eastern Himalayas, 257
eating, 173, 259-267
economic development, 37
economy, 5, 23 31, 157
education, 55, *114*, 115
Educational Enterprises, 296
eightfold path, 75
election, 18
electricity, 294
elephants, 46
Emperor of China, 90
endangered species, 46
Enlightened One, 75
environment, 48, 236
era, 89
erosion, 48
erotic art, 95
erotic carvings, *165*
ethnic groups, 57, 61, 68
evacuation, 295
Everest Base Camp, 221, 224, 225, 228, 290
Everest Cultural Society, 278
Everest, 41, 51, 228, 233, 234, 242, 257, 293
evergreens, 48
exports, 29
extinction, 48

F
family, 173
Falgun, 299
FAO, 31
farmers, 25, 54, 223
Father's Day, 86, 173
fertilisers, 24
Festival Calendar, 85
Festival of Khumbeshwar, *87*
Festival, 147
fields, 131
fishing, 189, *254*
Fishtail, *257*
Five Buddhas, 134
flags, 60
flora and fauna, 45-55
folk beliefs, 82
food production, 24
football, 151
foreign aid, 18, 31
foreign exchange, 26
Foreign Post Office, 275, 296
Foreign support, 16
forest reserves, 46
Four Noble Truths, 73

Freak Street, 107, 108
Fuhrer, RA, 188

G
Gai Jatra, 85, 162
gainis, 97
gajur, 94
galleries, 283
Ganesh Himal, 121
Ganesh Jatra, 86
Ganesh, *67*, 69, 81, 104, 126, 162, 230, 299
Ganga, 60, 94, 299
Gangapurna, 204
Ganges, 39, 135
Gangtok, 287
Gorkhalis, 175
Garuda, 69, 110, 113, 119, 147, 165, 278, 299
gateway, 284
Gauri Shankar, 121, *216*
Gautama Buddha, 141, 187
Gaya, 287
Gelugpa, 68, 76, 299
general election, 16
geography, 33-43, 45
Ghandruk, 62, *202*, 216, 216, 217, 218, 219, 220
ghanta, 76, 299
Ghaora Jatra, 87
Gharyal, 48
Ghasa, 213, 214
ghats, 79, 136, 163, 299
ghazal, 263
Ghora Tabela, 229
Ghorepani, 214, *251*
Giant Asian One-Horned Rhi noceros, 46
Godavari Kunda, 121
Godavari Marble, 120
Godavari Springs, 120
Godavari, 53, *119*, 120, 121, 149
goddesses, 69, 183
gods, 69
Gokyo Ri, 225
Gokyo Valley, 224
Gokyo, 51, 224, 225
Golden Gate, *149*, 157, 278
Golden Temple, 94, *139*
goldsmiths, 131
Gompa of Braga, *212*
Gompa, 127, 132, 135, 174, 204, 207, 212, 222, 223, 229,

285, 299
Gondwanaland, 41
Gorak Shep, 228
Gorakhapur, 283
Gorakhnath, 77, 124, 137, 299
Gorakhpur, 187, 285
Gorkarna Aunsi, 86
Gorkha Bazaar, *171*
Gorkha, 12, 12, 13, 80, 91, 157, 176, *177*, 177, 186, 201, 297
Gorkhalis, 126, 175
Gosainkund Lakes, 142, 230
Gosainkund, 230
goths, 231
Government Agricultural Farm, 211
government, 55, 220
Grakhnath, 299
green revolution, 24
green trekking, 233
greetings, 173
Grindley's Bank, 294
gubaju, 83
guerilla resistance, 211
Guhjeswari Temple, 95, 137
Gul Bhanjyang, 231
Gulmarg, 284
Gunakamadeva, 10, 11
Gunivihar Temple, 134
Gupha Pokhari, *228*, 235, 236
gupha, 235
Gurkha, 16, *19*, 19, *61*, 62, 64, 174, 182, 187, 217, 299
Guru Padmasambhava, 124
guru, 76
Gurung, 19, 62, 64, 83, 202, 204, 217, 218, 299
guthi, 65, 141, 299
Gyangtse, 290

H

haat, 235
Haka Bahal, 151
handicapped, 243, 294
Hanuman Dhoka, 15, 90, 94, 95, 104, 107, *108*, 111, 111, 112, 277
Hanuman, 69, 71, 111, 144, 299
Hanumante River, 153
Hanumante, 156
Hari Shanker Temple, 146
Harigau, 128
harijans, 73

harvesting, 202
Hastaka, 274
Hauz Khas Village, 283
health, 297
Helambu, 127, 230, 230, 231, 253, 280
helicopter evacuation, 242
herding, 64
heriche, 228
Hetauda, 297, 297
Hidden Valley, 212
highest point, 5
Hile, *19*, 234
hill castes, 213
hill groups, 61
hill people, 180
hill society, 58
hill tribes, 60
hill, 73, 123, 180
hill-walking, 280
Hillary, Edmund, 51, 222, 223
Himalayan Booksellers, 296
Himalayan Montane birds, 53
Himalayan Musk Derr, 48
Himalayan Rescue Association, 206, 243, 295
Himalayan Trust Hospital, 244
Himalayan Trust, 222, 223
Himalayan zone, 36
Himalayan, 33, 34, 36, 49, *117*, 153, 169, 179, 200, 219, 221, *230*, 232, 237
Himalayas, 5, 37, 41, 60, 257
Himalchuli, *172*, 176, 230
Himals, *125*, 170, 295
Hinayana, 76
Hindu epics, 147
Hindu Kingdom, 12, 68
Hindu temple, 73
Hindu trinity, 69
Hindu worship, 189
Hindu, 8, 12, 57, 58, 65, 68, 68, 73, 76, 79, 82, 84, 94, 94, 95, 115, 119, 121, 128, 136, 149, *167*, 183, 207, 210, 230, 259, 278
Hinduism, 2, 5, 58, 64, 70, 72, 77
Hinko, 219
Hiranyaksha, 129
history, 7-21, 176
hiti, 299
Hiunchuli, 217
Holi, 87

holy men, 173
Hongde, 204, 204
Horticulture Centre, 126
hot season, 293
Hotel Diyalo, 185
Hotel Himalaya, 274
Hotel Kailas, 185
Hotel River View, 186
Hotel Srinagar, 177
hotels, 115, 283
House of the Living Goddess, 277
Howard-Bury, 51
Humayun's Tomb, 283
Hunt, John, 51
Hwezog, Maurice, 213
Hyangja, 174
hydro-electric power, 223
hydro-station, 123
hydropower, 37

I

I Baha Bahal, 148
Ilam, 62, 236
Imja Khola, 227
Impeyan Pheasant, 227, 299
imports, 29
incarnation, 299
income distribution, 31
India, 18, 37, 42, 43, 90, 104, 134, 136, 189, *283*, *284*
Indian Airlines, 283, 287
Indian Embassy, 16
Indian Gurkha files, 19
Indian independence, 19
Indian influence, 89
Indian Mutiny, 189
Indian newspapers, 295
Indian subcontinent, 41
indigenous, 64
Indo-Aryan, 60, 65
Indo-Ganjetic Plain, 39
Indra Chowk, 104, *106*, 106, 113, 271, 272
Indra Jatra Festival, 69, 109, 110
Indra Jatra, 11, 13, 85, 106, 110, 111
Indra, 69, 80, 81, 110, 131, 299
Indrachowk, 81
Indrawati Khola, 231
Indresvara Mahadeva Temple, 95, 280
industry, 25, 28, 182

infrastructure, 157
inskilled labour, 25
International calls, 296
international cuisine, 213
international, 223
Inther-ethnic, 60
irrigation, 24
Islamic art, 95
Island Peak Base Camp, 227
Itahari, 182

J
Jagannath, 111, 299
Jagat Pal Vihara, 126
Jagat, 202
Jai Binayak Temple, 123
Jai Mai, 162, 163
Jain, 68
Jama Masjid, 283
Jamacho Forest Reserve, 126
Jamal, 274
Jamuna, 94
Janai Purnima, 85
janai, 59, 72, 299
Janaki Mandir, 183
Janaki Temple, *183, 184*
Janakpur, 71, 86, 180, *182*, 183
Jang Bahadur Rana, *9*, 15
janai, 299
Janai Purnima, 142
Japan, 76
Japanese, 126
Jatra, 110, 299
Jawalakhel, 27, 82, 151, 271, 277
Jaya Ranjit Malla, 158
Jayanagar, 184
Jayanti, 135
Jayasthiti Malla, 12
jelebis, 260
Jesth, 299
Jeth Ganesh, 162
Jeth, 85, 296
jewellers, 131
jhankris, 62, 77, 83, *87*, 142, 299
Jharkot, 207
Jiri, 221
jogini, 299
joint families, 65
Jokhang Temple, *291*
Jomosom, 43, 53, 71, 210, 211, 261
Jong Bahadur Rana, 9

Jorsale, 221
Juddha Shumsher Rana, 107
Jugal Himal, 231
Jugals, 121
Jumla, 236, 237, 244
Jumla-Rara lake, 237
Jung Bahadur Rana, 9, 19
jute, 182
jyapu, 65, 147, 299

K
ka, 264
kaalo daal, 259
kaamis, 73
Kaartik Tihar, 86
Kaartik, 296
Kabre, 213
Kagbeni, 210
Kagmara Lekh, 244
Kagyupa, 76
Kahun Danda, 175, 280
Kailashkut Bhavan, 9
Kaiser, 115
Kakani, 126, 278, 280
Kakarbhita, 182, 287, 297
Kal Bhairav, 112, 113
kala jamun, 260
Kala Pattar, 221, 228, 228, 253
Kali Gandaki River, 201
Kali Gandaki, 9, 42, 64, *167*, *174*, 177, 186, 210, 211, 214, 248, *254*
Kali, 69, 125, 300
Kalika Mandir, 176
Kalimati Clinic, 239
Kalimpong, 287
Kalopani, 213
Kalu Pande, 125
Kamlachi-Asan- Indrachowk, 104
Kampas, 211
Kanchenjunga, 41, 235, 234, 236, 244
Kangan, 284
Kanjiroba Himal, 244
Kantipath, 294, 296
Kantipurat, 11
Kanya Kumari, 109
Kapilvastu, 74
Kargiil, 285
Karkot, 151
karma, 72, 75, 300
Karnal Zone, 25
Karnali Chisapani Project, 37

Karnali, 42, 248
Karnataka, 11
Kartik, 300
Kashmir Valley, 284
Kashmir, 13, 107
Kasi Biswanath, 162
Kaski kings, 175
Kasthamandap (House of wood), 11, 67, 104, 110, *112*, 165, 277
Kathe, 105
Kathesimblu Stupa, *127*
Kathmandu agencies, 289
Kathmandu Kodari Road, 230
Kathmandu Valley, 3, 4, 5, 8, 12, 13, 18, 26, 27, 29, 31, 34, *36*, 38, 42, 58, 61, 62, 64, *77*, 80, 87, 101-115, 117, *112*, 113, 115, 117-137, 120, 123, 130, 134, 139, 141, 153, 157, 165, 167, 169, 174, 176, 180, 183, 185, 189, 219, 221, 223, 229, 230, 231
Kathmandu, *67*, *112, 113*, 201
Kawaguchi, Ekai, 130, 167
KC's Restaurant, 296
Kesang, 211
Keshab Narayan Chowk, 146
Keshar Mahal, 297
Khaireni, 176
Khalikot, 203
Khalna Tole, 163
Kham, 211
Khampas, 211
Khandbari, 234
Khangjung, 229
khapsay, 260
Khaptad, 49
Khas, 300
Khasa, 11
Khichapokhari, 107, 295, 296
Khimbu, 221
Khimrong Khola, 216, 218
khir, 264
Khokana, 121, 123
Khongma La, 234
Khudi Khola, 202
khukuri, 19, 61, 107, 272, 300
Khuldighar, 218
Khumbu Glacier, 228
Khumbu Himal, 223, 234
Khumbu region, 53
Khumbu, 85, 195, 221, 223, 227, 234

Khumjung, 51, 222, 224
King Ananda, 156
King Birendra, 87
King Bupatindra, 119, 156
King Mahendra, 204
King Malla, *13*
King of Nepal, 128, 204
King of Patan, 125
King Tribhuvan, 177
King Yaksha Malla, 161
King Yalambar, 71
King, 82
kingdoms, *10*
kinkinimall, 300
Kirantis, 231
Kirati, 61, 71
Kirkpatrick, 179
Kirtipur, 12, 112, 125, 126
Kitatis, 8
kite competitions, 79
Kobang, 212
Kodari Highway, 165
Kodari, 153, 253, 297
Koirala, BP, 16, 18, 21
kos, 297
Kosi Barrage, 52
Kosi Tapu, 48, 52
Kosi, 9, 42
Kot Massacre, 16, 113
kot, 15, 244
Krishna Jayanti, 85
Krishna Mandir, 85, 277
Krishna, 71, 85, 86, 105, 110, *143*, 146, 300
Krishnastami, 86
kshatriyas, 300
kumar, 151
Kumari Bahal, 108
Kumari, 10, 13, 77, *81*, 107, 109, 300
Kumbeshwar Mela, *80*, 85, 142
Kumbeshwar, 141
kunda, 121
kundalini, 300
Kunde, 222
Kupondole, 274
Kushinagar, 75
Kusma, 214
Kuti Bahal, 137
Kutumsang, 231
Kwa Bahal, 94, 141
kwati, 264
Kyangjin, 229

L
la, 300
Lachenal, Louis, 213
Ladakh, 284
Ladakhis, 133
ladus, 260
Lady Mountbatten, *14*
Lagankhel, 119, 139, 295
Lake Pokhara, *257*
Lakeside, 169
lakh, 300
Lakshmi, 69, 80, 300
laliguras, 49, 50, 300
Lalipur Tower, 108, 112
Lama Hotel, 229, 230
lamas, 62, 300
Lamjung District, 201
Lamjung Palace, 202
Lamjung, 62
land, 180
landlocked, 33
Landruk, 216, 217, 220
landscape, 33
Langang Village, 229
Langankhel, 149
Langtang Lirung, 229
Langtang National Park, 229
Langtang, 49, 126, 228, 229, 230, 233
language, 5, 57, 58, 64
Lanka, 71
Lantang Himal, 229, 230
Lapsang La, 236
lapsi, 264
Larjung, 210, 212
Lakshmi Puja, 142
Lasuntar, 128
Lattamarang, *43*, 203
Laurebina Pass, 231
Ledar, 206
Leh, 285
Lele, 121
Lhabarma, 225
Lhasa, 134, 289, *291*
Lho, 210
Lhotse, 41, 228, 257
Licchavi, 8, 10, 89, 127, 134, 141, 147, 278
Licchaviera, 119
life, 191
lightning goddess, 111
Limbini, 3
Limbus, 8, 60, *61*, 62
Limu, 231

lingam, 69, 136, 141, 142, 163, 300
Lingsren, *226*
liquor, 261
Loboche, 228
local courtesies, 173
local customs, 295
local laws, 295
Lohan Chowk, 112
Lokeswar, 119, 149
Lokeswara, 300
loo, 189
loongi, 233
Lord Mountbatten, *14*
Lord Pashupati, 87, 161
Loshar, *79*, 87, *130*, 133
lotus, 127
lower castes, 59, 115
Lubhu, 121
Lucknow, 19
Lukla, 221
Lumbini Development Scheme, 189
Lumbini Gardens Guest House, 189
Lumbini, 74, 180, 187, 297
Lumle, 38, 46
Lunchun Lun Bun Temple, 105
lungi, 238
Lupra, 210, 211
Luza, 224

M
Maagh, 87, 296
Macchendranath, 77, 82, 85, 300
Macchermo, 51
mace, 127
Machhapuchhre Base Camp, *220*, 220
Machhapuchhre, *170*, 170, 214, 216, 217, 218, 220
Machhendra, 151
Machherma, 224
madala, 300
Magar Kura, 64
Magar, 19, 64, *171*, 214
magazines, 295
Magh, 84
Magha, 300
magnolia, 221
Mahabaudha, 148, 277
Mahabharat Lekh, 42
Mahabharat middle hills, 34

Mahabharata, 3, 8, 11, 34, 38, 39, 42, 70, 71, 207, 300
Mahabodhi, 148
Mahabuddhas, 148
Mahadev, 135
Mahadevi, 69, 124
Mahaguthi, 146, 274
Mahal, 115
Maharaja Padma Shamsher, *14*
Maharajgunj, 295
Maharashthra, 12, 79
Mahayana, 76, 300
Mahendra, 16, 18, 73, 175
Main Central Thrust, 41
Maitreya, 300
Maju Deval, 110
Makalu, 41, *206*, 234, 235, 257
Makhan Tole, 107, 113
malaria, 41, 64
Malla kings, 13
Malla, 25, 65, 73, 91, 94, 104, 111, 112, 119, 134, 156, 278
Manadev, 8
Manang, 177, 203, 204, 206, 211, *212*, 218
Manangbhot, 38
Manangis, 38, *204*, *218*
Manaslu, 41, 121, 126, 170, 176
mandala, 76, 133, 134, 204
mandap, 300
mandir, 112, 300
Manga Hiti, 146
Mangal Bazaar, 143
mani, *7*, 300
Mani Rimbu, 85, 222, 300
mani wall, 300
Manjushri, 77, 104, *123*, 134, 300
manna, 297
Manohara River, 118
mantra, 76, 77, 95, 300
Mara, 74
Marg, 260, 263
Marga, 296
Marpha, 211
marriages, 64, 65
marshland birds, 52
Marsyangdi Khola, 201, 202
Maru Ganesh, 67
masks, *272*
Matthiessen, Peter, 50
maths, 165, 300
matwali, 58, 73
Maya Devi, 74, 188

measures, 297
medical assistance, 295
Mediterranean, 41
mela, 85, 300
Melamchi Khola, 231
Melamchi Phul Bazaar, 231
meningitis, 243
merit, 72
Mewa Gola, 26
microclimates, 45
Middle Hills, 47
migration, 57
migratory birds, 52
Milarepa, 50
millet, 24, 61, 261
Min Nath, 149
mini-hydro-electric projects, 218
Minimum Impact Code, 233
Ministry of Health, 182
Ministry, 115
Miristi Khola, 213
Mithila, 11
Modi Khola Gorge, 220
Modi Khola, 219
Moghul, 57
mohar, 294
moksha, 72, 300
momos, 223, 260, 264
monasteries, 131, 148, 151, 278, 285
Mongoloid, 34, 60, 62, 64, 65
monkeys, 52
monopsony, 37
monsoons, 54, 293
montane forests, 52
monuments, 117
Moslem population, 189
Moslem, 11, 12, 68, 77, 134, 176, 188, 189
Mother Theresa, 136
Mother's Day, 173
motorcycles, 295
mountain bike tours, 253
Mount Everest, 35, 41, 50, 53, 118, 223, 293
mountaineering, *249*
mountainous terrain, 33
mountains, 3, 45, 167, 169, 220, 251, *252*, 257, 277, 293
mountain flight, *256*
mudra, 95
Mughal Sheraton, 284
Mughal-like, 147

Mugling, 169, 186, 247
Mugu, 133
Muktinath, 71, 187, 195, 206, 207, 211
Mukwanpur, 13
Mul Chowk Durbar Square, 128
Mul Chowk, 112, 144
Mul Chowkat, 94
multi-cropping, 24
multi-purpose elections, 21
Mumtaz, 284
museums, 283
Musk deer, 50
Mustang, *174*, 210
muthi, 297

N
Na, 225
Nag Bahal, 141
Nag Pokhari, 115
Nagarjun, 7, 126
Nagarkot, 7, 117, 118, 253, 278, 280
naga, 85, *123*, 144, 151, 156, 300
Nagi Gompa, 127
Nagi, 127
Nagin Lakes, 284
Najra Jogini Temple, 134
Nakkatta, 126
namaste, 300
Namche Bazaar, 85, 221
Namche, 62, 223, 228
Namobuddha, 253
Nandi, 69, 136, 300
Narasingha, 146, 147
Narayan Shah, 176
Narayan, 69, 119, 124, 127, 134, 165, 300
Narayanghat, 186, *187*, 247, 248
Narayani, 83, 139, 186
Narsingha, 69, 111, 144, 300
Nasal Chowk, 111
Nasaleswar, 111
Nataraj, 69
National Art Gallery, 95
National Art Museum, 159
national bird, 5
National Census Bureau, 28
National Civil Code, 73
national colour, 5
national economy, 28
national flower, 5

national income, 23
National Museum, 94
National Park lodge, 229
National parks, 46 , 48, 54, 229
National Planning Commission, 31
National Tuberculosis Centre, 153
Natraj, 135
natural history, 51
natural resources, 49
Naudada, 175, 177, 216, 280
Nava Durga, 165
Nawab of Oudh, 189
Naxalbari, 182
Nayaphul, 216
Nepal Art Council, 274
Nepal Association of Rafting Agents, 250
Nepal Association of Travel Agents, 297
Nepal Bank, 294
Nepal Congress Party (NCP), 18, 21
Nepal Indo-Suez, 294
Nepal International Clinic, 239, 295
Nepal Television, 119
Nepal Tourist Service, 294
Nepal, 59, 130, 136
Nepal, central, 40, 47
Nepal-Arab Bank, 294
Nepal-Hindu, 135
Nepalese, *57*
Nepalgunj, *186, 188*, 189, 237
Nepali (parbate), 2
Nepali art, 272
Nepali citizenship, 29
Nepali life, 173
Nepali villagers, 48
Nepalis, 5, *61*, 117
New Delhi, 283, *286*
New Himalchuli Culture Group, 278
New Road, 107, 175, 271, 278
Newar Bazaar, 177
Newar brass, 177
Newar Buddhism, 135
Newar New Year, 80
Newar society, 65
Newar traditions, 12
Newari Calendar Year, 141
Newari language, 65
newari raksi, 261

Newaris, *65*, 89, 94, 97, 157, 300
Newars, 64, 76, 77, 83, 90, 109, 131, 151, 157, 231
newspaper, 295
Ngozumpa Gacier, 225
Nightingale Books, 26
Nilgiris, 211, 213
Nirula's Marina, 283
nirvana, 75, 76, 300
non-agricultural income, 49
non-governmental agencies, 31
non-Hindus, 136, 137, 158
Num, 232, 234
Nunkdhaki, 235
Nuptse-Lhotse Wall, 227
Nuwakot, 10, 12, 13
Nyatapola Cafe, 162
Nyatapola, 159, *160*, 161-162, 163
Nyesyang, 204
Nyingma sect, 223
Nyingmapa, 76, 300

O

occupational castes, 73
Ocheterlony, 13
Okreni, 127
Oldfield Henry, 104
Om Mani Padma Hum, 300
Om, 71
onithological cross-roads, 52
orchids, 120
oriflammes, 300
overpopulation, 38

P

paati, 266, 297
Padmasambhava, 207
pagoda, *160*, 162, 301
Pahalgam, 284
pahar, 38
paisa, 294
Pakistan, 19
Palace of Fifty-five Windows, 159, 278
Paleartic region, 52
Paliputra (see Patna), 8
Palkhu, *177*
Panauti, 95, 165, 253, 278
pancamakara, 95
Pancha Mukhi Hanuman, 111
panchayat, 18, 37, 301
Panchkaal, 231

Pandavas, 71
Pangboche Monastery, 227
Pangboche, 225, 227
Pangka, 224
Pangpema, 236
Parikrama, 184
parjna, 301
parks, 52
parliament, 18
Paro, 290, 291
Parsa, 48
Parvati, 69, 89, 109, 110, 121, 146, 301
pashmina, 272
Pashupati, 136, 301
Pashupatinath Temple, 58, 67, 136, *137*, 161, 278, 58
Pashupatinath, 12, 86 87, 95, 136
pastoral lifestyle, 61
Patan Dhoka, 141
Patan Hospital, 295
Patan Industrial Estate, *27*, 141, 149, 269
Patan Durbar Square, 274
Patan, 11, 12, *13*, 21, *80*, 82, 85, *87*, 94, *96*, 109, 121, 126, 139, 139-151, 149, 269, 271, *277*, 277
path, 301
pathis, 146
Pati Bhanjyang, 231
Patle Chhango, 170
Patan Industrial Estate, *27*
Patan, 287
Patta, 162, 163
pau, 297
paubha, 94
Pausch, 301
Peacock Window, 165
Pedas, 260
Peking, 13
People of Nepal, 65
people, 5, 57-65
peppers, *262*
per capita income, 23
Phaagun, 87, 296
Phanta, 48
Pharping, 123, 126
Phedi, 175, 206, 216
Pheriche, 227
Phewa Lake, *169*
Phewa Tal, 167, 170, 175
Phewa, 169

philosophy, 70
Phoksundo Lake, 244
Phortse, 224, 225
photography, 296
Phulchowki Mai, 120
Phulchowki, 7, 52, 119, 120, 121, 127
phulpati, 79, 80
Phunki, 225
Pie Alley, 108
Pilgrim Bookshop, 296
pilgrimage, 2, 183, 207
pilgrims, 3, 132, 186, 187
Pina, 244
pipal, 63, 97, 141, 151
pipits, 53
Pisang, 203, 204
plains people, 180
poetry, 97
Pokhara Valley, 97, 167-177
Pokhara, 27, 31, *38*, 171, 185, 201, 214, 216, 217, 220, 244, 247, 248, 251, 253, 261, 280, 295, 297
Pokhara-Gorkha, 253
Pokhari, 104, 235, 293, 301
Pompo Yartung, 207
Poon Hill, 214, 216, *222*
population, 5, 180
porters, 62, *191*, 200, 223, 237, 253, 301
postal services, 296
Poste Restante, 296
potatoes, 36, 61, 64
potes, 107, 272
pottery, 162
Poush, 86, 296
poverty line, 23
power shortage, 37
Prajna, 95
Prakriti, 95
prasad, 67, 301
Pratap Malla, 97, 104, 110, 111, 134
prayer flags, 60, *288*, 301
prayer-wheel, 271, 272, 301
pre-Buddhist, 244
prehistory, 64
priests, 173
printing, 296
Prithvi Highway, 176
Prithvi Narayan Palace, 176
Prithvi Narayan Shah, 12, 13, 33, 125, *176*

puja, 67, 137, 301
Pujari Math, 91, *92*, 165
Punakha, 291
Purusha, 95
Pushpapur, 8

Q
Quary, 120
Qutb Minar, 283

R
Raajbiraj, 35
Raato Machhendra, 121, 123, 147, 149
radio, 296
rafts, 248, 250, 251, 297
Rais, 8, 60, *61*, 62, 231, 235
Raja Harisimha (Hari Singh), 11
Rajasthan, 12, 58, 97, 176, 284
rakhsa bandhan, 142
raksi, 261, 301
Ram Bahadur Limbu, 19
Ram Ghat, 162
Ram, 69, 71, 86, 111, 183, 301
Rama Navami, 184
Ramayana, 2, 69, 70, 71, 161, 183, *184*
Rana, *14*, 16, *17*, 85, 87, 110, 113, 115, 124, 139, 146, *150*, 177
Rana, Schumsher JB, 115
Rani Pokhari, 104, 127, 293
Rapti River, 52
Rara Lake, 42, 237, 244
Rara National Park, 52, 237
Rara, 49
Rastriya Banijya Bank, 294
Ratna park, 293
Ratna Pustak Bhandar, 295
Rato, 82, 85
Rawana, 71, 301
Raxaul, 184
recipes, *262*
Reclining Vishnu, *136*
Red Cross Service, 295
Red Fort, 283, *286*
referendum, 18
regional market, 29
religion, 5, 67-77, 173, 223
Renaissance, 90
Resident, 126
restaurant, 260, 261, 263
restricted zones, 191
rhinos, *48*, 52

rhododendron, 48, *54*, 120, *195*, 195, 221, 229, 230
rice, 24, *25*, 61, 213, 259
rickshaws, 62
rimpoche, 301
Ring Road, 121, 128
Ringmo, 244
Rioimo Shar, *224*
ritual bathing, 183
ritual kidnapping, 60
river tours, 285
river, 33, 156, 167, 186, 199
River-running, 247
RNAC, 182, 257, 278
Roberts, Jimmy, 220
rodi, 62, 64
routes, 191
Royal Bardiya Wildlife Reserve, 189
Royal Bengal Tiger, 46
Royal Botanical Garden, 121
Royal Chitwan National Park, 185
Royal Family, 170
Royal Nepal Airline, 80, 236, 247, 283
Royal Palace, 80
Royal Trek, 280
Rumtek, 76
Rupa, 174
rupee, 294
Rupse Falls, 213
rural Nepal, 278

S
Sacred Garden, 188
sacred mountain, 220
sacrifice, 80
saddhus, *71*, 74, 87, *122*, 127, 135, 183, 301
Sagarmatha National Park, 53, 223
Sagarmatha, *34*, 49, *208*, 223, 257
Sajha, 186, 293
Sakya, 109
Sakyamuni, 148
Sakyapa, 76
sakyas, 65, 91
sal, 46
sale roti, 260
Sali Nadi, 87
Salpa Pass, 221, 234
salt trade, 212, 213

samsara, 72, 73, 76
Samye, 290
Sanagaun, 121
Sanasa, 224
Sanctuary, 48, *202*, 219, 220
sangha, 75
Sankhu, 87, 134, 253, 278
Sankhuwasaba, 133
Sanskrit, 77
Sanskritised, 60
Sarangkot, 175, 280
Saraswati Books, 296
Saraswati Kunda, 121
Saraswati, 69, 87, 135, 147, 301
sardar, 239
saringhi, 97
saris, 135
sarkis, 73
Schneider Series Map, 223
School, 120
sculptures, 269
seasons, 191, 194
Self, 72
Sesha, 124
Seti River, 174
Seti, 248
Seto Bhairav, 82, 110
Seto Machhendra, 105, 106
Seto Machhendranath, 87, *105*
Shah, 12, 65, 80, 111, 112, 176, 244
Shaiva Raatri, 87
Shavaite Sadhu, *4*, 165
shakti, 77, 95, 301
shaligrams, 210
Shalimar Express, 284
Shamanistic beliefs, 2, 68, 77, 79
shamans, 142
shamars, 83
Shanker, 115
shell, 127
Sheopuri Wildlife Reserve, 53
Shermathang, 231
Sherpas, *60*, 64, 83, 85, 223, 227, 231, 232
Shey-Phoksumdo, 49
Shey-Phoksundo National Park, 244
Shigatse, 290
shikhara-style, 148, 161
shikhara, 146
Shimbu, 105
shipping, 274, 275

Shipton La, 234
Shipton, Eric, 51
Shishapangma Base Camp, 290
Shiva festival, 230
Shiva Raatri, 136
Shiva, 8, 12, 68, 69, 77, 83, 86, 87, 110, 111, 112, 121, 124, 135, 136, 142, 146, 149, 161, 165, 302
Shivapuri, 127
shopping, 269-275, 283
Shresthas, 65
Shrinivasa Malla, 143, 147
Shukla, 48
Siddhartha Gautam, 3, 74
Siddharta on Kantipath, 274
Siddhi Lakshmi, 162
Siddhi Narasingha Malla, 143
Siddhi Pokhari, 156
Sikkim, 13, 76, 235, 287
Sikkimese, 133
Siklis village, *63*
Siliguri, 287
silver jewellery, *272*
Simikot, *232*
sindoor, 67
Sing Gompa, *230*
Singha Durbar, 113
Sinion La, 236
Sinja, 237
Sino-Indian War, 19
Sinwa, 214
Sirjana, 274
Sita Bibaha Panchami, 86
Sita, 71, 84, 183, 301
Sithinakha, 264
Siva, 95
Siwalik Hills, 39
Siwalik, 34, 42
Snow Leopard, 48, 50, 274
social control, 73
social divisions, 72
socio-economic status, 65
Solu Khumbu, *33*, 62, 97, *224*
Solu, 221
Sonamarg, 284
Songtsen Gampo, 9
soul, 70
South Asian Area Regional Council, 115
south India, 165
Southeast, 76
souvenirs, 271, *272*
speech, 173

spirit world, 77
spirit, 261
spiritual guidance, 95
sports, 247-**257**
Srawan Naga Panchami, 85
Srawan, 296, 301
Sri Lanka, 76
Srigha Chaitya, 105
Srinagar, 284, 285
St Xavier, 120, *150*, 151
stomach problems, 240
stupa, 8, 131, 132, 133, 173, 224, 301
sub-group, 65
subbha, 213
subsistence crop, *24*
subsistence economy, 37
subtropical forests, 48
subtropical climate, 24
Suddhodana, 74
sudra, 73, 301
Sugauli, 13
suggested itineraries, 277-287
Suikhet, 175
sukkha, 73, 294
Suli Gad River, 244
Sultan Shamsuddin (Bengal), 11
Sun Dhokha, 146, *153*, *157*, 159
Sun Kosi, 248
Sunauli, 283, 297
Sundara, 147, 148
Sundari Chowk, *96*, *144*
Sundarijal, 119, 127, 230, 231
sundhara, 301
superstitions, 82
Surjya, 124, 301
Swayambhu Hill, *120*
Swayambhu, 10, 97, 104, 134, 135
Swayambhunath, *8*, *74*, 85, 105, 134, 277
sweet, 264
Swiss Agency for Technical Assistance, 29
Syabru, 229, 230
Syabrubensi, 229

T

taatopaani, 43
Tachupal Tole, 163
Tadapani, 216
tahr, 224
Taj Mahal, *283*

Tal, 202, 203
Taleju Bell, 146
Taleju Bhawani, 11, 301
Taleju Chowk, 159
Taleju Temple, 95, 113, 144, 158
Taleju, 109, 110
Tallo Durbar, 176
Tamangs, 29, 62, 85, 97
Tamur Kosi, 236
Tandi Bazaar, 186
Tansen, 177, 214, 244, 297
tantra, 76, 95
tantric, 9, 76, 77, 109, 144, 165, 301
tantrika, 95
Taplejung, 26, 133
tara, 9, 77, 134, 301
tarkaari, 259
Tarkeghyang, 231
Tashi Palkhel, 174
Tashigang, 291
Tashigaon, 232, 234
Tashiling, 175
Tatopani, 214
Taudaha Lake, 123
Taumadhi Tole, 162, 163
Taumadhi, 83
taxis, 62, 296
tea leaves, 130
Teaching Hospital, 295
Teej, 59, 86, 137
teen momo, 260
Teka Pokhari, 153
telecommunications Office, 296
television, 296
temperatures, 45, 293
Temple of Akash Bhairav, 106
Temple of Annapurna, 104
Temple of Bajra Jogini, 278
Temple of Bhagbati, 159
Temple of Harati Ajima, 134
Temple of Hiranya Verna Mahabir, 277
Temple of Narayan, 109
Temple of Varahi, 170
temple, 10, 119, 126, 141, 148
Temples of Khajuraho, 287
tempo, 188
Tengboche Meadow, 227
Tengboche Monastery, 222
Tengboche, 85, 223, 227
Terai, 13, 14, 16, 19, 24, 25, 34,

39, 41, 45, 46, 52, 64, 71, 83, 107, 121, 177, 179, 247, 248, 294, 301
Terai, accommodation, 182, 183, 186
Tethys Sea, 41
Thahiti, 104, 105
Thaibo, 121
Thak Khola, 213
Thakali, 64, 213, *218*
Thakalis, 301
Thakuri Chhetri, 19
Thakuri kings, 10
Thakuri, 58, 72
Thamel, 108, 115, 167, 171, 237, 260, 263, 269, 269, 270, 271, 275, 278, 295, 296, 297
Thami Monastery, 85, 222
Thamserku, 225
thangka, 89, 94, 97, 113, 271, 274, 301
Tharepati, 231
thars, 62
Tharu, 64, 180
The Four Truths, 73
The Rising Nepal, 274, 294, 295
Theravada monastery, 189
Theravada School, 76
Thieves Market, *186*
Thimi, 85, 153
Thimpu, 291
Thinigaon, 211
thon, 111
Thorang La, 201, 206
Thorung La Pass, 253
Three Years in Tibet, 130
threshing, 202
thukpa, 260
Thulo Bheri River, 244
Tibet Ritual Art Gallery, 271
Tibet Travel Bureau, 288-289
Tibet, 13, 26, *39*, 59, 76, 90, 104, 130, 130, 131, 156, 202, 207, 210, 211, 212, 237, 244, 244, 253, 285, 288-290
Tibet-Nepal border, 41
Tibetan, *60*, *61*
Tibetan Buddhism, 124, 207, 223, 244
Tibetan Buddhist, *7*, *131*
Tibetan civilisation, 290
Tibetan cuisine, 223
Tibetan Gelugpa, *68*
Tibetan Handicraft Centre, 151

Tibetan houses, 132
Tibetan Marginal Chain, 41
Tibetan Marginal Range, 41
Tibetan monastery, 124
Tibetan plateau, 42, 48
Tibetan Refugee Camp, 151, 174, 271, 277
Tibetan refugees, 27, 131
Tibetan trans-Himalayan Desert, 36
Tibetan, 60, 61, 64, 68, 87, 126, 133, 189, 211, 223, 231, 271
Tibetan, cultural identity, 29
Tibeto-Burman, 65
Tibeto-Nepalis, 133
Tiger Mountain group, 189
Tihar Festival, 69
Tihar, 80, 199
tika, *80*, 109, 111, *273*, 301
Tikagarh, 183
Tilicho Peak, 204
Tilman, HW, 51
time, 296
tipping, 296
tips, 296
tola, 297
tole, 83, 156, 157, 301
tongas, 184
tongba, 235, 261
topis, 61, 67, 135, 213, 301
torana, 146, *149*, 301
tourism, 23, *26*
Tourist Guide Association, 297
tourist, 26, 130, 131, 291
tours, **10 days**, 280
tours, **15 days**, 280
tours, 297
tours, **3 days**, 277, 278
tours, **5 days**, 278, 280
tours, **7 days**, 280
town, 167
Trade and Transit Treaty, 31
trade balance, 31
Trade Treaty, 18
trade, 25, 36, 59, 104, 131, 223
trading partners, 31
trail, *39*, 43, 53, 127
training, 55
trans-Himalayan, 64
transit points, 31
travel tips, **293**
travel agent, 257, 277, 294
Treaty of Friendship, 13
treaty, 16

trees, 36, 48
trek times, 195
trek, choosing, 191-200, 294
trek, organising, 199-200
Trekkers' Aid Post, 228
trekkers, 3
trekking agent, 200, 223, 251, 233
trekking expenses, 239
trekking food, 201
trekking gear, 237
trekking maps, 200
trekking months, 191-194
trekking permits, 297
trekking tips, 237-243
trekking with children, 243
trekking, 26, 191, 284, 294
trekking, 8-14 days, 197
trekking, cultural diversity, 194
trekking, equipment, 223
trekking, healthy, 239
trekking, mountain scenery, 194
trekking, one week, 195, 197
trekking, popular treks, 194
trekking, remoteness, 194
trekking, spring rhododendrons and plant life, 194
trekking, two weeks, 197, 198
treks, 169, 290
Tribeni Mela, *84*, 84
Tribhuvan Jayanti, 85
Tribhuvan Museum, 111
Tribhuvan University, 126
Tribhuvan, 16, 177, 301
Trichandra College, 104
Tripureshwor, 26, 153
trisul, 69
Trisuli, 126, *167*, 186, 247, 229, 248
tsampa, 133
Tsethang, 290
Tukche Peak, 211
Tukche, 211, 213
Tumlingtar airstrip, 232
Tumlingtar, 221, 234, 235
Tundikhel, *9*, 80, 87, 127, 182
Tupek, 128
Turana, *90*
turquoise, 130
Tusha Hiti, *96*, *144*

U

Udaipur, 12
Ugratara Temple, 104

Uku Bahal, *90*, 148
Ulleri, 216
Ultimate Reality, 70
UNDP, 31
UNESCO, 94, 112, 117
UNICEF, 3
United Nations, 31
Upanishads, 70, 72, 76
Upaya, 95
upper Lantang, 195

V

Vaisha Dev, *83*, 105
vaisya, 73
Vajracharya caste, 77
Vajrayana Buddhism, 77
Vajrayana, 76, 77, 95
Valley, 19, 109, 113, *125*, 125, 139, 141, 149, 161, 165, 167, 199, 207, 231, 247, 277
Varanasi, 285
Vayadoot, 283, 287
Vedas, 69, 70, 72, 76
veena, 69
vegetation, 33
verbal arts, 97
Victoria Cross, 19
vihara, 301
Vijaya Dashami, 80
Vikram Sambat Calendar, 296
Vilas Mandir, 112
Vilas, 112
Village Life, 62
vipassana, 75
Vipaswi Buddha, 7
Vipaswi, 134
visa, 293, 297
Vishnu, 12, 68, 69, 89, 111, 119, *121*, 127, 128, 129, 135, 144, 210, 278, 301
volleyball, 151

W

Waddell, WA, 51
waders, 53
Wakupati Narayan, 165
Wangdi, 211
Wangdiphodrang, 291
warblers, 53
water taps, 147
wealth, 223
wedding, *173*
weights, 297
Wencheng, 9

west Nepal, 236
western Tibet, 290
wetlands, 52
wheat, 24, 61
whitewater, 247, *248*, 251
WHO, 31, 41
Wild Asiatic Elephant, 48
wildlife reserves, 48
wildlife, 46, 189
wo, 264
women in economy, 28
Woodcarving Museum, 165
woodcarving, 269
World Bank, 31
World Heritage List, 117
World Wildlife Fund, 217
worship activities, 183

Y

Yak and Yeti, 115, 297
yaks, *39*, *45*, 51, 229, 244
Yaksha Malla, 12, 163
Yala Peak, 229
Yalung Glacier, 236
Yamambar, 8
yantra, 95
Yarlung Valley, 290
Yashodhara, 74
Yeh-tch, 51
Yellow-hat monks, 133
yeti, 51, 222
yidams, 95
yoghurt, 260
Yogi, 69, 301
York, 283

Z

zamindars, 180
Zanskar, 285

NOTES

NOTES

NOTES